SOCIAL POLICY REVIEW 27

Analysis and debate in social policy, 2015

Edited by Zoë Irving, Menno Fenger and John Hudson

First published in Great Britain in 2015 by

Policy Press
University of Bristol
1-9 Old Park Hill
Bristol BS2 8BB
UK
t: +44 (0)117 954 5940
e: pp-info@bristol.ac.uk
www.policypress.co.uk

North American office:
Policy Press
c/o The University of Chicago Press
1427 East 60th Street
Chicago, IL 60637, USA
t: +1 773 702 7700
f: +1 773-702-9756
e:sales@press.uchicago.edu
www.press.uchicago.edu

© Policy Press/Social Policy Association 2015

British Library Cataloguing in Publication Data
A catalogue record for this book is available from the British Library.

Library of Congress Cataloging-in-Publication Data
A catalog record for this book has been requested.

ISBN 978-1-4473-2277-1 hardback
ISBN 978-1-4473-2280-1 paperback SPA members' edition (not on general release)

The right of Zoë Irving, Menno Fenger and John Hudson to be identified as editors
of this work has been asserted by them in accordance with the Copyright, Designs and
Patents Act 1988.

Cover design by Policy Press
Front cover: photograph kindly supplied by www.alamy.com
Printed and bound in Great Britain by CPI Group (UK)
Ltd, Croydon, CR0 4YY
Policy Press uses environmentally responsible print partners

MIX
Paper from
responsible sources
FSC® C013604

Contents

Part Three: 25 years after *The three worlds of welfare capitalism*: a retrospective

List of tables and figures

Tables

Figures

Notes on contributors

Graham Bowpitt is Reader in Social Policy at Nottingham Trent University, UK. His research is concerned with homelessness and related aspects of deep social exclusion, and with faith-based responses to social issues, mainly focusing on the UK. He currently manages a local evaluation in Nottingham of Fulfilling Lives, a national programme seeking better outcomes for adults with multiple and complex needs.

Menno Fenger is Associate Professor of Public Administration at Erasmus University Rotterdam. His research focuses on processes of institutional change in welfare states in the Netherlands and in comparative perspective. He is project manager of the European Union-funded INSPIRES research project about innovations in labour market policies and social policies.

Jon Glasby is Professor of Health and Social Care and Director of the Health Services Management Centre, University of Birmingham, UK. From August 2015, he will take up a new role as Head of the School of Social Policy. A qualified social worker by background, Jon carries out regular research, teaching, consultancy and policy advice around the future of adult social care and health services.

Joe Greener is Lecturer in Social Policy at Liverpool Hope University, UK. His research focuses on how political and economic processes shape the quality of care for older people in the UK. He is also editor for the *Journal of Critical and Radical Social Work* and part of the H2020-funded project Re-inVEST, aimed at developing new policies and perspectives to combat poverty and inequality across the European Union.

Chris Grover is Senior Lecturer in Social Policy at Lancaster University, UK. His research interests primarily focus on the political economy of social security policy. He has written extensively about the loaning of social security and disability benefits, and is co-editor with Linda Piggott of *Disabled people, work and welfare* (Policy Press, 2015). He is currently working on a book for Palgrave Macmillan that examines historical and contemporary debates about, and the practice of, the state supplementing wages.

John Hudson is Senior Lecturer in Social Policy at the University of York, UK. He has published widely in the areas of comparative social policy and the policy process, and is currently researching social policy in global cities. Together with Stuart Lowe he is co-author of *Understanding the policy process* (Policy Press, 2009) and co-author with Stefan Kühner and Stuart Lowe of *The short guide to social policy* (Policy Press, 2nd edn forthcoming 2015).

Gyu-Jin Hwang is Senior Lecturer in Social Policy in the Department of Sociology and Social Policy, University of Sydney, Australia. His research fuses theoretically informed debate with its practical application to the field of public sector policy reform. He is editor of *New welfare states in East Asia: Global challenges and restructuring* (Edward Elgar, 2011) and author of *Pathways to state welfare in Korea: Interests, ideas and institutions* (Ashgate, 2006).

Zoë Irving is Senior Lecturer in Comparative and Global Social Policy at the University of York, UK. Her current research interests are in the politics of economic crisis and austerity, and also in the development of comparative welfare theory that accounts for population size. She is co-editor with Kevin Farnsworth of the *Journal of International and Comparative Social Policy*, and *Social policy in challenging times* (Policy Press, 2011), and co-author with Michael Hill of *Understanding social policy* (Wiley Blackwell, 2009).

Stefan Kühner is Senior Lecturer in Social Policy at the University of York, UK. His main academic interest centres on comparative and international social policy with emphasis on the politics of welfare state change. His research has explored the effect of government ideology on welfare reforms in historical perspective and discussed the notion of welfare productivism as backdrop for comparing social policies across high, middle and low-income economies. He is also co-author of *The short guide to social policy* (Policy Press, 2nd edn forthcoming 2015).

Hannah Lambie-Mumford is Research Fellow at the Sheffield Political Economy Research Institute (SPERI), University of Sheffield, UK. Her research focuses on food poverty, the rise of emergency food provision in the UK, and the human right to food. She has previously worked as a researcher at the Department of Sociology, University of Warwick, and the Applied Research Centre in Sustainable Regeneration at Coventry University.

Stuart Lowe is Senior Lecturer at the University of York, UK. He has written extensively on housing policy and both his books have been well received by students and practitioners: *Housing policy analysis* (Palgrave/Macmillan, 2004) and *The housing debate* (Policy Press, 2011).

Jed Meers is a research student at York Law School, and teaches there and in the Department of Social Policy and Social Work, University of York, UK. His research has a socio-legal focus and is currently concerned with legal responses to the coalition government's welfare reform agenda, and its impact on tenants living in social housing.

Deborah Rice is Research Associate in the COPE Project at the Department of Social Sciences, CvO University Oldenburg, Germany. Her research interests focus on labour market policy and activation policies, multi-level governance, networks and (micro-)institutionalist theory.

Dominic Richardson has recently been appointed to the UNICEF Office of Research as a Senior Education Specialist where he will be working on issues of equity in education and measurement of school outcomes. Previously, he worked in the OECD Social Policy Division on issues of child and family well-being. Dominic has been a contributor to UNICEF Innocenti Report Cards 7 and 9 on child well-being in rich countries, and recently completed projects at the OECD include an evaluative report of the efficiency and effectiveness of cash versus social service benefits for family and child outcomes.

Jay Wiggan is Lecturer in Social Policy and Administration in the School of Social and Political Science at the University of Edinburgh, UK. Jay's research interests include comparative analysis of public employment services and social security administration and the political economy of active labour market policy.

Fiona Williams is Emeritus Professor of Social Policy at the University of Leeds, UK and Honorary Professor in the Social Policy Research Centre at the University of New South Wales, Australia. Her recent research has been on migrant care workers. She has written widely on gender and ethnicity in social policy, and on a political ethic of care.

Introduction

Part One: Continuities and change in UK social policy

Zoë Irving

Traditionally, Part One of *Social Policy Review* draws together chapters concerned with the key 'pillars' of the welfare state. This edition follows this tradition in spirit, but with contributions that underscore both the continuities and change that shape these pillars. In Chapter One, Hannah Lambie-Mumford discusses an issue that, while central to any debate on human needs, and historically significant in the development of social assistance transfers, has been largely subsumed in wider analyses of poverty and social exclusion. The rapid emergence of 'food banks' and their usage has placed the existence of 'hunger' in the global North under a policy spotlight. Although not a UK-specific phenomenon, and not necessarily one that has only emerged in the post-2008 context, the rise of food banks in the UK has occurred in tandem with the austerity project pursued by the coalition government. Chapter One seeks to demonstrate how food banks and their charitable status are symptomatic of wider and longer-term developments in welfare state development, and represent both an immediate challenge to meeting needs, an ongoing challenge to the quest for 'joined-up' policy-making, as well as a disciplinary challenge to those engaged in social policy research.

Chapter Two considers another dimension of social policy that has been gradually buried under the recent avalanche of policy attention given to benefit recipients without work: the question of wage subsidies for those in work. Chris Grover's analysis highlights the shift in justification for the existence of subsidies for low wages, and the ideological anomalies they can be argued to represent. With a focus on the introduction of Universal Credit (UC) and its historical precedents, the discussion in this chapter reminds us that the question 'who benefits' remains core if we are to properly understand the complexities of contemporary social protection mechanisms and their relationship to labour market discipline. This is a particularly pressing concern given that the 'recovery' from the great recession is largely reliant on the expansion of precarious, part-time and low-paid work, that outside the voluntaristic notion of 'employment portfolios' is incapable of providing security. Chris Grover's chapter contrasts the goals and outcomes of UC with alternative avenues for achieving social security, notably the idea of the 'living wage', which currently has momentum but not yet traction.

The third chapter in this part directs attention to the place of 'housing' as an everyday practice within both the wider global process of financialisation and the neoliberal quest for a smaller state through the responsibilisation of individuals. The role of housing finance markets in the global economy (and its meltdown) is widely known, but in the post-financial crisis world the sociopolitical dimensions of being an asset-bearing citizen are as deeply significant as the economic. In this chapter, Stuart Lowe and Jed Meers outline the links between the macro economic and the 'everyday' through an assessment of the relationship between the global financial market and the place of housing equity in the support of welfare needs. Their discussion then focuses on developments in UK housing policy under the coalition government, specifically financial responsibilisation within social housing, the 'Bedroom Tax' and discretionary housing payments in particular. Their analysis draws attention to the varied use of financial imperatives in the reconfiguration of the welfare state, the greater insecurities produced, and the implications of these for the discipline of financial subjects.

The final chapter in this part represents a slightly different 'take' on the 'pillars' of the welfare state with examination of the current policy dilemmas of adult social care provision. Thanks to feminist contributors to scholarship over the last few decades, care has been firmly located at the core of social policy research and debate, but in more recent times, the macro concerns preoccupying many analysts in the post-crisis world have somewhat overshadowed the policy reform realities in day-to-day delivery of services. In the care sector, Cinderella has continued to toil at the mercy of less charming siblings – currently austerity measures and the science of muddling through. Jon Glasby's chapter presents a commentary, informed by direct involvement in the muddling through process, which outlines key areas of contention in contemporary adult social care services and their relationship to policy aims and implementation – some organised under previous Labour governments, and some emergent in the years since 2010. The chapter concludes that there is promise in some dimensions of reform in terms of moving towards a modernised system of care delivery, but that given the challenges inherent in matching increasing needs with diminishing resources, the scope for more radical solutions remains wide.

Part Two: Contributions from the Social Policy Association Conference 2014

Menno Fenger

The financial and economic crisis that has held Europe in its grip since 2008 has triggered a wide variety of austerity measures in welfare states throughout the world, including the UK. These measures have given rise to protests in many countries. In some cases, these protests have taken the shape of 'traditional' forms of resistance such as general strikes and demonstrations, usually closely linked to or organised by traditional institutions such as trade unions or political parties. In other cases, we can observe the emergence of new forms of resistance: more global, making extensive use of social media, and less organised and institutionalised. 'Resistance, Resilience and Radicalism' was the central theme of the 2014 Social Policy Association Annual Conference. This theme invites reflection on 'old' and 'new' forms of resistance and their impact on the transformation of social policies in in the UK and beyond.

Part Two begins with Chapter Five by Fiona Williams, which is based on her plenary lecture at the Annual Conference. She explores how the critical perspectives on social policies that have been developed in the 1970s and 1980s have further evolved. In its original shape, the key critique of social policies was that they were normatively constructed towards the needs of white, able-bodied, heterosexual, male breadwinning families as central welfare subjects. The critical perspective in the early days focused the attention on the representation and voice of individuals that do not fit within the normative role model that allegedly dominated the construction of social policies. In response to the neoliberal agenda of the 1990s, the critical perspective brought forward the importance of agency, identity and personal experiences of (potential) welfare recipients. It articulated that social policy concerns addressing the 'real' needs of 'real' people, rather than running an efficient managerial process. Finally, it is argued that in the 21st century the critical perspective focuses on the relational elements in social policies. It does not concern individuals as 'atomised subjects of an inexorable neoliberal capitalism, but of people who are connected to each other and to their environment'. Therefore, social policies might be considered as a common-pool resource, the sustainability of which depends on the interrelated actions of those people involved, including care providers and recipients. Contributing to the social commons is the main challenge for a critical perspective in the 21st century. This chapter clearly illustrates how radically not only social policy, but also its critical followers, have changed in the last decades: resistance and radicalism have not disappeared, but changed shape. This is also illustrated by the other contributions to this part.

Chapters Six and Seven both embrace a street-level perspective on the implementation of social policy, thereby bringing the personal experiences of welfare subjects to the foreground. In Chapter Six, Graham Bowpitt focuses on the relationship between re-offending and homelessness. His discussion centres on a prisoner rehabilitation project that combines planned post-release accommodation with intensive personal support. Through a series of qualitative in-depth interviews with released offenders and staff members, he provides insight into the needs of released offenders. His work suggests that without adequate shelter on release, prison itself feels like a 'safe' place to many, which leads to a 'nothing to risk' attitude in the further conduct of criminal offences. From his evaluation of this small-scale rehabilitation project, he distillates various conditions that are important for the successful prevention of re-offending: consistency of support through the prison gate; direct accompaniment both to pre-arranged accommodation and everything else needed to make it habitable; a day centre base; and the relationship between the offender and the support officer. In relation to the general theme of this section, Bowpitt underlines the importance of 'caring' in social policies and their delivery.

In Chapter Seven, Joe Greener reports from his participant observation experiences in a privatised elderly residential care home. The home in which he conducted his study was part of the Southern Cross Healthcare Group, one of Europe's largest private providers of elderly residential care which was forced to end its operations through financial problems in 2011. He explores the potential impact of privatisation on the delivery of day-to-day care services. In his chapter, Greener primarily shows how the managerial control of resident records leads to a gap between care delivered 'on paper' and care delivered 'in reality'. Supervision and quality control are reduced to the administration of resident records that represent demonstration of adequacy in the receipt of care. This leads to a strong pressure to have the records in order, when, as Greener shows, service delivery in reality was not in order at all: understaffing and, consequently, failing continence care and food assistance were all too common. By providing insights into the determinants of service quality, and in the way this quality is affected by processes of managerialism and privatisation, Greener portrays the challenges of balancing financial profits and high-quality care.

In the final chapter of Part Two, Jay Wiggan discusses the marketisation of employment services in Ireland. Whereas marketisation is sometimes considered as a general and uniform trend, Wiggan claims that the specificities of the way marketisation is implemented to a large extent determine its consequences. Many public services have been turned into quasi-markets rather than 'proper' markets. Wiggan concludes that in the Irish case, a so-called 'private power market' has been created in employment services, although the level of direction from the state is bigger than in some other cases of private power markets. In terms of maintaining the quality of service delivery, the Irish government has stipulated requirements for the interaction between the service provider and the client, thereby again illustrating the delicate balance between economic rationality and social goals in the current framework of welfare states.

Part Three: 25 years after *The three worlds of welfare capitalism*: a retrospective

John Hudson

Few texts can genuinely claim the mantle of 'ground breaking'. On the basis of the sheer number of citations it has gathered alone – some 20,759 at the start of 2015[1] – Esping-Andersen's 1990 book, *The three worlds of welfare capitalism*, must surely be one of them. The year 2015, of course, marks a quarter of a century since its publication, and the four chapters in this part mark this anniversary by offering a (mini) retrospective on the ongoing influence of the text on social policy scholarship.

It is tempting to deploy the line that a work of such prominence 'needs no introduction' in order to dodge the tricky task of summarising *The three worlds of welfare capitalism* in this introductory note. Such is the breadth of contemporary social policy scholarship, and the myriad of specialisms within it, that even ground-breaking texts may remain unfamiliar to at least some readers of *Social Policy Review*, in this instance, particularly so for those working outside the realm of comparative analysis. We therefore refrain from playing this card, and provide a brief summary.

A book does not garner 20,000+ citations, nor sustain a debate spanning a quarter of a century, without offering a rich set of arguments. While *The three worlds of welfare capitalism* is chiefly known for its claim that welfare systems in high-income countries centre around three ideal types, this typology rested on a fresh conceptualisation of the welfare state and innovation in the measurement of welfare state effort. In short, the book offered new insights into the classification, conceptualisation and measurement of welfare states.

With regard to the *conceptualisation* of welfare, Esping-Andersen built on core theoretical contributions to the field in order to suggest that welfare states – or welfare state regimes, as he then termed them – may be distinguished from each other according to how they operate in three key areas: the strength of social rights (or, more technically, the degree to which labour is decommodified); the impact on social stratification; and the roles allocated to the state, market and family in providing welfare.

In terms of *measurement*, Esping-Andersen (1990, p ix) somewhat ruefully noted in the preface that 'It may not show, but this is a book that stands on a veritable mountain of data and years of endless statistical manipulation.' Crucially, at a time when robust cross-national datasets covering social policy activity were thin on the ground, the book built on a mountain of newly assembled data too. The text eschewed dominant social expenditure measures of welfare state effort, arguing that they told us little about how money was spent. Instead, the text drew on a range of indicators concerning policy detail, including a bespoke 'decommodification index' – compiled via analysis of the detail of key social security benefits such as their payment rates, qualification rules and payment mechanisms – which permitted Esping-Andersen to rank countries on the strength of their social rights.

Finally, in terms of classification, the book proposed – as its title suggests – that three distinct welfare regimes could be found in the high-income countries: a social democratic regime (strong social rights, egalitarian, dominant role for state, Sweden the key example); a liberal regime (weak social rights, high inequality, dominant role for the market, the US the key example); and a conservative-corporatist regime (strong social rights, modest redistributional intent, strong role for family, Germany the key example).

Crucially, however, the book extended beyond offering a mere classification, providing a theoretical explanation for the development of the three clusters too. Rather than representing short-term ephemeral differences in policy choices, Esping-Andersen suggested that membership of a particular type was rooted in historical processes, and that each type represented a different path of welfare state development. Again, with a nod to earlier work in the field, he pointed to three key factors in explaining the variation in outcomes: the degree of working-class mobilisation; the extent of cross-class coalitions; and historical-institutional legacies. So, simplifying a huge deal: the presence of a strong church might be key in fostering a conservative/corporatist pathway; the absence of a strong working-class political movement might point towards a liberal pathway; and a strong working-class political movement able to forge cross-class alliances might point towards a social democratic pathway.

This potted summary of *The three worlds of welfare capitalism* naturally simplifies the core arguments hugely, but hopefully sets the scene for what is to follow in the chapters in this part. We should make clear at the outset that the retrospective does not seek to offer a comprehensive 'state-of-the-art' style review of studies that have followed in the wake of *The three worlds of welfare capitalism* (for such reviews, see Arts and Gellisen, 2002; Powell and Barrientos, 2011). Nor do we attempt to challenge the veracity of Esping-Andersen's thesis or challenge its status as a foundational text in (comparative) social policy analysis. While inevitably, after the passage of much time and such widespread debate, many valid criticisms have been made of the text and some important weaknesses identified, we approach the retrospective from the viewpoint that *The three worlds of welfare capitalism* is indeed a ground-breaking text and one that merits such a mantle. Instead, the aim here is to reflect on the ways in which the book has shaped the nature of debate in comparative social policy analysis over the past 25 years.

In the opening chapter to this part, Deborah Rice suggests that widespread adoption of Esping-Andersen's empirical typology has often resulted in sub-optimal usage of purely analytic ideal types in comparative research, not only because researchers often presume that his classification of actual countries can fruitfully be applied in a wide array of contexts, but also because it prevents them from developing their own potentially fruitful, purpose-specific, and theoretically rooted ideal types afresh. She makes the case for an alternative approach to the use of types in comparative social policy research.

Stefan Kühner's chapter takes as its point of departure Esping-Andersen's suggestion in *The three worlds of welfare capitalism* that expenditure-based measures of welfare state activity can be misleading. While Esping-Andersen broke new ground in the statistical analysis of welfare state effort in his text, he did not have the benefit of the wealth of data now available to social policy scholars specialising in cross-national analysis. Nor did he have data that was as timely as scholars tend to have nowadays: although published in 1990, *The three worlds* largely relied on data relating to 1980, and so predated many of the major socioeconomic pressures that have shaped social policy reform agendas in the past 25 years. Kühner explores whether the passage of time and explosion in data alter the best approaches for the measurement of welfare state activity. He notes that different measures of welfare state effort can produce significantly different findings, and that the arguments against using expenditure-based measures of welfare state effort may be less compelling now than in 1990. His analysis also suggests that regime-level analysis may risk missing important programme-level changes taking place in individual countries, and that more nuanced approaches that exploit the finer-grained data available today might be the best way forward.

Gyu-Jin Hwang's chapter explores the impact of *The three worlds of welfare capitalism* on a research agenda that has flourished in recent decades, but that was in its infancy in 1990: social policy in East Asia. One of the earliest critiques of *The three worlds of welfare capitalism* came from scholars arguing it omitted consideration of a distinctive fourth world of welfare found in East Asia. As Hwang notes, a considerable amount of energy has been expended since then, debating whether a distinctive fourth world exists, what such a world might look like, and whether the countries in the region have similar social policy frameworks in practice. While much important scholarship has addressed these questions, Hwang asks whether the focus on the 'fourth world' question has ultimately served to displace the arguably more important task of understanding how and why specific welfare state frameworks have developed in the region.

Finally, Dominic Richardson's chapter approaches the legacy of *The three worlds of welfare capitalism* from a policy-maker perspective, reflecting on the ways in which a key agency for the distribution of international data and its analysis, the Organisation for Economic Co-operation and Development (OECD), has made use of regime typologies in its cross-national social policy work. The bottom line here is that the typologies have not had the same impact in policy-making circles as in academic ones, and indeed, that classification of countries into social policy types has been rare in the OECD's work. He suggests that the level of data available today opens the potential for policy-relevant ideal types to be used in policy work. However, echoing the earlier chapter by Rice, he also suggests these types need to be constructed afresh for each study, and be viewed as dynamic rather than fixed if they are to appeal to policy-makers keen to identify areas of policy that might benefit from reform.

This retrospective will be by no means the only one devoted to *The three worlds of welfare capitalism* this year, and it seems right that there should be considered reflection on the impact of a text of such import. Taken together, what might be the key messages to take home from the collection of chapters here?

Perhaps the first is that *The three worlds of welfare capitalism* continues to influence contemporary debate in comparative social policy analysis in many fruitful directions. Indeed, we can probably take this as a given, the text still gathering hundreds of citations in 2014 alone.[2] However, a second key message may be that the strong focus on Esping-Andersen's trichotomous classification of welfare types has often squeezed other potentially productive agendas in comparative social policy research. Physicists suggest the creation of a supernova is accompanied by the creation of a black hole, with a gravitational pull that overwhelms other forces to such a degree it prevents all other objects from escaping. Might the 'stellar black hole' be a metaphor for the impact of *The three worlds of welfare capitalism* on comparative welfare state scholarship? Has it shone so brightly that darkness has been inadvertently cast over other important agendas that the academy might have pursued more deeply than has been the case? The chapters presented here indicate that this may be the case in particular with respect to the *classification* element of its argument: always only one element of *The three worlds of welfare capitalism*, but the aspect that appears to have been taken forward with the greatest fervour.

This ties to the third and final key message, which is that the chapters in the retrospective invite us to look beyond the 'three worlds' element of *The three worlds of welfare capitalism* and, in essence, to revisit the analytic approach presented in the text itself. That is, to continue to seek afresh the best ways to conceptualise, measure, classify and theorise welfare systems from a comparative perspective. In some ways, the chapters are an invitation to read more deeply into the arguments of the book as a whole: to go beyond the headline argument captured in the book's title. Indeed, perhaps the greatest testament to the enduring value of *The three worlds of welfare capitalism* some quarter of a century on is that, even for those who have read it numerous times, it still holds the capacity to stimulate, inform and generate new ideas on each re-reading.

References

Arts, W. and Gelissen, J. (2002) 'Three worlds of welfare capitalism or more? A state-of-the-art report', *Journal of European Social Policy*, vol 12, no 2, pp 137-58.

Esping-Andersen, G. (1990) *The three worlds of welfare capitalism*, Cambridge: Polity Press.

Powell, M. and Barrientos, A. (2011) 'An audit of the welfare modelling business', *Social Policy & Administration*, vol 45, no 1, pp 69-84.

Notes

[1] According to Google Scholar, 3 January 2015.

[2] According to Google Scholar, 3 January 2015.

Part One

Continuities and change in UK social policy

Part One

ONE

Britain's hunger crisis: where's the social policy?

Hannah Lambie-Mumford

Introduction

The issue of hunger, whether referred to as such or in related terms such as 'food poverty' or 'food insecurity', has remained largely on the periphery of social policy research in the UK despite notable interjections (Joffe, 1991; Dowler, 2002). In so far as the experience of limited access to food is addressed, it is often done so within the context of wider poverty research, rather than as a site of investigation in and of itself. Yet, what we have seen in the UK since 2010 in particular is the increasingly high public and political profile of the issue, manifest in the rise in the number of people attending charitable food bank projects for help with food. The nature of hunger in the UK today, and the 'food bank phenomenon', raise particular questions both of and for social policy, including how social policies themselves have affected these experiences, and the role social policies and social policy research could have in shaping progressive ways forward.

This chapter presents a case for rethinking hunger in relation to the current and future welfare state and the role social policy analysis and research could play. Its premise lies in evidence suggesting that people are finding it harder to eat well in the so-called 'era of austerity', and the fact that the main response to this is through the provision of emergency food parcels by charities, outwith the state. Recently published Poverty and Social Exclusion (PSE) survey data reveal that in 2011, 4 million adults could not afford 'food basics', with 3 per cent of adults not able to afford two meals a day (up from less than 1 per cent in 1999) and 7 per cent not able to afford fresh fruit and vegetables (PSE, 2012). Other surveys and research also indicate that people have been finding it more difficult to access food since the turn of the decade (Save the Children, 2012; Shelter, 2013). The key drivers of the shifting nature of hunger lie in the fact that wages and social security incomes have been growing at a slower pace relative to costs of living, including housing, food and fuel (Davis et al, 2014; Padley and Hirsch, 2014; see also Dowler and Lambie-Mumford, 2015). This has been putting considerable pressure on household budgets, and evidence tells us that households have been changing their shopping and eating habits, trading down or eating less in response (Save the Children, 2012; Defra, 2014). At the same time, we have seen a rise of food banks as a charitable response. Drawing on the national Trussell Trust Foodbank Network in particular, these initiatives have proliferated since their establishment at the beginning of the 2000s.[1] The growth of this network has been especially marked in recent years, with the largest growth in number of food bank projects between 2011/12 and 2012/13 (with 221 projects established in that time) and numbers of parcels provided rising particularly sharply, by 566,146 between 2012/13 and 2013/14 (The Trussell Trust, no date, b). These projects are not-for-profit charitable initiatives for people experiencing an income crisis, which provide people with free parcels of food to take away, prepare and eat.

The rise of food banks has captured significant attention in the media and among politicians: 2012 was declared by a prominent columnist in *The Guardian* to be the 'year of the food bank' (Moore, 2012; The Trussell Trust, no date, a); in December 2013 the first parliamentary debate on food banks was held (*Hansard*, 2013); and in February 2013 the Department for Environment, Food and Rural Affairs (Defra) commissioned a review of food aid in response to increasing numbers of parliamentary questions and widespread reporting of the rising rates of people turning to food aid (Lambie-Mumford et al, 2014). In 2013, an All-Party Parliamentary Group (APPG) on Hunger and Food Poverty was established, and in 2014 it commissioned a Parliamentary Inquiry into Hunger and Food Poverty in Britain which reported in December 2014 (Food Poverty Inquiry, 2014b; Register of All-Party Groups, 2014). The nature of the political reaction to this growth is interesting to note because on the one hand, the rise of food banks has been said to represent the success of the Conservative Party's 'big society' (Cabinet Office, 2010) policy and to embody calls for more responsibility to be held in local communities; on the other hand, the rise in numbers visiting food banks is attributed to socioeconomic failures, unmanageable increases in the cost of living and ultimately a wider growing 'hunger' problem (Conservative Home, 2012; Butler, 2014).

This chapter explores hunger as a key issue in contemporary social policy research. It argues that not only is the relationship between food and poverty an important site for social policy investigation in and of itself, but that the relationship between charitable food banks and the welfare state is particularly important to understand because it embodies wider shifts in the welfare state, including retrenched social security provision and increasingly mixed economies of welfare. The chapter progresses from here in four parts. First, it explores what hunger is in the UK, and how it has changed since the financial crisis of the mid-2000s. Second, it explores the lack of policy ownership of the hunger 'problem' and how this works to hinder the realisation of progressive solutions. Third, the response of food banks to rising levels of hunger is discussed, and the ways in which this non-state response is a consequence of a longer trajectory of changes in welfare provision including diversification and retrenchment. Finally, the chapter looks to progressive ways forward in the face of this rising hunger, and argues that developing solutions in terms of the *human right to food* (see Riches, 2011) could be particularly productive, as this provides a framework for progressive policies that facilitate action by all stakeholders – government, civil society and the food industry – towards the progressive realisation of the human right to food for all in the UK.

Hunger and food poverty in times of austerity

A key problem in exploring and arriving at a better understanding of limited access to food in the UK is the fact that terminology and conceptualisation are not well established or widely understood. The terms of reference of the parliamentary inquiry into hunger and food poverty in Britain, which was launched in April 2014, illustrate this fact well. The words 'hunger', 'food poverty' and 'household food security' are all used in these 'terms of reference' without corresponding definitions or authoritative use of one particular term over the others (Food Poverty Inquiry, 2014a). Such differing terminology can cause confusion, but what this vocabulary has in common is reference to how well people are able to eat and participate in the socially accepted food culture within the means available to them.

This chapter adopts a conceptualisation of 'food poverty' to frame the analytical discussion. Food poverty has been chosen over hunger because, like malnourishment or nutrition insecurity, hunger is a concept often tied up with physical, biological states, and given the importance of social dynamics and processes inherent within the experience under study, food poverty is favoured instead. The food poverty concept highlights the importance of examining food experiences broadly defined, and incorporates the role of food in social interactions and holistic lived experiences. People's ability to access adequate, appropriate food and socially acceptable food experiences are at the heart of 'food poverty' (Riches, 1997; Dowler et al, 2001; Lang et al, 2010). Food experiences as a whole, as opposed to specific dietary intakes or the composition of shopping baskets, are the focus with an emphasis placed on minimally acceptable *food experiences*, not minimum *diets*. Such a conceptualisation recognises the important ways in which food facilitates or prevents social interaction at numerous life stages and in various social settings. It also draws attention to issues of social acceptability in relation to both the types of food acquired and consumed, and the acceptability of the methods of that acquisition – for example, shopping for food (Dowler et al, 2001).

This conceptualisation mirrors contemporary poverty research more generally, which incorporates notions of acceptable standards of living and experiences of social exclusion (Gordon and Pantazis, 1997; Gordon et al, 2000; PSE, 2012). Like poverty, food poverty is a dynamic concept, a lived experience which importantly can be 'defined objectively and applied consistently' in relative terms (Townsend, 1979, p 31). Historically, UK social policy research has addressed hunger as one element, albeit an important one, in the definition, measurement and lived experience of poverty. Having the resources to access a customary diet was at the forefront of Townsend's 1979 definition of poverty (Townsend, 1979, p 31), and questions relating to types of diet and food experiences (such as being able to invite friends or family over for a meal) are established measures in surveys such as Breadline Britain and the PSE survey (Gordon and Pantazis, 1997; Gordon et al, 2000; PSE, 2012). Importantly, these surveys measure food experiences as much more than minimum diet and nutritional intake, incorporating the facilitative social dynamics embodied in food experiences such as sharing food with others, reciprocating food-based activities and eating similarly to others – in other words, being able to take an active part in a socially embedded food culture.

In arriving at a definition of food poverty from this broader conceptualisation, the chapter draws on that provided by Dowler et al (2001, p 2):

> The inability to acquire or consume an adequate quality or sufficient quantity of food in socially acceptable ways, or the uncertainty that one will be able to do so.

This definition provides the opportunity to study not only the different dimensions of food poverty (access, availability and social acceptability, for example), but also notions of scales of severity such as mild, moderate and acute experiences. The latter aspect is particularly important here given the emphasis placed on 'crisis' experiences by food bank providers, with food bank provision being designed to assist people experiencing acute crises (Lambie, 2011). Adopting a broader definition and conceptualisation of food poverty therefore enables these acute crisis experiences to be placed on a wider experiential context, opening up policy and research discussion over issues of prevention, not just alleviation.

Of particular relevance to social policy research is evidence relating to experiences of food poverty and hunger which draw attention to structural determinants (see Dowler, 2002; Hitchman et al, 2002; Caraher, 2008). In particular, structures influencing household income, food prices, housing (including the adequacy of food storage and cooking facilities) and retail and transport infrastructure have been identified in this part of the food poverty literature as playing an important role in determining the physical and economic accessibility of adequate food experiences. These structures have been found to each influence different aspects of food poverty, determining: what kinds of foods are available from where (and at what cost); how these outlets can be accessed by transport; and whether people have enough money to afford this transport and the food available and how easily they can keep and prepare food when they get home.

While this structural interpretation is prominent in food poverty research, practitioner and policy responses have tended to focus instead on behavioural interventions, concerned with whether people are budgeting, shopping and cooking well enough (Dowler and Caraher, 2003, p 59; Caraher, 2008, p 4). This behavioural approach is powerful in policy discourse, and has found special favour in much community-based health work promoting healthy eating, despite limited evidence of its effectiveness (DH, 2005; Dowler, 2008).

Importantly, when looking at these structural determinants of food poverty and how they have changed over time (especially income levels and income security, food prices and transport costs), evidence suggests that circumstances have worsened in the last few years (see Hirsch, 2013). Relative to wages and benefit levels, prices have risen, and access to services and other forms of publicly funded support have been restricted as a result of public finance austerity. This, together with evidence which suggests that when under financial pressure households will cut back on food budgets, perceived to be the most flexible element of household spending (Dowler, 1997; Hossain et al, 2011; Goode, 2012), means that the nature of food poverty is likely to have changed for the worse over recent years.

Statistics produced by Defra (2014, p 20) highlight that falling income and rising costs of living, including rising food prices, have meant that food is now over 20 per cent less affordable for those living in the lowest income decile in the UK compared to 2003. Recent work by Hossain et al (2011, p 5) highlights that during the recession, households were shopping and cooking differently to reduce expenditure, and increasingly relying on social networks for support. A survey commissioned by the national housing charity, Shelter (2013), found that in the year leading up to the survey, 31 per cent of the 4,000 respondents had cut back on food in order to meet housing costs. Minimum Income Standards research is also particularly helpful here and highlights the issue of current income *in*adequacies in terms of minimum wages and benefit levels in particular (Davis et al, 2014; Padley and Hirsch 2014). According to Padley and Hirsch (2014), the recession has 'created additional hardship' in particular for young people, single people and those living in privately rented accommodation. In 2012, a report by Save the Children (2012, p 4) found that 60.8 per cent of families surveyed with incomes up to £16,999 were cutting back on how much they spent on food, 39.1 per cent were eating less fruit and vegetables, and 25.5 per cent were serving smaller portions.

When we look at the nature of income crises leading to food bank use it appears that there has also been an increase in vulnerability to these shocks in the last few years. Impacts of reduced or insecure incomes and problems associated with social security appear to be leaving increasing numbers of people without income or with a reduced level of income, leading to food bank uptake (Lambie-Mumford, 2014; Lambie-Mumford and Dowler, 2014). In particular, delays in benefit payments, sanctions, problems with disability benefits and tax credit payments are reported as key triggers of food bank use (see Perry et al, 2014).

This body of evidence indicates that food poverty has worsened over the so-called 'age of austerity', with the effects of lagging incomes relative to other costs of living forcing households to cut back or trade down on the food they purchase and eat. Moreover, the situation appears to have worsened across the scale of severity, with acute experiences of food poverty, induced by income crises, also increasing particularly in the context of welfare reform.

Policy neglect of food poverty

As the nature and extent of food poverty changes in the UK, the question of the role of policy becomes more urgent. As food poverty has risen in visibility, there has been a considerable level of political reaction in the form of parliamentary debates, comments to the media and most significantly, the parliamentary inquiry (Wallop, 2009; *Hansard*, 2013; Food Poverty Inquiry, 2014a), but as yet, there has been little tangible policy response in the shape of targeted interventions or strategies. This policy void occurs in the context of a general lack of policy ownership of the issue of food poverty. Traditionally in the UK, approaches to ensuring everyone has access to healthy food has been left to the operation of efficient markets in retail and employment, appropriate consumer choice and a social welfare system which is meant to enable those lacking employment to be able to purchase food (Dowler et al, 2011). However, the evidence of rising food poverty and increasing numbers of people turning to charitable food sources questions the efficacy of these mechanisms in protecting people from hunger, and, moreover, suggests that they may ultimately have failed.

Responsibility for household-level 'food security' is currently situated within the remit of Defra (Defra, 2006).[2] However, the notion of food security has only relatively recently been applied by policy makers to the household level in the UK, with the development of limited indicators in the late 2000s (MacMillan and Dowler, 2011). While the issue of household access to food is located formally within Defra's remit, it nonetheless intersects with areas of responsibility in other Whitehall departments, therefore opening up the possibility of cross-Whitehall commitment and working. For example, food poverty relates to the work of the Department for Work and Pensions (DWP) on social security levels and tax credits; the Department of Health's (DH) work on the consequences of poor diet on health; and community access to adequate shops as part of the Department for Communities and Local Government's (DCLG) role in planning guidelines. Despite these intersections, there has been little formal engagement with developing cross-governmental approaches to addressing the structural root causes of food poverty to date.

The lack of a definition and measurement of food poverty is also likely to be hindering more effective policy ownership and action. Without embracing a conceptualisation and subsequent definition, as outlined above, which clearly identifies drivers and determinants – and therefore possibilities for cross-government policy interventions – the issue will continue to be seen as one for markets and policies related to shoring up imports and food supply. Second, there is currently no measurement of hunger, and therefore no clear idea of how many people are experiencing it now or may be vulnerable to it in the future, making effective preventive and protective responses difficult to identify. Both defining and measuring the food poverty policy problem will be critical to establishing a policy framework that facilitates effective interventions.

A rights-based approach to food (see Riches, 2011; Dowler and O'Connor, 2012; Lambie-Mumford, 2013) could provide an important blueprint for progressive ways forward, prioritising, as it does, policy responses and the involvement of all stakeholders in pursuing socially acceptable and appropriate food experiences for all. In terms of the human right to food, states are duty bearers, and have the obligations of respecting, protecting and fulfilling the right to food (UNESC, 1999). There is a clear proactive role set out for governments in progressively realising this right, and they are also required to 'provide an environment that facilitates implementation' of the responsibilities of other actors, including the private and civil society sectors (UNESC, 1999). Policy frameworks built to ensure that the right to food is realised – established through legal and institutional frameworks and the implementation of a national right to food strategy (De Shutter, 2010) – would be a particularly helpful way forward in the context of the UK's food poverty policy void.

Food bank response

Within this policy void, and set against the backdrop of recession, austerity and welfare reform, a particular response to hunger has gained dominance – the food bank. The group of charitable initiatives now popularly referred to as food banks, are projects where people in need (usually defined as being in some kind of acute income crisis) can collect a parcel of emergency food to take away, prepare and eat (Lambie-Mumford et al, 2014). These projects fit within a broader category the UK government has termed 'food aid', which refers to a range of different types of short-term assistance with food, beyond the provision of food parcels, to include, among others, onsite and home-based meal provision (see Lambie-Mumford and Dowler, 2014).

While local projects that help people meet food needs in various ways have long been in existence (McGlone et al, 1999), the growth of the food bank response in particular to contemporary hunger in the UK has been especially notable since 2010. This growth has included the proliferation of one particular national network of food banking projects – The Trussell Trust Foodbank Network. This is a network of not-for-profit 'foodbank' franchises that operate in local communities across the UK (including Scotland, Wales and Northern Ireland). After an initial foodbank was set up in Salisbury in 2000, the first franchise was opened in Gloucester in 2004 (Lambie, 2011). Since then, the network has grown substantially to 58 projects helping 61,468 people in 2010/11, and to 405 projects helping 913,138 people in 2013/14 (The Trussell Trust, no date, b). While independent food bank initiatives do exist across the country, there is, as yet, no systematic research into the number of these projects, making The Trussell Trust Foodbank Network an instructive case study.

The food bank response has, to date, been characterised by its charitable nature – situated outwith the state. However, the charitable food bank response has been defined and influenced in important ways by the state and what it provides in terms of poverty prevention and alleviation. Both the contemporary experience of food poverty and the food bank response are a result of wider shifts in social policy in recent decades (especially since the mid-2000s) and the changing nature of the welfare state, in particular, changes in what the state provides in welfare (through services and social security) and the changing role and shape of the voluntary and community sector (VCS).

While there has been a long trajectory of evolving welfare policies, shifts seen since the 1990s have been especially formative, giving rise to a leaner, more conditioned welfare state (see Ellison and Fenger, 2013). Farnsworth and Irving (2011, p1) have described the most recent period of change in welfare policy as the 'age of austerity'. As a defining era of welfare state development, 2010 marked the end of 13 years of New Labour governments and the arrival of a Conservative-led coalition government (in coalition with the Liberal Democrat Party). Coming into government in the wake of the economic crash of the mid-2000s and in the middle of a recession, the government introduced stringent austerity measures including some of the largest cuts in public finance ever seen, and some of the most extensive welfare reforms since the introduction of the welfare state (see Taylor-Gooby and Stoker, 2011; Beatty and Fothergill, 2013).

Reforms to welfare processes and entitlements have affected the need for food banks in several ways (see Lambie-Mumford, 2014; Lambie-Mumford and Dowler, 2014; Perry et al, 2014). Changes to levels of entitlements such as capping benefit income and introducing conditions on the size of housing for which people can claim support (often referred to as the 'Bedroom Tax') have reduced incomes overall. But at the same time, and significantly, processes including benefit sanctions and administrative delays in payments are leaving people without any income at all – factors which have been identified as key triggers to food bank use (Perry et al, 2014).[3] Public spending cuts to services are also associated with the need for food banks. There have been extensive spending cuts since 2010 which, even in 2011, meant that practitioners were referring people to food banks where before they may have had discretionary funds for social assistance – for example, cash to buy food or fuel (see Lambie, 2011; Lambie-Mumford, 2013).

Other factors in the changing welfare state have also influenced the nature of the response in the form of charitable food banks. Over the last 17 years, welfare diversification under successive New Labour governments, and more recently coalition government 'Big Society' policies, have resulted in the professionalisation and expansion of the role of the voluntary sector (see Alcock, 2010). This has meant that both the nature of voluntary organisations and the expectations that government and society has of them has changed. These organisations are increasingly professional and business-like, and there are increased expectations that the voluntary sector will meet needs in local communities where the state may not. Charitable food banking in the form of The Trussell Trust Foodbank Network is an embodiment of this: operating as a not-for-profit franchise and assuming increasing amounts of responsibility for alleviating hunger in the absence of adequate state-based responses. Overall, the changing dynamics of hunger and the rise of a charitable response to it appear to be influenced in important ways by wider shifts in social policy. Experiences of hunger are being shaped by the pulling back of state social security, and civil society – in the form of food banks – is increasingly assuming responsibility for responding to crisis needs in the absence of adequate state support.

The proliferation of food banks as a response to crisis experiences of food poverty present a number of issues of concern for social policy research, especially when drawing on a human rights-based perspective. In the first place, food charity is not a population-wide response and also, critically, is not an entitlement. There are also issues of the accessibility to this provision in relation to both how access to food charity is managed (for example, whether people have to be referred), thresholds of need and qualifying criteria, and the accessibility of charitable provision when access is granted (location, opening times and limitations on usage). Critically, charitable food banking initiatives and other emergency food projects like them are – necessarily, given their capacity – only able to provide relief from the symptoms of food poverty, not to address the underlying drivers (see Lambie-Mumford et al, 2014).

These issues raise important questions relating to how to adequately protect people from food poverty when it occurs, and what kind of policies and provisions are required to do that effectively and universally. At the same time, however, we must also look at what progressive and appropriate *prevention* looks like – alongside this focus on alleviation. These are issues that stretch beyond the UK, however, as across Europe there is a similar growth of emergency food initiatives that is raising questions about the adequacy of social policy provision (Food Poverty Inquiry, 2014c; Nielsen et al, 2015).

Where next for addressing food poverty in the UK

In the face of the changing dynamics of contemporary food poverty and the rise of the charitable food banking response, three key actions will be required: agreeing a definition of the policy 'problem'; initiating a systematic measurement of food poverty; and focusing on food poverty prevention through developing a clear framework for progressive solutions. In the first instance, the lack of an effective and agreed upon conceptualisation and definition of the problem of food poverty is highly problematic, making it difficult for social policy researchers and policy-makers to engage with the topic. A key question for social policy in particular relates to the utility of separating 'food poverty' from the wider experience of poverty. Framing the issue specifically as one of 'food poverty' could, on the one hand, serve to describe a particularly complex policy problem, and could represent an acknowledgement of the numerous stakeholders and sectors involved in its resolution, from the food industry to the voluntary sector, and from social security policy to retail planning policy. Conceptualised this way, 'food poverty' could become an identifiably important site for social policy investigation, where social, economic and food-related policies converge and are manifest in a particular experience of exclusion. On the other hand, however, separating food poverty out from broader poverty research could potentially have the opposite effect, serving to create a food silo where the problem is framed as one of a lack of food, to be solved by the provision of food (Tarasuk, 2001) and in doing so, these complexities overlooked.

The lack of systematic data relating to food poverty is also problematic for both researchers and policy-makers. Not knowing how many people experience food poverty and the kind of households that are particularly vulnerable to it hinders policy-makers' and researchers' ability to assess what the most effective responses might look like. In the absence of available statistics relating to levels of hunger, the numbers of people accessing food banks are increasingly being used as a proxy measure. This is problematic for several key reasons: these numbers only account for those visiting projects, not those in equal need who did not or could not access such provision; and a cumulative figure cannot account for repeat visits, so cannot show how many individuals were helped or the extent of unmet need where the number of visits to a single provider is limited (see Lambie-Mumford and Dowler, 2014). Moreover, where need is defined as 'crisis' or 'acute' food poverty, food bank statistics also do not take account of people experiencing mild or moderate food poverty, and in doing so, can draw attention away from the broader structural determinants of these experiences, inhibiting more preventative-focused responses. But what hunger measures would be, and the validity of different methods of measurement, remains open for discussion and requires further detailed debate. Within the context of the global debate on how best to measure hunger, including the merits of objective nutrient-based measures versus more subjective, experience-based measures (Webb et al, 2006), some countries in the global North have adopted measures (of food insecurity) which capture the subjective lived experience of hunger (see, for example, Bickel et al, 2000). Capturing the subjective aspects of the food poverty experience would be particularly important for a UK-based measure as this provides a richer understanding of the experience and its specific determinants.

Definitions and measurements are necessary pre-requisites to determining what effective responses and solutions will look like. When building policy responses, however, whether or not they come from social policy specifically, a focus on prevention is required. The conceptualisation of food poverty outlined in this chapter has highlighted that socially acceptable food experiences – including, but not exclusively related to, nutritional intake – are of principal concern. Preventative measures are therefore required to ensure the active participation of all in socially acceptable food experiences. Structural factors are key determinants of food poverty, including income levels, housing, retail and transport infrastructure (Caraher et al, 1998; Dowler et al, 2001; Hitchman et al, 2002). Preventative measures will therefore involve ensuring that incomes are adequate, that food is made available to all at affordable prices through retail, and that transport to shops is accessible and affordable.

Framing responses in terms of the human right to food could enable progressive, prevention-focused approaches to overcoming food poverty in the UK. The human right to food was ratified in the mid-1970s by the UK as part of the International Covenant on Economic, Social and Cultural Rights (ICESCR) (UN, 2014). While the role and responsibilities of other stakeholders are acknowledged, the state is still seen as the duty-bearer for the progressive realisation of the right (UNESC, 1999). Operationalising the right to food in the UK would require establishing legal and institutional frameworks and the implementation of a national right to food strategy (De Schutter, 2010). These processes would involve a review of current legislation and policy initiatives relating to access to food, the development of programmes for intervention in all aspects of the food system (including production, distribution and consumption), and a focus on anti-poverty agendas that specifically look at access to food.

Conclusion

The issue of food poverty is increasingly visible and urgent in the UK today. Evidence suggests that experiences of food poverty have worsened as incomes, for those both in and out of work, have lagged behind rising costs of living. This indicates that when faced with wider sociopolitical and economic shifts having an impact on household incomes and expenditures, traditional hands-off policy approaches to food poverty, relying on markets to regulate the affordability and economic accessibility of food, are not adequate.

Social policy specifically has played and will continue to play a significant role in shaping experiences of food poverty and the responses to it in the UK. The retrenchment and reimagining of welfare in the recent 'age of austerity' has played an important part in determining the need for and the shape of the charity food bank response, particularly in terms of increasingly conditioned and reduced social security entitlements, and through greater expectation on voluntary and charitable initiatives to respond to community needs.

While there is a lack of policy ownership over the issue of food poverty in social policy terms, social policy research could be at the forefront of informing more progressive policy responses and ways towards addressing the structural determinants of these experiences. This could start with work towards a definitive definition of food poverty, initiating a regular national measurement of food poverty and focusing on human rights-based approaches to frame policy responses focused on both effective prevention and alleviation of food poverty.

Notes

[1] 'Foodbank' is the name of The Trussell Trust project. The term 'food bank' refers to the wider group of similar projects that provide food for people to take away, prepare, cook and eat at home.

[2] Defra (2009, p 6) defined food security as 'ensuring the availability of, and access to, affordable, safe and nutritious food sufficient for an active lifestyle, for all, at all times.'

[3] Sanctions are reductions in the amount of social security payments for set periods of time 'as a result of a failure to comply with prescribed requirements' (Gov.uk, 2014).

References

Alcock, P. (2010) *Partnership and mainstreaming: Voluntary action under New Labour*, Working Paper 32, Birmingham: Third Sector Research Centre, University of Birmingham (www.birmingham.ac.uk/generic/tsrc/documents/tsrc/working-papers/working-paper-32.pdf).

Beatty, C. and Fothergill, S. (2013) *Hitting the poorest places hardest: The local and regional impact of welfare reform*, Sheffield: Centre for Regional Economic and Social Research, Sheffield Hallam University (www.shu.ac.uk/research/cresr/sites/shu.ac.uk/files/hitting-poorest-places-hardest_0.pdf).

Bickel, G., Nord, M., Price, C., Hamilton, W. and Cook, H. (2000) *Guide to measuring household food security*, Alexandria, VA: US Department of Agriculture, Food and Nutrition Service (www.fns.usda.gov/fsec/files/fsguide.pdf).

Butler, P. (2014) 'Hunger is a "national crisis", religious leaders tell Cameron', *The Guardian*, 16 April (www.theguardian.com/society/2014/apr/16/million-people-britain-food-banks-religious-leaders-faith-groups).

Cabinet Office (2010) *Building the Big Society*, London: Cabinet Office (www.gov.uk/government/publications/building-the-big-society).

Caraher, M., Dixon, P. and Lang, T. (1998) 'Access to healthy foods: part 1. Barriers to accessing healthy foods: differentials by gender, social class, income and mode of transport', *Health Education Journal*, vol 57, pp 191–201.

Caraher, M. (2008) 'Food and health promotion: lessons from the field', *Health Education Journal*, vol 67, no 1, pp 3–8.

Conservative Home (2012) 'Food banks ARE part of the Big Society – but the problem they are tackling is not new', 19 December (www.conservativehome.com/localgovernment/2012/12/council-should-encourage-food-banks.html).

Davis, A., Hirsch, D. and Padley, M. (2014) *A Minimum Income Standard for the UK in 2014*, York: Joseph Rowntree Foundation.

Defra (Department for Environment, Food and Rural Affairs) (2006) *Food security and the UK: An evidence and analysis paper*, London: Defra (http://archive.defra.gov.uk/evidence/economics/foodfarm/reports/documents/foodsecurity.pdf).

Defra (2009) *UK food security assessment: Our approach*, Defra: London (http://archive.defra.gov.uk/foodfarm/food/pdf/food-assess-approach-0908.pdf).

Defra (2014) *Food statistics pocket book: In year update*, London: Defra (www.gov.uk/government/uploads/system/uploads/attachment_data/file/307106/foodpocketbook-2013update-29apr14.pdf).

De Schutter, O. (2010) 'Countries tackling hunger with a right to food approach', Briefing note 01, May 2010 (http://www2.ohchr.org/english/issues/food/docs/Briefing_Note_01_May_2010_EN.pdf).

DH (Department of Health) (2005) *Choosing a better diet: A food and health action plan*, London: DH.

Dowler, E. (1997) 'Budgeting for food on a low income: the case of lone parents', *Food Policy*, vol 22, no 5, pp 405-17.

Dowler, E. (2002) 'Food and poverty in Britain: rights and responsibilities', *Social Policy & Administration*, vol 36, no 6, pp 698-717.

Dowler, E. (2008) 'Food and health inequalities: the challenge for sustaining just consumption', *Local Environment*, vol 13, no 8, pp 759-72.

Dowler, E. and Caraher, M. (2003) 'Local food projects: the new philanthropy?', *Political Quarterly*, vol 74, no 1, pp 57-65.

Dowler, E. and Lambie-Mumford, H. (2015) 'How can households eat in austerity? Challenges for social policy in the UK', *Social Policy and Society*, doi:10.1017/S1474746415000032.

Dowler, E. and O'Connor, D. (2012) 'Rights-based approaches to addressing food poverty and food insecurity in Ireland and UK', *Social Science & Medicine*, vol 74, pp 44-51.

Dowler, E., Turner, S. and Dobson, B. (2001) *Poverty bites: Food, health and poor families*, London: Child Poverty Action Group.

Dowler, E., Kneafsey, M., Lambie, H., Inman, A. and Collier, R. (2011) 'Thinking about "food security": engaging with UK consumers', *Critical Public Health*, vol 21, no 4, pp 403-16.

Ellison, M. and Fenger, M. (2013) 'Social investment, protection and inequality in the new economy and politics of welfare in Europe', *Social Policy and Society*, vol 12, no 4, pp 611-24.

FAO (Food and Agriculture Organisation) (2005) *Voluntary guidelines to support the progressive realisations of the right to adequate food in the context of national food security*, Rome: FAO (ftp://ftp.fao.org/docrep/fao/009/y7937e/y7937e00.pdf).

Farnsworth, K. and Irving, Z. (2011) 'Varieties of crisis', in K. Farnsworth and Z. Irving (eds) *Social policy and challenging times: Economic crisis and welfare systems*, Bristol: Policy Press, pp 1-30.

Food Poverty Inquiry (2014a) 'Terms of reference' (http://foodpovertyinquiry.org/terms-of-reference/).

Food Poverty Inquiry (2014b) *Feeding Britain: A strategy for zero hunger in England, Wales, Scotland and Northern Ireland. The report of the All-Party Parliamentary Inquiry*, The Children's Society.

Food Poverty Inquiry (2014c) *An evidence review for the All-Party Parliamentary Inquiry into Hunger in the United Kingdom*, The Children's Society.

Goode, J. (2012) 'Feeding the family when then the wolf's at the door: the impact of over-indebtedness on contemporary foodways in low-income families in the UK', *Food and Foodways: Explorations in the History and Culture of Human Nourishment*, vol 20, no 1, pp 8-30.

Gordon, D. and Pantazis, C. (1997) *Breadline Britain in the 1990s*, Bristol: Summerleaze House Books (www.poverty.ac.uk/sites/default/files/attachments/Breadline%20Britain%20in%20the%201990s%20%28Gordon%20%20Pantazis%201997%29_0.pdf).

Gordon, D., Levitas, R., Pantazis, C., Patsios, D., Payne, S., Townsend, P., Adelman, L., Ashworth, K., Middleton, S., Bradshaw, J. and Williams, J. (2000) *Poverty and social exclusion in Britain*, York: Joseph Rowntree Foundation (www.jrf.org.uk/sites/files/jrf/185935128x.pdf).

Gov.uk (2014) 'Chapter 34 – JSA sanctions', vol 6, Amendment 39, February (www.gov.uk/government/uploads/system/uploads/attachment_data/file/373189/dmgch34.pdf).

Hansard (2013) 'Food banks' debate (www.publications.parliament.uk/pa/cm201314/cmhansrd/cm131218/debtext/131218-0003.htm).

Hitchman, C., Christie, I., Harrison, M. and Lang, T. (2002) *Inconvenience food: The Struggle to eat well on a low income*, London: Demos.

Hirsch, D. (2013) *A Minimum Income Standard for the UK in 2013*, York: Joseph Rowntree Foundation (www.jrf.org.uk/sites/files/jrf/income-living-standards-summary.pdf).

Hossain, N., Byrne, B., Campbell, A., Harrison, E., McKinley, B. and Shah, P. (2011) *The impact of the global economic downturn on communities and poverty in the UK*, York: Joseph Rowntree Foundation (www.jrf. org.uk/sites/files/jrf/experiences-of-economic-downturn-full.pdf).

Joffe, M. (1991) 'Food as a social policy issue', in N. Manning (ed) *Social Policy Review 1990-91*, Essex: Longman, pp43–59.

Kneafsey, M., Dowler, E., Lambie-Mumford, H., Inman, I. and Collier, R. (2013) 'Consumers and food security: uncertain or empowered?', *Journal of Rural Studies*, vol 29, pp 101-12.

Lambie, H. (2011) *The Trussell Trust Foodbank Network: Exploring the growth of foodbanks across the UK, Final report*, November, Coventry: SURGE, University of Coventry (www.trusselltrust.org/resources/ documents/Our%20work/Lambie-(2011)-The-Trussell-Trust-Foodbank-Network---Exploring-the-Growth-of-Foodbanks-Across-the-UK.pdf).

Lambie-Mumford, H. (2013) '"Every town should have one": emergency food banking in the UK', *Journal of Social Policy*, vol 42, no 1, pp 73-89.

Lambie-Mumford, H. (2014) 'Food bank provision and welfare reform in the UK', SPERI British Political Economy Brief No 4, Sheffield: Sheffield Political Economy Research Institute (http://speri.dept. shef.ac.uk/wp-content/uploads/2014/01/SPERI-British-Political-Economy-Brief-No4-Food-bank-provision-welfare-reform-in-the-UK.pdf).

Lambie-Mumford, H. and Dowler, E. (2014) 'Rising use of "food aid" in the United Kingdom', *British Food Journal*, vol 116, no 9, pp 1418-25.

Lambie-Mumford, H., Crossley, D., Jensen, E., Verbeke, M. and Dowler, E. (2014) *Household food security: A review of food aid*, Report to the Department for Environment, Food and Rural Affairs (www.gov.uk/ government/publications/food-aid-research-report).

Lang, T., Barling, D. and Caraher, M. (2010) *Food policy: Integrating health, environment and society*, Oxford: Oxford University Press.

MacMillan, T. and Dowler, L. (2011) 'Just and Sustainable? Examining the Rhetoric and Potential Realities of UK Food Security', *Journal of Agricultural and Environmental Ethics*, vol 25, no 2, pp 181–204.

McGlone, P., Dobson, B., Dowler, E. and Nelson, M. (1999) *Food projects and how they work*, York: Joseph Rowntree Foundation (www.jrf.org. uk/sites/files/jrf/1859354165.pdf).

Moore, S. (2012) '2012 has been the year of the food bank', *The Guardian*, 19 December (www.theguardian.com/commentisfree/2012/ dec/19/2012-year-of-the-food-bank).

Nielsen, A., Bøker Lund, T. and Holm, L. (2015) 'The taste of "the end of the month", and how to avoid it: coping with restrained food budgets in a Scandinavian welfare state context', *Social Policy and Society*, doi:10.1017/S1474746415000056.

Padley, M. and Hirsch, D. (2014) *Households below a Minimum Income Standard: 2008/9 to 2011/12*, York: Joseph Rowntree Foundation (www.jrf.org.uk/publications/households-below-minimum-income-standard).

Perry, J., Sefton, T., Williams, M. and Haddad, M. (2014) *Emergency use only: Understanding and reducing the use of food banks in the UK*, Oxfam (http://policy-practice.oxfam.org.uk/publications/emergency-use-only-understanding-and-reducing-the-use-of-food-banks-in-the-uk-335731).

PSE (Poverty and Social Exclusion) (2012) 'Going backwards: 1983-2012' (www.poverty.ac.uk/pse-research/going-backwards-1983-2012).

Register of All-Party Groups (2014) *Hunger and food poverty* (www.publications.parliament.uk/pa/cm/cmallparty/register/hunger-and-food-poverty.htm).

Riches, G. (1997) 'Hunger, food security and welfare policies: issues and debates in First World societies', *Proceedings of the Nutrition Society*, vol 56, pp 63-74.

Riches, G. (2011) 'Thinking and acting outside the charitable food box: hunger and the right to food in rich societies', *Development in Practice*, vol 21, pp 768-75.

Save the Children (2012) 'Child poverty in 2012: it shouldn't happen here', Save the Children: Manchester (www.savethechildren.org.uk/sites/default/files/documents/child_poverty_2012.pdf).

Shelter (2013) '4 out of 10 families cut back on food to stay in their homes' (http://england.shelter.org.uk/news/march_2013/4_out_of_10_families_cut_back_on_food_to_stay_in_their_homes).

Tarasuk, V. (2001) 'A critical examination of community-based responses to household food insecurity in Canada', *Health Education & Behavior*, vol 28, pp 487-99.

Taylor-Gooby, P. and Stoker, G. (2011) 'The coalition programme: a new vision for Britain or politics as usual?', *The Political Quarterly*, vol 82, no 1, pp 4-15.

Townsend, P. (1979) *Poverty in the UK*, Middlesex: Pelican.

Trussell Trust, The (no date, a) 'In the news', Salisbury: The Trussell Trust (www.trusselltrust.org/media-coverage).

Trussell Trust, The (no date, b) 'Trussell Trust foodbank stats', Salisbury: The Trussell Trust (www.trusselltrust.org/stats).

UN (United Nations) (2014) *International Covenant on Economic, Social and Cultural Rights* (https://treaties.un.org/pages/viewdetails. aspx?chapter=4&lang=en&mtdsg_no=iv-3&src=treaty).

UNESC (United Nations Economic and Social Council) (1999) *Substantive issues arising in the implementation of the International Covenant on Economic, Social and Cultural Rights: General Comment 12, Twentieth session, 'The right to adequate food' (Article 11)*, Geneva: UN.

Wallop, H. (2009) 'Thousands of people rely on food handouts as recession bites', *The Telegraph*, 26 May (www.telegraph.co.uk/finance/ recession/5387484/Thousands-of-people-rely-on-food-handouts-as-recession-bites.html).

Webb, P., Coates, P., Frongillo, E.A., Lorge Rogers, B., Swindale, A. and Bilinsky, P. (2006) 'Measuring household food insecurity: why it's so important and yet so difficult to do', *The Journal of Nutrition*, pp 14045s–1408s.

TWO

Social security policy and low wages in austere times

Chris Grover

Introduction

This chapter considers state responses to low wages. It develops from the view that low wages are economically problematic for both individuals and the state, as they create dilemmas related to social reproduction, and financial incentives to take waged work. As the solutions to these dilemmas have been expressed differently at various moments in England and later in the UK, the chapter places policies aimed at addressing low wages in their historical context. It traces concerns with wage supplementation under the Elizabethan Poor Law to the now infamous Poor Law Commission report of 1834, and the consequential prohibition of such forms of poor relief in the Poor Law Amendment Act 1834. The chapter demonstrates how those concerns with wage supplements cast a long shadow over social security policy-making until the 1970s, since when, the arguments of the 1834 Poor Law Commission have been reversed. No longer are wage supplements defined as being economically and socially problematic. In contrast, they are now seen as being beneficial to individuals and wider society, encouraging people into (albeit low) paid work, and helping to flexibilise late modern capital accumulation in Britain.

It is within this context that the chapter considers the coalition government's new form of social assistance – Universal Credit (UC) – that arguably brings to its logical conclusion trends begun in the 1970s. While UC might be seen as representing a break with post-1834 poor relief and post-Second World War social assistance, as it removes distinctions between the employed and unemployed, this chapter argues that the lasting influence of the 1834 Poor Law Commission's concerns can be seen in UC's extension of conditionality to people in waged work to ensure that they earn as much money as possible.

Finally, the chapter considers the potential alternative to wage supplements – a *living wage* – an idea that is currently enjoying a revival in Britain. It is argued that living wages have a great deal of potential. However, that potential is limited by an economic orthodoxy that frames hegemonic approaches to living wages and which means that, in a time of public spending austerity, they have arguably become little more than a means of reducing the cost to the state of wage supplements.

Wage supplements in the *longue durée*

Under the Elizabethan Poor Law (1601) forms of relief developed which were heavily criticised in the Poor Law Commission report of 1834 (Checkland and Checkland, 1974). According to Poynter (1969, p xx), the 'three injunctions of the Elizabethan Poor Law' – the relief of the impotent, the employment of the able-bodied and the correction of the 'wilfully idle' – were 'interpreted, obeyed or neglected in a bewildering variety of local circumstances.' Most important for this discussion, the 'three injunctions' facilitated the spread of wage supplements in the 18th century. While events – in particular, the adoption of the Speenhamland Scale by Berkshire magistrates in 1795, and Henry Whitbread's wage regulation bill the year after – have come to dominate discussions about how wage poverty, at least in the late 18th century, was, and might have been, addressed, it is the case that wage supplements in cash and/or in kind were widespread by the 18th century.

This observation should not be surprising, for in feudal times, 'work and poverty went hand in hand' (Quigley, 1996, p 75). Even as the last vestiges of feudalism were being laid to rest and industrial capitalism was in the ascendency, work and poverty continued to be closely related. Hence, while the Speenhamland Scale, mainly because of its appearance in a number of notable publications (for example, Eden, 1797; Webb and Webb, 1929; Polanyi, 1957 [1944]), is often portrayed as the first example of wage supplementation (or allowances in aid of wages) provided by parishes, it should more correctly be understood as systematising 'a practice which, because it was becoming widespread, needed to be conducted on some regular plan' (Fay, 1928, p 339; see also Neuman, 1969).

The Speenhamland Scale should be understood as the best known, but by no means the first or unique, system of allowances in aid of wages. It allowed that:

... every Poor and Industrious Man should have for his own Support 3s weekly, either produced by his or his Family's Labour, or an Allowance from the Poor rates, and for the support of wife and every other of his Family, 1s 6d.... When the Gallon loaf shall cost 1s 4d then every Poor and Industrious Man shall have 4s Weekly for his own, and 1s and 10d for the Support of every other his Family. And so on in proportion as the price of bread rises or falls. (cited in Grover and Stewart, 2001, p 124[1])

The Speenhamland Scale was introduced in the mid-1790s, as a response to rural distress caused by a combination of factors. These included longer-term issues, such as population growth, the erosion of opportunities in cottage industries due to industrialisation in northern Britain, and the increasing rapidity of the enclosure movement.[2] The cumulative effect of these factors was chronic unemployment and underemployment, particularly in the rural south, and stagnant real wages (Hammond and Hammond, 1920; Thompson, 1963; Deane, 1965). Shorter-term factors included the Napoleonic Wars (1793–1815) and a succession of poor harvests (1792–93, 1795–96), which also placed downward pressure on the real wages of agricultural labour (see Hobsbawm and Rudé, 1969).

Despite such reasons for the development of allowances in aid of wages, the 1834 Poor Law Commission report (Checkland and Checkland, 1974) was particularly critical of them. First, they were held to erode the liberal virtues – hard work, thrift and honesty – that framed the Victorian ideal of the independent and morally upstanding, or as the Poor Law Commission put it, the guaranteed income provided by allowances in aid of wages meant labourers lose 'all that sweetens labour, its association with reward' (Checkland and Checkland, 1974, p 167). 'What motive', questioned the Commission's report:

... has the man who is to receive 10s every Saturday, not because 10s, is the value of his week's labour, but because his family consists of five persons, who knows that his income will be increased by nothing but by an increase of his family, that it has no reference to his skill, his honesty, or his diligence – what motive has he to acquire or to preserve any of these merits? (Checkland and Checkland, 1974, p 145)

Second, the Poor Law Commission report argued that allowances in aid of wages allowed employers to reduce the wages paid to labourers in the knowledge that the parish would make them up to a subsistence minimum:

> The employers of paupers are attached to a system which enables them ... to reduce wages to a minimum, or even below a minimum of what will support an unmarried man, and to throw upon others the payment of a part, frequently of the greater part, and sometimes almost the whole of the wages actually received by the labourers. (Checkland and Checkland, 1974, p 135)

Given such observations, Block and Somers (2003) argue that there are essentially two competing understandings of the Speenhamland Scale that, while having different explanations, are equally devastating in their critique. For the new breed of political economists of the late 18th and early 19th centuries, the Speenhamland Scale:

> ... created new and perverse incentives that led to increasing pauperization. Exponential increases in childbirth and illegitimacy, declining wages and productivity, assaults on public morality and personal responsibility, and the development of a culture of indolence were only some of the effects attributed to Speenhamland. (Block and Somers, 2003, p 287)

This version of the effects of wage supplementation by the state has since been used by the political right to criticise such forms of poverty relief and social security policy more generally (see, for example, the comments of Enoch Powell, House of Commons Debates, 1970; and Block and Somers, 2003, on American neoconservative versions of such arguments).

Critiques of wage supplementation that emanate from the 1834 Poor Law Commission report are not, however, the preserve of the political right. Block and Somers (2003) also point to 'Leftist critics' of allowances in aid of wages. They cite (Block and Somers, 2003, p 289), for example, Engels, *The condition of the working class in England* (1958 [1845]):

> As long as the old Poor Law survived it was possible to supplement the low wages of the farm labourers from the rates. This, however, inevitably led to further wage reductions since the farmers naturally wanted as much as possible of the cost of maintaining their workers to be borne by the Poor Law. The burden of the poor rates would, in any case, have increased with the rise in

population. The policy of supplementing agricultural wages, of course, greatly aggravated the position.

Accepting the arguments of the Poor Law Commission, Engels' view was that allowances in aid of wages encouraged employers to reduce wages in the knowledge that they would be made up to the locally defined minima by the parish.

According to the 1834 Poor Law Commission report, the problem with allowances in aid of wages was that the supplementation of wages was counter-productive because it either (or both) encouraged working people to work less hard or less hours, or it encouraged employers to pay lower wages. In both instances, and this was the Poor Law Commission's real concern, the payment of allowances in aid of wages were held to degrade working poor people so that they became morally and socially akin to the pauper or indigent. In brief, the distinction between the 'independent' and the indigent was being removed, leading to mass pauperisation, the economic and social consequences of which could only be to the detriment of both the elite and the masses.

The Poor Law commissioners' concerns were reflected in the principle enshrined in the Poor Law Amendment Act 1834, and reinforced through various Orders later in the 19th century, that the wages of labourers should not be subsidised by the state (Poor Law Boards of Guardians at the time). While this was always easier to state than to implement in practice (in reality, the supplementation of wages continued throughout the Victorian Poor Law), the Poor Law Commission's critique of allowances in aid of wages cast a long shadow over poverty relief in a number of countries. Block and Somers (2003), for example, note the influence of such arguments on the 1969-74 Nixon government, and in critiques in the 1980s and 1990s of Aid to Families with Dependent Children in the US. Similarly, they point to its influence in Canada in 2000 in relation to the possible introduction of a 'comprehensive anti-poverty programme based on a guaranteed income for all Canadians' (Block and Somers, 2003, p 284). In Britain, like these other countries, concerns about wage supplements continued to haunt social security policy debates regarding the efficacy (or otherwise) of providing financial support for people in waged work (Grover and Stewart, 2001; Grover, 2015: forthcoming).

The rediscovery of (in-work) poverty

The previous section indicates that from the 1830s there was concern the supplementation of low wages was so economically and socially damaging that the state at a local level should not subsidise such wages via poor relief. So powerful were such arguments that in Britain, it was not until some 140 years later, that legislation reintroduced a direct supplementation to wages. Introduced in 1971, Family Income Supplement (FIS) was small in scale and targeted on those households defined as being the most in need through means testing. It aimed to address the problem of below poverty level incomes in households with dependent children that were excluded from receiving social assistance (then Supplementary Benefit) because they were in paid employment.

The antecedents of FIS lie in the 'rediscovery of poverty' in the mid-1960s. Abel-Smith and Townsend's (1965) *The poor and the poorest* indicated that a significant proportion (34.6 per cent in 1953/54 and 41 per cent in 1960) of households that might be considered as living in poverty (those with incomes below 140 per cent of National Assistance levels) contained someone in full-time employment.

The debate that followed the publication of *The poor and the poorest* and the setting up of the Child Poverty Action Group (CPAG) centred on how such households might be supported through the social security system. Labour's Wilson governments (1964-70) were criticised as being both slow in developing a response, and it being inadequate when they did (an increase in Family Allowance accompanied by a decrease in tax allowances for people on higher incomes). This 'claw back' policy was criticised as being an attack on universalism and for not addressing the poverty of all income-poor households (Grover, 2015: forthcoming). Indeed, it is argued (Banting, 1979; McCarthy, 1986) that the difficulties that the Wilson governments had in addressing family poverty was a factor in Labour losing the 1970 General Election to a parliamentary Conservative Party government.

Given the problems that Labour faced, particularly in-Cabinet disagreement over the way poor working households should be supported, the Conservatives' introduction of FIS in 1971 was rapid and painless. However, it could not be done without addressing concerns that the introduction of FIS would break the principle established in 1834, that the wages of those people in full-time work should not be supplemented by the state. In Parliament, for example, backbench Conservative MP, Enoch Powell, suggested that:

> The reformers in the 1830s were hard, harsh and, it seems to us, unimaginative men.... But at least they re-established a principle, a principle from which the [FIS] bill decisively departs. It is the principle that it is an act of fateful consequence to pay relief – cash supplementation of income – to persons in full time employment; that it is something which is bound profoundly to distort the wage system and to frustrate the ambition – which seems to me to be almost indissoluble from the idea of a free society – that a man should receive as near as may be the full value of his work in cash. (House of Commons Debates, 1970, cols 264-5)

Powell was an economic liberal of the traditional political economic kind. Hence, his argument that the supplementation of wages was an undesirable development, essentially for reasons similar to those previously outlined in the 1834 Poor Law Commission report. However, in arguing the case for FIS, the then Secretary of State for Social Services, Sir Keith Joseph (before his conversion to a brand of economic thinking that was close to that of Powell's), had a number of reasons to explain why FIS was not like the Speenhamland Scale. These included the limited scope of FIS – 'Speenhamland came to affect the majority of rural workers.... The contrast with this Bill is startling. It will bring help to well under 1 per cent of working households...' – and the fact that in the 1970s 'the trade union movement is strong' (House of Commons Debates, 1970, col 225). Hence, it was 'highly unlikely that the small extra payment which we are providing will in total enter into wage negotiations or calculations' (House of Commons Debates, 1970, col 225).

More importantly for this discussion, however, is the fact that FIS was framed by qualifying criteria that were designed to ensure that it did not provide disincentives for people to work at all, or to work harder to increase their wages. These included, for example, having a minimum working hours qualification (people had to work at least 30 hours per week to qualify), providing only 50 per cent of the difference between the prescribed amount (below which people would qualify) and normal gross income, and a maximum weekly payment, initially set at £3 per week[3] (Barker, 1971). While such criteria might be explained with reference to the Conservative government's preference for tax cuts over social spending (McCarthy, 1986), it is also the case that they acted to ensure there were differences between 'independent' and unemployed workers. That said, FIS represented a (albeit very small) step in the direction of blurring that distinction, which was to culminate in the contemporary coalition government (in which the Conservative Party is the senior partner) removing, at least at first glance, any notion of a distinction between 'independent' and unemployed people through the introduction of UC.

There is not the space here to recount the history of the intervening policies – Thatcherite governments' Family Credit and Labour's Tax Credits – that came between FIS and UC. Suffice to note that while the (re)introduction of direct wage supplementation in 1971 was seen as a measure that would only affect the few – Joseph estimated 180,000 households (House of Commons Debates, 1970, col 217) at a cost of £8 million per annum (House of Commons Debates, 1970, col 222) – by the time the coalition government was constructed in 2010, some 3 million households[4] (including 482,000 childless households) (HMRC, 2011, Table 1A) received a supplement to their wages at a cost of £27.6 billion per annum (DWP, 2013, p 9).

This massive expansion of wage supplementation in Britain occurred alongside a shift from Keynesianism to neoliberalism, the distinguishing features of which, it might be expected, would have acted against such an increase in state support. What is particularly intriguing is that Conservative governments have been as responsible for the expansion of wage supplements as Labour governments have, when their ideological forebears, the views of whom were visible in the 1834 Poor Law Commission report, were opposed to wage supplements. Tomlinson (2012, p 221), for instance, argues that the trend to supplement wages can be understood as a 'startling return to the eighteenth-century-style Speenhamland system of "outdoor relief", a reversal that would have early nineteenth-century economic liberals rotating in their graves'.

Such arguments, however, miss the political economic significance of the role of social policy interventions in reproducing capitalist accumulation (see Jessop, 1994a, 1994b, 2002). Along with the deepening of conditionality and its extension to groups of claimants (for instance, lone mothers and people who are chronically sick and/or who are disabled) who, before the 1990s were seen as having legitimate reasons for not partaking in waged work, wage supplementation became understood in the 1980s as a means of incentivising people to take low-paid waged work.

In the 1980s, in the context of mass unemployment, and for under-valued workers, stagnating wages (Balls, 1993; Gregg and Wadsworth, 1995), wage supplements lost their association with disincentivising people from doing waged work. In contrast, they were held to encourage people to do such work by attempting to address the unemployment and poverty 'traps' (Secretary of State for Social Services, 1985, para 4.46). Such a view continued under the 1997-2010 Labour Party governments which replaced Family Credit (FC) with Working Families' Tax Credit (WFTC) in 1999 (and then replaced it with Child Tax Credit [CTC] and Working Tax Credit [WTC] in 2003) (see, for example, Grover and Stewart, 2001, chapter 3). However, the existing labour market concerns with wage supplements were bolstered in 1999 by the then Prime Minister, Tony Blair's (1999, p 7) announcement that committed Labour to 'end child poverty forever' by 2020. This was because the primary way of addressing child poverty was to be to move workless people into waged work. The idea that was heavily pushed at the time and continues to be so – that work is the best route out of poverty – could only be realised by the increasing supplementation of wages.

Furthermore, in the late 1980s and into the 1990s, given the levels of unemployment and worklessness more generally, the objection – that wage supplementation encouraged employers to reduce wages – was redefined as a potential merit. The idea was that wage supplements would reduce the reservation wage at which people were willing to work (Grover and Stewart, 1999, 2001), which would mean more competition for waged work. In turn, given orthodox economic theory, this would mean that there would be downward pressure on wage levels as more people would be competing for waged work, an approach that was extended by Labour governments between 1997 and 2010 through the idea of the 'effective labour supply' (Grover and Stewart, 2001; Grover, 2005).

Despite the expansion of wage supplementation in the 1990s and 2000s, the qualifying criteria for FC and later Tax Credits was still concerned with maintaining a distinction between employed and unemployed people by adding 'credits' to the wages of the former and paying 'benefits' to the latter (see also Dean, 2012; Jordan, 2012). Although reduced, primarily to facilitate the employment of lone mothers,[5] to 16 hours per week, there remained an hours qualification for FC that Labour governments kept for Tax Credit purposes,[6] and the tapered withdrawal of the supplements was supposed to maintain at least some financial incentive to increase wages. In the contemporary reforms, however, such distinctions are arguably removed by UC.

Universal Credit

The reasons for introducing, and an outline of UC, were contained in the coalition government's Green and White Papers on social security policy published in 2010 (Secretary of State for Work and Pensions, 2010a, 2010b). Wiggan (2012, p 400) argues that those two papers portrayed the extant social security system for working-age people as an 'expensive, well meaning system of state support' that was 'ineffective ... reinforcing social problems by permitting people to make the "wrong" choices, due to poor incentives in the benefit system, with devastating consequences for poor families'. Essentially, the coalition government's critique of the 1997–2010 Labour Party governments was that while the cost of social security benefits had increased, the outcomes were poor – a complex system that, because of the interaction of several means-tested benefits, provided claimants with little financial incentive to take paid employment. This analysis would not have looked out of place in the 1834 Poor Law Commission's report, and repeated concerns that were also central to the development of FC and Tax Credits – that there must be clear financial benefits if people receiving out-of-work benefits are to be incentivised to take waged work.

The difference to those earlier concerns, however, is in the suggested solution to end what Iain Duncan Smith (Secretary of State for Work and Pensions, 2010a, p 1) describes as 'the culture of worklessness'. Rather than suggesting, as was the case, for example, in the 1980s, that social security spending should be severely curtailed – this has been left to the Treasury's austerity measures, discussed below – the focus is on the development of a new form of social assistance (UC) that will 'simplify the benefits system in order to improve incentives to work' (Secretary of State for Work and Pensions, 2010a, p 4). The importance of UC in this discussion is that the waged work status of recipients is immaterial to entitlement to it. What determines entitlement to UC is whether household income is low enough to qualify, whether its cause is worklessness or low wage income. In this sense, UC is held to be the solution to the coalition government's claim that existing 'distinct in-work benefits have failed to convince many people to make the transition to work' (Secretary of State for Work and Pensions, 2010b, p 8).

While some (for example, Jordan, 2012) see UC as being the (albeit low) road to a basic income whereby Britons are entitled to an income by virtue of their citizenship, such an argument removes UC from its political economic antecedents in wage supplementation. The coalition government's idea of UC is not that people will remain reliant on it for long periods of time, but that they will use it to metaphorically climb the wage labour ladder (Secretary of State for Work and Pensions, 2010b). In addition, UC is held to be to the advantage of Britain's variant of neoliberal capital accumulation:

Establishing a single withdrawal rate, and eliminating the hours rules currently present in Working Tax Credit, has the potential to create a much more flexible labour market. Workers will be able to work the number of hours that most suits their needs and those of their employer, without being constrained by the structure of the benefits system. Employers will find that their workforces become more flexible and open to opportunities for progression. (Secretary of State for Work and Pensions, 2010b, p 55)

The views of the coalition government are hedged with the potential benefits of UC for working people. However, it can also be understood as being framed by productivist concerns that subordinate the potential social objectives of social security policy to economic concerns and ends. In brief, it can be understood as being more concerned with facilitating the process of capital accumulation than it is concerned with the needs of low-paid working people.

UC extends the economic rationale for wage supplementation which in the past was related to 'full-time'[7] jobs to *all* jobs. Hence, it could be argued that the distinction between people in and out of paid work, the need for which was so forcefully put in economic and moral terms in the 1834 Poor Law Commission report, has finally been abolished. To make this argument, however, would be to ignore the role that is assigned to the extension and strengthening of conditionality in UC. The Green Paper, *21st century welfare* (Secretary of State for Work and Pensions, 2010a, p 29), notes that removing the distinction in UC between in- and out-of-work benefits would lead to an 'enabling [of] a new approach to conditionality that aimed to incentivise people to enter work and progress – increasing hours and earnings until they move off benefits altogether'. What this means is that people who are already in paid work can, if they are deemed not to be working enough hours, at a high enough wage, be mandated to engage in activities that will increase one or both of these.[8]

For Dwyer and Wright (2014, p 33), the extension of conditionality to people in waged work is something that is new and acts to further limit social citizenship by 'offloading the welfare responsibilities of the state and employers onto citizens who are in receipt of *in work* and *out of work* social security benefits'. In this reconfiguration of social citizenship it is within the individual/social assistance nexus that the explanation for unemployment, underemployment, or, of most interest here, low-paid employment, is found. In brief, UC could not operate without the introduction of conditionality to people working for hours and wages that are deemed by the state to be too low, because the belief, as was argued in the 1830s, to remove the distinction between the unemployed and employed would lead to a disincentivising of paid work.

The extension of conditionality in UC extends this view to contemporary society where the state is grappling with tensions between, on the one hand, a desire to increase labour market flexibility (through, for example, 'mini-jobs'), and, on the other hand, a desire to ensure that people strive for independence from the state-sponsored benefits. Hence, distinctions between, in 19th-century language, the 'independent' and indigent have shifted. The conditionality regime of UC suggests that the 'independent' are those who are making the greatest effort in work, while the indigent are unemployed people and those who really could work harder, but choose not to do so, just as recipients of allowances in aid of wages were condemned.

Given the current precariousness of contemporary labour markets for many (Standing, 2011), and the lack of any recognition of the quality of waged work in UC, it has been suggested by Dean (2012, p 358) that UC can be understood as a policy aimed at 'pimping the precariat'. This is because, Dean (2012, p 358) argues, such wage supplements are implicated in a 'breach of the right to just and favourable conditions of work[9] insofar as they enable employers to hire workers at below poverty level wages'. It is at this juncture that we might consider that element of waged work – wages – through which the value of individuals in capitalist countries are judged. Of particular importance is the notion of a 'living wage'.

A living wage?

Like any social policy, the state supplementation of wages is affected by a range of factors that can have an impact on their social and economic objectives, for instance, the political priority placed on maintaining their value, particularly in the context of wider economic trends, such as those in wages and inflation. These considerations make the payment of wage supplements potentially unstable. In Britain the Social Mobility and Child Poverty Commission[10] (2013a, p 6) makes the point, for example, that in the late 1990s and early 2000s, '[h]igher tax credits subsidised stagnating earnings and propped up living standards ... they were the only substantial source of growth in real incomes for those in the bottom half.' However, the report goes on to argue that austerity 'removes that prop. The taxpayer alone can no longer afford to shoulder the burden of bridging the gap between earnings and prices' (p 6). Hence, it concludes that the 'Government will need to devise new ways of sharing that burden with employers, without damaging employment' (p 7).

The Commission suggests, among other things, that this might be done by encouraging 'employers who can afford it to pay the living wage on a voluntary basis', and 'paying the living wage more widely in the public sector (since there are savings to be made on tax credits)' (Social Mobility and Child Poverty Commission, 2013b, p 5). In recent years, however, it is not just the Social Mobility and Child Poverty Commission that has suggested a living wage – 'an hourly rate of income calculated according to a basic cost of living ... and defined as the minimum amount of money needed to enjoy a basic, but socially acceptable standard of living' (Living Wage Commission, 2014, p 5) – as a means by which low pay and household poverty might be addressed. Indeed, Bennett (2014, p 46) suggests that the living wage is 'enjoying a renaissance', and in recent years, politicians of many persuasions have 'compete[d] to associate themselves with the idea [of the living wage]' (Lawton and Pennycook, 2013, p 4).

Bennett (2014, p 49) argues that there are several reasons for the current interest in the living wage that include renewed concerns with the 'sweating' of labour and the 2008 economic crisis that has provided 'a catalyst for new ideas' for delivering higher incomes to households where wage earners are low-paid. Here, for example, the effects of austerity measures introduced as a politically mediated response to 2008 economic crisis might be highlighted. The Social Mobility and Child Poverty Commission (2013a) estimate that £5.5 billion per annum in spending on Tax Credits has been removed through austerity cuts to social security spending. In this context, it is perhaps not a surprise that Conservative Prime Minister, David Cameron, has described the living wage 'as an idea "whose time has come"' (cited in Lawton and Pennycook, 2013, p 8), as has leader of the Labour Party, Ed Miliband. For Miliband, support for the living wage is a consequence of the argument that 'we cannot carry on with ever-spiralling costs of billions of pounds of subsidies for low pay'. The important issue here is how the idea of the living wage might be related to long-term policy concerns about households containing people who are poorly paid. A cursory glance suggests that the living wage has much to offer. First, it might, as politicians hope, be understood as a means of bolstering household income at a time of austerity. The living wage does shift some responsibility from public spending to employers. There are arguments for such a move from both the left and the right. In the case of the left, for instance, it could be argued, given that employers profit from the application of the labour power of employees, enterprises should take more responsibility for the costs of the social reproduction of that labour power; and that for too long, the costs of social reproduction have been socialised, while profit, that is dependent on such reproduction, has been privatised. In the case of the right, the desire for individuals to be more independent from the state might indicate that employers should pay higher wages.

Second, given that austerity measures are having a disproportionate affect on poorer neighbourhoods (Hancock et al, 2012), the living wage has the potential to support spending in neighbourhoods that have been the hardest hit. As was argued by Henry Brailsford and colleagues (1926, p 8) as part of the Independent Labour Party's 'Socialism in Our Time' campaign: 'low wages mean a limitation of a home market.' A living wage, therefore, has the potential to stimulate demand for goods and services, a potentiality that is particularly important at the neighbourhood level (cf Living Wage Commission, 2014).

Third, and related to Figart et al's (2002, p 5) notion of wages as a social practice – 'a means of reinforcing or changing cultural understanding of workers' appropriate "places"' – it is clear that wage supplements do not 'compensate for the injustices or adverse effects of ... precarious and inadequately paid work' (Dean, 2011, p 1). In his qualitative work with WTC recipients, Dean (and his colleague, Gerry Mitchell, 2011) found that while few of their respondents recognised WTC as a subsidy for poorly paying employers, a 'lot of them felt devalued at work or locked in to menial jobs' (Dean, 2011, p 1). Hence, it can be argued that a living wage, rather than wage supplementation, might help to address feelings of stigma associated with the receipt of such supplements.

The idea of a living wage has much to commend it. However, it can also be argued that the notion of the living wage is constrained by its location within orthodox conceptualisations of wages. Here, for instance, we can point to what Figart et al (2002) describe as 'wages as a living', for which notions of subsistence are central. Rothschild (1954, p 4) argues that notions of subsistence, linked to concerns with population reproduction, were central to the 'first coherent wage theory'. This, the subsistence theory of wages, was associated with the physiocrats in France and later Adam Smith and other classical political economists (for instance, Thomas Malthus and Karl Marx) in Britain. For Rothschild (1954, p 4), it was a 'rather simple theory ... that, *in the long run*, wages would tend towards that sum which is necessary to maintain a worker and his [sic] family'. Rothschild (1954, p 4) explains:

It was assumed that every increase in wages above the subsistence minimum would at once induce workers to have larger families. The consequent increase in the supply of labour would bring wages back down to the old level. On the other hand, a wage level that fell below the subsistence minimum would mean that starvation, increased infantile mortality, postponed marriages, all resulting in a reduced supply of labour which would ultimately lead to an increase in wages.

Living wages can be understood in this context because some analysts equate them with '[w]ages as subsistence' (Bennett and Lister, 2010, p 10). Bennett (2014) also notes Anker's (2011, p 14) work for the International Labour Office on estimating living wage levels in which he uses a family of four as their basis, because such a family 'roughly represents population replacement and it is reasonably consistent with fertility rates found in many developing countries.' Anker directly links living wages to population reproduction. In Britain, the calculation of living wages in London (see GLA Economics, 2013) and outside of it (see Hirsch, 2011) are not directly linked to population reproduction. They are, nevertheless, concerned with social reproduction (Wills and Linneker, 2014). In both approaches, however, and in a somewhat more culturally sensitive way compared to 18th- and 19th-century political economists, living wages are conceptualised as a subsistence wage concerned with physical and social reproduction. In this context, the criticism of living wages made in the 1920s by the Communist Party in still relevant. Dutt (1927, pp 95-6), for example, suggested that they were merely a means of supporting 'wage-slavery and of the buying and selling of labour power', a means, in other words, of buttressing rather than challenging the social relations of capitalism.

It is also the case that the living wage is heavily framed by what Figart et al (2002) describes as 'wages as a price'. Here, wages are understood as a second classical wage theory – as part of marginal productivity theory. Rather than the needs of workers being central (as in subsistence wage theories), it is the commodified market value of the worker – as defined, for instance, by supply and demand, the productivity of the worker and the profitability of the enterprise for which they work – that determines wage rates (cf Rothschild, 1954). Such an approach is clear, even among living wage supporters, in resistance to making such a wage a statutory requirement (Pennycook, 2012; Living Wage Commission, 2014). This resistance is driven by orthodox economic concerns with the ability of enterprises to afford living wages,[12] and with possible 'unintended consequences', particularly increases in unemployment if employers were legally obliged to pay all workers living wage. Essentially, such concerns suggest that there are sectors of the economy where workers are justifiably paid a low wage because the market is held to be unable to bear any more than this. For a living wage to apply to all workers, its roots in orthodox economic theory would have to be challenged. However, even the most ardent supporters of the living wage do not seem willing to do this.

Furthermore, because of orthodox economic concerns, the hegemonic conceptualisations of living wages in Britain 'do not precisely do what they say on the tin' (Lawton and Pennycook, 2013, p 4). As noted, the living wage is calculated in relation to a basic, but socially acceptable, standard of living. The assumption in the calculation of this standard is that the hourly living wage is net of any entitlement to wage supplements and other benefits that can be claimed by people if their incomes are low enough. GLA Economics (2013) explains that such an approach is taken because 'the tax and benefit system is, by design, redistributive.' However, in previous years it argued (for example, GLA Economics, 2005, p iii) that in addition to the redistributive factor, existing wage supplements and means-tested benefits are taken into account to ensure 'that disadvantages are not placed in the way of securing employment.' Once again, orthodox economic concerns help to frame (and ultimately reduce) the level at which the living wage is set. Such an approach to the living wage is, however, inconsistent with other approaches that suggest people should be paid high enough wages so that they do not have to rely on means-tested wage supplements to make up their income, even to a basic income level (see, for example, UNISON and the Low Pay Unit, 2002; and Bennett, 2014, on the US).

Conclusion

This chapter has focused on long-term concerns with low incomes in households where there is at least one person in paid work. Over the past two centuries the approach of the state in Britain to wage supplementation has shifted from one in which such a policy was criticised as being responsible for economic and social degradation to one where it is thought to have both individual and societal benefits. This can clearly be seen in the development of UC that, although plagued by technical difficulties, should eventually be payable to all people, whether in or out of work, providing their income is low enough (and they do not possess more than modest savings). This essentially denotes a return to allowances in aid of wages, exemplified in the Speenhamland Scale, that were so fiercely criticised by the Poor Law Commission in 1834.

It would, however, be wrong to suggest that UC loses the concern with denoting the employed from the unemployed. The extension of conditionality to those already employed highlights that there is continuing concern that people will do the least amount of work possible in order to claim UC. UC, therefore, is still constructed around the idea, outlined in the 1834 Poor Law Commission report, that the work ethic is easily subverted by the provision of collectively provided financial support for people in low-paid work. Hence, these employees need to be disciplined into working as many hours they as they are deemed capable of.

It is the case, however, that for many low-paid workers, the trend towards supplementing low wages is not particularly helped by the way the main alternative to wage supplements – the living wage – is conceptualised in Britain. Because the living wage is ultimately framed by economic orthodoxies, it is arguably reduced to a means of decreasing the financial cost of wage supplements, and strengthening capitalist social relations at a time when, in the context of the 2008 economic crisis, and subsequent austerity, they have been weakened.

Notes

[1] The original material relating to the Speenhamland Scale is available at the Berkshire Record Office, catalogue reference BRO QS/07.

[2] It is often assumed that the 18th-century enclosure movement involved the demarcating of land with physical boundaries (such as hedges and fences), but it did not necessarily involve such developments. Enclosure was, in fact, a legal, rather than physical, means of excluding people from using land. In this sense, 'enclosure involved the removal of communal rights, controls or ownership over a piece of land and its conversion into "severalty", that is a state where the owner had sole control over its use, and of access to it' (Kain et al, 2004, p 1).

[3] Compared to average male manual earnings of about £54 per week (Paul Bryan MP, House of Commons Debates, 1971, col 562).

[4] The figure excludes those households receiving only or below the Family Element of Child Tax Credit. If those household were included, the figure would be 4.76 million receiving Tax Credits.

[5] See, for example, the comments of Tony Newton, then Secretary of State for Social Security (House of Commons Debates, 1990, col 731).

[6] When, in 2003, single people and childless couples were able to claim Working Tax Credits, they had to be working at least 30 hours per week.

[7] There have been various hour thresholds – 30, 24, and then 16 hours for couples and single people with dependent children, and 30 hours for childless couples and single people – governing the claiming of wage supplements since the introduction of FIS in 1971. None have been related to the actuality of hours worked by people in full-time employment, which, for example, in 2013 was 44 for men and 40 for women (ONS, 2013).

[8] UC contains a 'conditionality threshold' that is equivalent to a 35-hour working week at the relevant National Minimum Wage. So, for example, from October 2014, if a single person aged 30 earns a gross wage of less than £227.50 (£6.50 x 35), s/he will have to engage with compulsory activities, which is supposed to increase the amount that they earn (see Pennycook and Whittaker, 2012).

[9] As, for example, in the Council of Europe's Social Charter and the European Union's Lisbon Treaty.

[10] In 2012, the Social Mobility and Child Poverty Commission was created by the British government 'as an independent and statutory body to monitor and report on what is happening to child poverty and social mobility' (Social Mobility and Child Poverty Commission, 2014, p iii).

[11] For the full text, see http://labourlist.org/2014/07/full-text-ed-milibands-npf-speech-a-new-settlement-for-a-new-era/

[12] In October 2014, the UK's National Minimum Wage (NMW) for employees aged 21 years or over was £6.50. In comparison, the living wage was £9.15 per hour in London and £7.85 outside of London. The NMW is a statutorily enforceable wage for all employees. Its level is age- and employment status-dependent, with young people (£5.13 an hour for 18- to 20-year-olds and £3.79 per hour for those aged under 18) and apprentices (£2.73 per hour) receiving less than the rate payable to those workers aged 21 years or over. The living wage, in contrast, is paid only to those workers whose employers voluntarily commit to paying such a wage. The Living Wage Foundation estimates that there are just over 1,000 living wage employers in the UK (see www.livingwage.org.uk/employers).

References

Abel-Smith, B. and Townsend, P. (1965) *The poor and the poorest: A new analysis of the Ministry's of Labour's 'Family Expenditure Surveys' of 1953-54 and 1960*, London: Bell.

Anker, R. (2011) *Estimating a living wage: A methodological review*, Conditions of Work and Employment Series No 29, Geneva: International Labour Office.

Balls, E. (1993) 'Danger: men not at work', in E. Balls and P. Gregg, *Work and welfare: Tackling the jobs deficit*, London: Institute for Public Policy Research, pp 1–30.

Banting, K. (1979) *Poverty, politics and policy*, London: Macmillan.

Barker, D. (1971) 'The Family Income Supplement' in D. Bull (ed) *Family poverty: Programme for the seventies*, London: Gerald Duckworth, pp 70–82.

Bennett, F. (2014) 'The "living wage", low pay and in work poverty: rethinking the relationships', *Critical Social Policy*, vol 34, no 1, pp 46-65.

Bennett, F. and Lister, R. (2010) *The 'living wage': The right answer to low pay?*, London: Fabian Society.

Blair, T. (1999) Beveridge Speech, Toynbee Hall, 18 March, published as 'Beveridge revisited: a welfare state for the 21st century', in R. Walker (ed) *Ending child poverty: Popular welfare in the 21st century*, Bristol: Policy Press.

Block, F. and Somers, M. (2003) 'In the shadow of Speenhamland: social policy and the old Poor Law', *Politics & Society*, vol 31, no 2, pp 283-323.

Brailsford, H., Hobson, J., Creech Jones, A. and Wise, F. (1926) *The living wage*, London: Independent Labour Party.

Checkland, S. and Checkland, E. (1974) *The Poor Law report of 1834*, Harmondsworth: Penguin.

Dean, H. (2011) 'Wage top-up schemes are an attractive way for policy makers to address income inequalities, but they may well be corrosive to those they are aiming to help' (http://blogs.lse.ac.uk/politicsandpolicy/wage-top-up-schemes/).

Dean, H. (2012) 'The ethical deficit of the United Kingdom's proposed Universal Credit: pimping the precariat?', *Political Quarterly*, vol 83, no 2, pp 353-9.

Dean, H. and Mitchell, G. (2011) *Wage top-ups and work incentives: The implications of the UK's Working Tax Credit scheme. A preliminary report*, London: London School of Economics and Political Science.

Deane, P. (1965) *The first Industrial Revolution* (2nd edn), Cambridge: Cambridge University Press.

Dutt, R. Palme (1927) *Socialism and the living wage*, London: Communist Party of Great Britain.

DWP (Department for Work and Pensions) (2013) *Tax Credit expenditure in Great Britain*, London: DWP.

Dwyer, P. and Wright, S. (2014) 'Universal Credit, ubiquitous conditionality and its implications for social citizenship', *Journal of Poverty and Social Justice*, vol 22, no 1, pp 27-35.

Eden, F. (1797) *The state of the poor*, London: B. and J. White.

Engels, F. (1958[1845]) *The condition of the working class in England*, translated by W. Henderson and W. Chaloner, Oxford: Basil Blackwell.

Fay, C. (1928) *Great Britain from Adam Smith to the present day*, London: Longmans, Green & Co.

Figart, D., Mutari, E. and Power, M. (2002), *Living wages, equal wages: Gender and labour market policies in the United States*, New York: Routledge.

GLA (Greater London Authority) Economics (2005) *A fairer London. The Living Wage in London*, London: GLA.

GLA Economics (2013) *A fairer London. The 2013 Living Wage in London*, London: GLA.

Gregg, P. and Wadsworth, J. (1995) 'Making work pay', *New Economy*, vol 2, issue 4, pp 210-13.

Grover, C. (2005) 'Living wages and the "Making Work Pay" strategy', *Critical Social Policy*, vol 25, no 1, pp 5-27.

Grover, C. (2015: forthcoming) *Social security and wage poverty: Historical and policy dimensions of subsidising wages in Britain and beyond*, Basingstoke: Palgrave Macmillan.

Grover, C. and Stewart, J. (1999) '"Market workfare": social security and competitiveness in the 1990s', *Journal of Social Policy*, vol 24, no 1, pp 73-96.

Grover, C. and Stewart, J. (2001) *The work connection: The role of social security in regulating British economic life*, Basingstoke: Palgrave.

Hammond, J. and Hammond, B. (1920) *The village labourer*, London: Longmans, Green & Co.

Hancock, L., Mooney, G. and Neal, S. (2012) 'Crisis social policy and the resilience of the concept of community', *Critical Social Policy*, vol 32, no 3, pp 343-64.

Hirsch, D. (2011) *Detailed calculation of out of London living wage: Method, rationale, data sources and figures for the 2010/11 calculation*, Loughborough: University of Loughborough.

HMRC (Her Majesty's Revenue and Customs) (2011) *Child and Working Tax Credits statistics. Finalised annual awards 2009-10. Geographical analysis*, London: HMRC.

Hobsbawm, E. and Rudé, G. (1969) *Captain swing*, London: Lawrence & Wishart.

House of Commons Debates (1970) Family Income Supplements Bill, 10 November, vol 806, cols 217-340.

House of Commons Debates (1971) Average weekly wage, 1 July, vol 82, col 562.

House of Commons Debates (1990) Child maintenance, 29 October, vol 178, cols 729-49.

Jessop, B. (1994a) 'The transition to post-Fordism and the Schumpeterian workfare state', in R. Burrows and B. Loader (eds) *Towards a post-Fordist welfare state?*, London: Routledge, pp 13-37

Jessop, B. (1994b) 'Post-Fordism and the state', in A. Amin (ed) *Post-Fordism. A reader*, Oxford: Blackwell, pp 251–79.

Jessop, B. (2002) *The future of the capitalist state*, Cambridge: Polity.

Jordan, B. (2012) 'The low road to basic income? Tax-benefit integration in the UK', *Journal of Social Policy*, vol 41, no 1, pp 1-17.

Kain, R., Chapman, J. and Oliver, R. (2004) *The enclosure maps of England and Wales 1595-1918* (http://assets.cambridge.org/97805218/27713/excerpt/9780521827713_excerpt.pdf).

Lawton, K. and Pennycook, M. (2013) *Beyond the bottom line: The challenges and opportunities of a living wage*, London: Institute for Public Policy Research and Resolution Foundation.

Living Wage Commission (2014) *Work that pays. The final report of the Living Wage Commission*, York: Living Wage Commission.

McCarthy M. (1986) *Campaigning for the poor*, London: Croom Helm.

Neuman, M. (1969) 'A suggestion regarding the origins of the Speenhamland Plan', *The English Historical Review*, vol 84, no 331, pp 317-22.

ONS (Office for National Statistics) (2013) *Full report – women in the labour market*, London: ONS.

Pennycook, M. (2012) *What price a living wage?*, London: Resolution Foundation.

Pennycook, M. and Whittaker, M. (2012) *Conditions uncertain: Assessing the implications of Universal Credit in-work conditionality*, London: Resolution Foundation.

Poynter, J. (1969) *Society and pauperism. English ideas on poor relief 1795-1834*, London: Routledge & Kegan Paul.

Polanyi (1957 [1944]) *The great transformation*, Boston, MA: Beacon Press.

Quigley, W. (1996) 'Five hundred years of English poor laws, 1349-1834: regulating the working and nonworking poor', *Akron Law Review*, vol 30, no 1, pp 73-128.

Rothschild, K. (1954) *A theory of wages*, Oxford: Blackwell.

Secretary of State for Social Services (1985) *Reform of social security: Programme for change*, Cmnd 9518, vol 2, London: HMSO.

Secretary of State for Work and Pensions (2010a) *21st century welfare*, Cm 7913, Norwich: The Stationery Office.

Secretary of State for Work and Pensions (2010b) *Universal Credit: Welfare that works*, Cm 7957, Norwich: The Stationery Office.

Social Mobility and Child Poverty Commission (2013a) *State of the nation 2013: Social mobility and child poverty in Great Britain*, London: Social Mobility and Child Poverty Commission.

Social Mobility and Child Poverty Commission (2013b) *Social mobility: The next steps*, London: Social Mobility and Child Poverty Commission.

Social Mobility and Child Poverty Commission (2014) *State of the nation 2014: Social mobility and child poverty in Great Britain*, London: Social Mobility and Child Poverty Commission.

Standing, G. (2011) *The precariat: The new dangerous class*, London: Bloomsbury.

Thompson, E. (1963) *The making of the English working class*, London: Penguin.

Tomlinson, J. (2012) 'From "distribution of industry" to "local Keynesianism": the growth of public sector employment in Britain', *British Politics*, vol 7, no 3, pp 204-23.

UNISON and the Low Pay Unit (2002) *Justice, not charity: Why workers need a Living Wage*, London: UNISON.

Webb, S. and Webb, B. (1929) *English Poor Law history: Part II: The last hundred years*, Volume 1, London: Longmans, Green & Co.

Wiggan, J. (2012) 'Telling stories of 21st century welfare: the UK Coalition government and the neo-liberal discourse of worklessness and dependency', *Critical Social Policy*, vol 32, no 3, pp 383-405.

Wills, J. and Linneker, B. (2014) 'In-work poverty and the living wage in the United Kingdom: a geographical perspective', *Transactions of the Institute of British Geographers*, vol 39, no 2, pp182-94.

THREE

Responsibilisation of everyday life: housing and welfare state change

Stuart Lowe and Jed Meers

Introduction

In this chapter we focus on the unfolding narrative of social change instigated through 'housing' and its central connection to welfare reform. We couch this commentary in terms of two closely related concepts – 'responsibilisation' and 'financialisation' – both of these implying that citizenship in 21st-century UK is defined largely in terms of individuality, risk-taking and self-management. These concepts have been associated with homeownership, but are now surfacing in social housing too, dramatically illustrated in the period under consideration in this review. Our central argument is that housing, for a long time marginal to key debates about welfare state change, is now at the forefront of welfare reform and the wider reconstitution of 21st-century welfare states. The idea behind this chapter is to show in detail how 'housing' has an impact on and through institutional structures, and how the discourse around 'responsibilisation' and 'financialisation' is increasingly common ground in both the owner-occupier and social housing sectors, that these concepts bleed across what were once thought of as discrete housing tenures. In this chapter we use what might appear to be two very disparate examples – the rise of asset-based welfare very largely derived from housing equity and re-mortgaging, and the interface between the welfare reform agenda and social housing. What binds them together is the increasingly shared discipline of a welfare system that preaches freedom, responsibility and self-provisioning, but in the context of rules and institutional structures that citizen-consumers do not control. In the realm of 'everyday life', households behind their front doors are faced with decisions about how to react to sometimes very stark choices regarding their welfare needs, often risking financial insecurity, and always with a lonely burden of responsibility. Housing and home is the place, but increasingly also at the centre of the *process* through which household budgets shape decision-making on welfare needs.

Even the most casual political observer would appreciate that 'responsibility' has been a buzzword in British political discourse surrounding UK welfare reform. From the Third Way's central tenet of 'no rights without responsibilities' (Dwyer, 2004, p 265) to the coalition government's fostering of 'social responsibility' through the 'Big Society' (Ellison, 2011, p 55; Bulley and Bulley, 2014, p 455), a focus on the changing boundaries of individual responsibility for welfare or life outcomes has provided ample fuel for rhetoric and policy-making throughout successive governments. In a previous edition of *Social Policy Review*, Lister goes as far as proclaiming that we are in the 'age of responsibility' (Lister, 2011, p 63).

Rather more recently, the exponential growth of capital markets, the increasing connectivity of the global financial system, and its subsequent crisis and re-invention, has created new streams of research across the disciplines about the role of *finance* capital. Financialisation is the bedfellow of the responsibility agenda. Financialisation also has quite a long gestation in the literature. In his influential book, *A theory of capitalist regulation* (1979), Aglietta argued that a nascent form of finance-driven capital was rapidly overtaking the Keynesian mixed economies. In similar vein, more recently French regulationist theorists, for example, argued that an understanding of the regime of capital accumulation based on industrial production was flawed because the institutional structures of modern capitalism were, in fact, substantially finance-led (Froud et al, 2000; Jurgens et al, 2000). For our purpose it is sufficient to acknowledge that these interdisciplinary streams of research show that 21st-century citizens have become, as Watson describes it, 'financialised economic agents' (Watson, 2009, p 49). This involves new ways of thinking about personal assets, notably housing and pensions. As van der Zwan argues,

> By participating in financial markets, individuals are encouraged to internalize new norms of risk-taking and develop new subjectivities as investors or owners of financial assets. (van der Zwan, 2014, p 102)

Here in this discussion, the wide-angle lens of macro-economics and politics zooms in to focus on the impacts on families of the waves of finance capital that swept the globe for more than three decades before the system partially broke down in 2007. It is here that our themes of responsibilisation and financialisation coalesce, because financial products and the democratisation of finance after the deregulation of the banking system in the 1980s made finance capital available to people in ways previously unimaginable. In tandem with this, narratives about citizenship shifted from the Beveridge 'cradle-to-grave' welfare states to emphasise individual responsibility, risk-taking and willingness to engage with new financial products and the industry they spawned. This system grew exponentially, with the invention and embedding of the internet into family life (Davis, 2009). The focus on the 'everyday' means looking in detail at individual practices, at how globalisation and specifically global capital literally 'came home'. With its powerful agenda of self-management, the 'home' become a super-financialised domain (Lowe, 2011).

The first substantive section of this chapter discusses arguments about the role that homeownership has played in facilitating the transition towards what has loosely been called 'asset-based' welfare (Sherraden, 1991), which is basically sustained by personal asset accumulation and specifically through mortgage markets and the ability of homeowners to trade their property in exchange for goods and services. As Smith and Searle observe, releasing housing equity through re-mortgaging makes it possible to literally 'bank on housing' as a cushion in adversity and to meet welfare needs (Smith and Seale, 2010). The second case involves a more subtle intrusion of the responsibilisation agenda into the social housing domain, marking a significant change in how we should think about provision for housing need. Since 2010, the UK coalition government's welfare reform agenda, especially through the so-called 'Bedroom Tax' and its approach to discretionary housing payments (DHPs), has shifted the frontier of self-regulation, risk-taking and family budgeting into the heart-land of the old welfare state. Financialisation and reponsibilisation are long-standing norms for owner-occupiers, but are now burrowing away in social housing too. This chapter may be rather ambitiously viring from the consequences of the globalisation of housing finance markets through to how UK local authorities operationalise DHPs, but it is our firm belief that the macro and micro levels are increasingly bound together, and one way to understand this is though being conceptually rooted.

Financialisation of the everyday

For more than three decades after the deregulation of the banking system in the 1980s, the world was immersed in a financial revolution, of which expanding housing markets were a central part. The mortgage market in the US led this process particularly through the invention of secondary markets arising from the securitisation of mortgage debt. In other words, the process of originating home loans through brokers and on the high street was increasingly separated from the treatment of the loans as long-term investments. By bundling these loans into mortgage-backed securities (MBS), investors reduced their risk of exposure to interest rate changes and defaulting. Banks and building societies were enabled to take these loans off their books and to create new capital. In theory, MBS are secure long-term investments very attractive to pension funds and life insurers because repayments gradually amortise the loans. As Schwartz and Seabrooke (2008) observed, the institutional connection between housing and pension funds was a key complementarity of the period between deregulation in the 1980s and the banking crisis of 2007.

The problem, as we now know, is that the scale of mis-selling of mortgages in the sub-prime market in the US was of enormous dimensions. As house prices surged in the US, the 'private-label' mortgage market grew from US$586 million in 2003 to US$1.2 trillion in 2005 (England, 2006). The fraudulent selling of tempting, short-term low-interest loans to low-income families was a key root cause of the crisis that broke in the summer of 2007, because the value of some MBS deteriorated very quickly as millions of families defaulted on their loans. By this time, these risk-laden bonds had been sold on into the global financial markets, very detached from their source, and with investors simply not knowing how toxic these investments had become.

However, for three decades before 2007, huge amounts of capital were created through MBS and other types of bonds. Securitisation was the process through which the housing market connected to the global capital markets. As Renaud and Kim (2007, p 6) suggest, 'Securitization is now a major pillar of the structured debt finance revolution in modern finance.' At its peak in the third quarter of 2003, a staggering US$952 billion of refinancing was originated in the US housing market (Case and Quigley, 2010). Indeed, during the boom in the years leading up to the bubble bursting, three-quarters of mortgage lending was for refinancing *in situ*, which was pouring money into the US consumer market, and, to a large extent, sustaining it. Housing markets were not the only source, but this massive wave of global capital surged across the planet, having an impact on and changing people's behaviour (Lowe, 2011). The UK's mortgage market was particularly vulnerable because its institutional structures were very open and under-regulated. Huge amounts of new debt were created as banks underwrote new capital sourced in the securitised circuit of finance. The ill-fated financial model of Northern Rock was largely based on the purchase of capital from the wholesale money market. The scale of this flow of capital, and particularly its international reach, created, for the first time, a *global* surge in house prices and accompanying mortgage debt (Kim and Renaud, 2009).

Re-mortgaging and welfare change

The ability to release housing equity through the mortgage market meant that housing wealth became more fungible than ever before. Evidence of this had been seen in the 1980s in the early days of the deregulation of the banking system. As Lowe pointed out, families were using housing equity to sponsor access to services at all stages of the life cycle. As he observed, 'It is the ability to move flexibly between the public and private sectors that is in part sponsored by decisions on debt and equity in home ownership' (Lowe, 1990, p 58). In other words, households with access to housing equity were not dependant on public services, but had wider choices. This observation was the precursor to a much bigger scale of 'equity leakage' from private housing. The globalisation of mortgage markets through internet trading in the weightless economy intensified this process, as the 'financialisation of the everyday' took hold in advanced economies around the world, albeit mediated through different institutional systems (Lowe, 2011; van der Zwan, 2014, p 111).

The very open mortgage market in some countries, such as the UK, witnessed the creation of thousands of products enabling re-mortgaging to occur, through which owner-occupier households became connected to global capital markets on a very large scale. By 2008 in the UK, the net mean value of homeowner wealth was £208,000, mostly held in the form of housing and pensions, totalling in each sphere net assets of £3.5 trillion. *In situ* re-mortgaging – taking on a new, higher mortgage without moving – enabled homeowners to access their newly inflated housing equity. Smith and Seale's interrogation of the British Household Panel Survey (BHPS) found that one-third of homeowners had withdrawn equity through re-mortgaging peaking in 2007 at a mean amount of £22,600. In a low interest environment, this enabled spending to be advanced at relatively low cost. Smith and Searle revealed that re-mortgaging was accessed mostly by 25- to 34-year-olds. The circumstances most likely to trigger equity withdrawal were a divorce, redundancy, change of job, or having children. Housing equity was not being used for binging on consumer products, new cars or high days and holidays consumerism, but at moments of particular need in the life course or during a family crisis. During their interviews, Smith and Searle found respondents talking about their housing as a 'financial buffer', a 'shield', a 'comfort zone', basically as a safety net against adversity and, as they concluded, '… governments recognize that housing wealth has acquired a de facto role as an asset-base for welfare' (Smith and Searle, 2010, p 351).

The financialisation of everyday life thus becomes more and more familiar, and part and parcel of how homeowners calculate the balance of their welfare needs and those of their family. There is strong evidence of intergenerational behaviour – for example, first-time buyers have sourced deposits from their families, usually in the form of parents re-mortgaging their own property. Wilcox (2010) showed that 80 per cent of first-time buyers between 2005 and 2010 borrowed or were given most of their deposits by family members. Meanwhile, elderly homeowners are increasingly using housing equity to sponsor their access to care support, and are forced to sell their properties to pay for residential care/nursing home fees once savings have been used. The financial buffer offered through long-term homeownership has unlocked funds at particular points of need or choice – switching children to fee-paying independent schools for sixth form is commonly underpinned by re-mortgaging (20 per cent of sixth formers attend fee-paying schools). There is strong evidence that homeowners buy second homes in university towns to avoid paying housing costs for their children by letting rooms to other students. All sorts of lifestyle and care needs are now sponsored through the reach of re-mortgaging, and although lenders are more cautious, and the number of mortgage products far fewer than at their peak in the early 2000s, private medical care, drug treatments unavailable on the NHS, private transport, home renovations of older properties to meet environmental standards and so on are all examples of the fungibility of housing equity. Asset-based welfare is the reality in which millions of homeowners live as they plug into global finance and homes become increasingly financialised.

This process has been openly supported by The Treasury for some time. In essence, what the Treasury argued was that the state can no longer guarantee a minimum income level or even core services, but *instead* guarantees equal opportunity to accumulate private assets in a culture in which a savings habit is normal (HM Treasury, 2001). Supported at the time by Gordon Brown, the Labour government backed the Treasury's view that the housing market should be a central feature of welfare reform – responsible citizens needed to garner their assets and were clearly required to think of their housing wealth as a core of this now highly individualised asset-based approach to welfare. This approach is replete with moral overtones. Gurney points out that the word 'home' became strongly associated with homeownership against social renting, so that the language fostered a normalising discourse in which being a tenant of a social landlord became subtly associated with a form of homelessness, as though being 'at home' could only be truly experienced as an owner-occupier (Gurney, 1999). As will be shown in the next section of this chapter, this idea can easily morph into the terms in which welfare reform has been conducted by the coalition government, notably through its imposition of the so-called 'Bedroom Tax' in which under-occupation of social housing is deemed to be a subsidy provided by taxpayers in general. It is not only homeowners who must calculate the financial value of their homes. The agenda of financial responsibility has trickled down even to social housing, and those households who are the poorest by income. Financialisation and responsibilisation has surfaced in another context.

Responsibilising social housing

Housing, and particularly the social rented sector, has always been linked, to some extent, with questions of responsibility (Flint, 2006, p 21; Robinson, 2013, p 1491), with the idea being firmly 'embedded in housing policy discourse' (Malpass, 2008, p 9). Walker and Chase go as far as to suggest that the roots of the responsibilisation agenda took hold in over four centuries of history (Walker and Chase, 2014, p 137). However, the coalition's welfare reform programme has marched hand-in-hand with a significant 'deepening of personal responsibility' (Patrick, 2012, p 315). The idea of welfare recipients bearing more 'responsibility' for their own life outcomes, and the implied social threat of a dependency culture, speaks to the key assumption behind current welfare reforms that the benefits system itself strongly influences the behaviour of those it intends to assist (Lindsay and Houston, 2013, p 4). This thinking has become increasingly important in justifying the broad range of reforms to Housing Benefit introduced following the Welfare Reform Act 2012 and subsequent secondary legislation (McNeill, 2014, p 182), such as the 'benefit cap' (see below) and the Removal of the Spare Room Subsidy (RSRS) – known as the 'Bedroom Tax', alongside policies established beforehand that have begun to bite more forcefully as the parliamentary term has progressed, such as cuts to Housing Benefit claimed in the private rented sector under Local Housing Allowance, by reducing its ex-ante allowances to the 30th rather than the 50th percentile of reference rents (Ferrari, 2014, p 19).

These changes have not occurred in a vacuum. This well-documented process of responsibilisation in social housing goes hand-in-hand with the processes of financialisation discussed above. This link has recently been drawn by others. Rolnik and Rabinovich align the financialisation of homeownership, and the consequent commodification of all forms of housing (2014, p 86), with the resulting emphasis on the extension of 'market discipline' into areas previously covered by 'basic institutional welfare' (2014, p 57). André and Dewilde go further, highlighting the link between increasingly financialised housing systems and levels of support for redistribution (2014, pp 19-20), a point echoed by Watson when he suggests that a key off-shoot of the processes of financialisation is the construction of a 'responsible citizenry' to provide the basis for a 'moral platform' for welfare reform (Watson, 2009, p 46).

These links chime strongly with the current welfare reform agenda. In line with the 'financialisation of the everyday' and associated political support for allocation of resources through competitive markets (Moloney, 2012, p 129), the welfare reforms detailed above subscribe to this thinking. They use financial penalties and reforms designed to nudge tenants into making more responsible choices, either in the housing market generally, or specifically in the social housing sector. The RSRS introduces a fixed penalty based on the level of eligible rent to households deemed to be 'under-occupying' their property (a 14 per cent penalty for one bedroom, 25 per cent for two or more), the benefit cap introduces a 'maximum' amount of total benefit a household can currently receive (set at £500 per week for families, and £350 for single people), and changes to the uprating of Local Housing Allowance constrains the increase in money available for those claiming Housing Benefit for properties in the private rented sector.

Unsurprisingly, these developments have maintained a high profile. Raquel Rolnik, the United Nations (UN) Special Rapporteur for the Right to Adequate Housing, tuned into the responsibilisation agenda when she undertook her analysis of the realisation of the right to adequate housing during her mission to the UK in 2013. She suggested that 'the welfare State has been transformed from a system centred on State provision into one in which the individual bears more responsibility for his or her welfare and social security' (Rolnik, 2013, p 6), and following concerns about the disproportionate impact of the RSRS, suggested that the policy be suspended immediately (Rolnik, 2013, p 20).

As an example of responsibilisation in the coalition government's welfare reform agenda, the RSRS provides the focus for this section of the chapter. The controversial policy was introduced in April 2013, and was designed with the intention of both saving money and decreasing levels of under-occupation in social housing. However, it would appear that neither of these aims has been met, and its main impact has been to unsettle the lives of a wide range of tenants (see below). By definition these are some of the lowest income families, and the attempt to cut back the Housing Benefit bill has created serious consequences for them. According to Ipsos MORI research on behalf of the National Housing Federation, of the 550,000 households affected by the Bedroom Tax, nearly two-thirds are in rent arrears, and nearly 40 per cent of tenants affected by the size criteria are in arrears due to their failure to pay the shortfall since implementation of the policy (Ipsos MORI, 2014).

The RSRS raises a number of pressing issues, and its responsibilising effect could be explored from many different angles. However, to demonstrate that 2013/14 has seen new developments in the incoming tide of responsibilisation, the discussion here focuses on the use and function of the key discretionary exemption mechanism for the policy – discretionary housing payments (DHPs). It outlines their position in the RSRS scheme, and then deals with their role within the responsibilising agenda.

Responsibilising exemption: the importance of discretionary housing payments

'Responsibilising' reforms to the benefits system, such as the RSRS, are immediately presented with a challenge – how best to filter out those who are too vulnerable, too politically sensitive, or lack capacity to take 'responsibility' for the sanction imposed on them, from those who are the target of the policy. In other words, where to draw the line to identify where the 'sharp division between deserving and undeserving groups' lies (Taylor-Gooby, 2013, p 37). This is a difficult task for policy-makers for two key reasons. First, attempting to operationalise concepts of 'vulnerability' or 'deservingness' is problematic, both in terms of codifying characteristics in legislation or policy documents, and in guiding their interpretation and application to factual cases by frontline workers (Brown, 2012, p 49). Second, as has been well-established by Schneider and Ingram (2005, p 3), the target populations of welfare interventions are inherently socially constructed groups – in this case, they are the 'demons' of 'lifelong renters' in social housing (Hodkinson and Robbins, 2013, p 69), who are congesting a system that could be better used by more 'deserving' households on waiting lists. Membership of this socially constructed group is hard to cast onto a great deal of households in the social rented sector, particularly given the high level of disadvantage and vulnerability (due to disability, for instance) which pervades what is a heavily residualised sector (Robinson, 2013, p 1495). Sorting between those who fit the target group and those deserving of exemption, in other words, determining the 'magnitude of deservedness' of those affected (Drew, 2013, p 620), becomes intensely fact-sensitive – for example, determining the level of disability required for exemption or the number of foster children permitted in the regulations is a difficult factual assessment.

The solution in the case of the RSRS is to offer very limited statutory exemptions within the regulations themselves for small and easily identifiable groups,[1] and to use a discretionary exemption mechanism to deal with the majority of cases. Those statutorily exempted include adults who require 'overnight carers', those on service in the armed forces and, following legal challenges,[2] those with children who are unable to share a bedroom due to a disability. The discretionary mechanism is achieved through the previously small, locally administered, 'low expenditure' (Walker and Niner, 2005, p 64) DHP scheme, to assist tenants who fall outside of exempted groups. Under the new system, DHPs have received somewhat of a second coming – they are cast as the 'panacean payments' (Meers, 2014) for problems presented by the policy. A total of £165 million has been distributed to local authorities in line with a formula based on certain impact indicators and previous DHP expenditure, to assist with plugging the gaps left by the social sector size criteria, benefit cap and changes to Local Housing Allowance (Wilson, 2014, p 2). Tenants who are receiving benefit and who are struggling to pay their rent are able to apply to their local authority for a DHP, which is then paid at their discretion from the capped fund provided by the Department for Work and Pensions (DWP).

When considering the 'responsibilising' function of this scheme, the key consideration here is the discretion given to local authorities in administering these payments. There is a smorgasbord of statutory instruments that deal with payment of DHPs and the various controls on their use imposed on local authorities,[3] and these impose certain limitations on the amount of each award or criteria, which must be met by the applicants. For instance, in cases where the local authority is meeting an ongoing rent liability (as would be the case in awarding a DHP in response to the SSSC), then the total awarded by DHPs cannot exceed the eligible rent for the property, and payments cannot cover certain exempted areas (such as benefit sanctions, increases in rent due to arrears or service charges).[4]

However, aside from these controls and a stream of guidance flowing out of the DWP, local authorities are left to their own devices to decide how to make DHP awards bound only by the general principles of public law. The payment of DHPs is not the payment of Housing Benefit. Although there is a right to a written decision with stated reasons and to seek review, the payments fall outside of para 6 of Schedule 7 to the Child Support, Pensions and Social Act 2000, and are therefore outside of the jurisdiction of a first-tier tribunal.

Discretionary housing payments as a tool of responsibilisation

Although at first glance the utilisation of a discretionary exemption mechanism administered through local authorities instead of a statutory exemption may seem a rather dry distinction, the operation of these payments by local authorities has resulted in a starkly responsibilising scheme. There are three issues that serve to demonstrate this.

The first point is consistent with what has been described as the evolution of a 'new localism' (Jacobs and Manzi, 2012, p 41) often tied with the development of the 'Big Society' agenda (Harrison and Sanders, 2014, p 16), which sees the decentralisation of aspects of welfare provision as engendering a more democratically accountable and efficient alternative to a central command and control approach (Clarke and Cochrane, 2013, p 11). However, the discretion given to local authorities in making these DHP decisions to achieve this can lead, in some instances, to the application of overtly moral criteria or the attachment of conditionality onto the awards. The most widely publicised examples are councils refusing to make DHP awards to those who smoke or who have satellite television (DWP, 2014, p 44), or councils helping those who demonstrated that 'they were making a serious attempt to remove themselves from the situation, either by finding work or moving home' (DWP, 2014, p 44). These conditions align themselves well with the findings of Valentine and Harris on the 'moral evaluation' of those receiving benefits, with key indicators of being a 'shirker' being premised on ways of living (such as smoking and gambling) and economic worth (2014, p 91). Although as highlighted by Harrison and Sanders, separating out these behavioural characteristics from assumptions related to factors such as intra-class demarcations and disability is difficult (2014, p 7), a point perhaps underscored by DWP findings that 75 per cent of local authorities include Disability Living Allowance (DLA) in the means testing for DHP payments (DWP, 2014, p 42).

Second, an issue that presents itself when using an application based discretionary exemption mechanism is that the onus for attaining an exclusion from the policy falls onto the tenant themselves. In line with fostering responsibility for the 'individual provision of welfare' (Lister, 2014, p 12), it is effectively a form of 'bounce-back exemption' – local authorities assess applications they receive; if the tenant does not fulfil their responsibility to apply and put their case for exemption, they are not considered, and the mechanism cannot do its work. This point is particularly pertinent given recent empirical evidence collected on rates of DHP applications by those affected by the RSRS. Twenty-two per cent of tenants had applied for a DHP payment (and consequently the main form of exemption) over the course of the financial year, compared with 26 per cent who had borrowed money to pay the penalty or 60 per cent who had cut back on household expenditure (DWP, 2014, p 39). Those who did not apply expressed concerns that others would be in greater hardship and needed the money more than them, and many affected tenants had simply never heard of the DHP scheme (56 per cent of those who had not applied in the DWP report) (DWP, 2014, p 48).

Third, as the RSRS penalty is financial, DHPs are designed to meet this cost instead of offering a straight exemption – namely, the penalty is paid by DHPs rather than being removed altogether. This is important, as it offers far more shades of grey in comparison to the binary finding of fact that often results from a statutory exemption, where an applicant either meets the criteria to warrant exemption from the measure or does not. The end result is a form of exemption which is far less secure and predictable, with a whole spectrum of different options available for local authorities, which can triangulate between the amount of money awarded, the period it is awarded for, and any conditionality attached. Consequently, local authorities can decide to partially exempt a household by awarding a payment that does not meet the full cost of the penalty, award an exemption for a time-limited period, or provide an exemption conditional on performing an action.

Tying the strands together

In looking at the development of financialisation and responsibilisation in both owner-occupation and the social rented sector, this chapter does not seek to simply observe a mere correlation between the two – rather, it argues that financialisation and responsibilisation work in parallel, and trends in one tenure can bleed into others. Recent research has attempted to investigate this link by examining the connection between financialised housing systems and welfare state support. André and Dewilde have discovered, using data from 43,602 respondents to the European Social Survey 2004-05 across 24 countries, that there is a significant negative correlation between more financialised housing systems and support for government redistribution, and this is true for both homeowners and renters (2014, pp 19-20). This counteracts the intuitive argument that in more financialised housing systems homeowners bear higher risks and have more to lose, and therefore would be willing to support higher levels of government redistribution contrary to the demands of 'responsibilisation'. Instead, it supports the premise that financialisation of housing systems breeds increasing responsibilisation in the welfare state, or, with reference to the examples in this chapter, developments in the owner-occupied sector can win hearts and minds in a way that supports developments in the social rented sector.

This dual relationship has been explored elsewhere, particularly with reference to how the government and the media engrain the process of 'financialising welfare' (Lundström, 2013, p 639) by rendering it as 'common sense' (Greenfield and Williams, 2007, p 420), and subject those who fail to meet the resulting obligations to the 'moral scorn of the state' (Beggs et al, 2014, p 189), or become labelled as 'shirkers' or 'skivers' (Whitworth and Carter, 2014, p 108). This ongoing narrative linking 'financialisation' and 'responsibilisation' does not show many signs of slowing.

However, in the field of housing, the linking of these two policy trends is an inherently ironic exercise. As highlighted by Trnka and Trundle, the same responsibilising and financialising processes that encourage 'freedom, choice, and autonomy ... simultaneously constitute new relations and dependencies' (2014, p 140). Namely, by encouraging people to engage with globalised mortgage markets, or to provide more of their own welfare safety net through asset-building or otherwise, they become dependent and governed by the same structures designed to give them the autonomy to take responsibility for themselves. In the words of Mahmud, a 'discourse of responsibility furnished the grounds for the symbiosis between debt and discipline' (Mahmud, 2012, p 482) – those who are engaging with financial markets need to play by the rules they set. Kear epitomises this problem when he re-casts the so-called rationally acting 'homo economicus' into what he describes as the 'homo subprimicus' – a financial subject whose dependencies render them 'eminently governable by financial means' (Kear, 2013, p 941).

The RSRS provides an example from a different angle. A tenant's conduct is financialised in the form of a penalty based on their level of eligible rent, and they are given the responsibility to either make their case for exemption by applying for a DHP payment, find money to pay the penalty, or attempt to find somewhere else to live. Although those subject to the policy are supposedly given the responsibility and associated autonomy to make their own decision, the government are inherently compromising their ability to do so through the imposition of the penalty. Mik-Meyer and Villadsen describe this contradiction as the process of 'managing free-subjects' (Mik-Meyer and Villadsen, 2013, p 24). Finally we come back to the core of our argument: that housing has become a key domain for the ideational and practical out-working and reconfiguration of the 21st-century welfare state.

Notes
[1] Contained within Regulation B13 in the amended Housing Benefit Regulations 2006.
[2] See *Burnip v Birmingham City Council* [2012] EWCA Civ 629.
[3] See Council Tax Benefit Abolition (Consequential Provisions) Regulations 2013/458, Discretionary Housing Payments Grants Amendment Order 2008/1167, Discretionary Financial Assistance Amendment Regulations 2008/637, Discretionary Housing Payments Grants Amendment Order 2005/2052, Discretionary Housing Payments Grants Amendment Order 2004/2329, Discretionary Housing Payments (Grants) Order 2001/2340, and Discretionary Financial Assistance Regulations 2001/1167.
[4] See Regulation 3, Discretionary Financial Assistance Regulations 2001/1167.

References
Aglietta, M. (1979) *A theory of capitalist regulation: The US experience*, London: Verso.

André, S. and Dewilde, C. (2014) 'Home ownership and support for government redistribution', *Comparative European Politics*, 30 June (www.palgrave-journals.com/cep/journal/vaop/ncurrent/full/cep201431a.html).

Beggs, M., Bryan, D. and Rafferty, M. (2014) 'Shoplifters of the world unite! Law and culture in financialized times', *Cultural Studies*, vol 28, pp 976-96.

Brown, K. (2012) 'Re-moralising "vulnerability"', *People, Place & Policy*, 6, pp 41-53.

Bulley, D. and Bulley, B. (2014) 'Big Society as big government: Cameron's governmentality agenda', *The British Journal of Politics & International Relations*, 16, pp 452-70.

Case, K.E. and Quigley, J.M. (2010) 'How housing busts end: home prices, user costs and rigidities during down cycles' in S.J. Smith and B.A. Searle (eds) *The Blackwell companion to the economics of housing: The housing wealth of nations*, Chichester: Wiley-Blackwell.

Clarke, N. and Cochrane, A. (2013) 'Geographies and politics of localism: the localism of the United Kingdom's coalition government', *Political Geography*, vol 34, pp 10-23.

Davis, G.F. (2009) *Managed by the markets: How finance re-shaped America*, Oxford: Oxford University Press.

Drew, R. (2013) 'Constructing homeownership policy: social constructions and the design of the low-income homeownership policy objective', *Housing Studies*, vol 28, pp 616-31.

DWP (Department for Work and Pensions) (2014) *Evaluation of removal of the spare room subsidy*, Research Report No 882, London: The Stationery Office.

Dwyer, P. (2004) 'Creeping conditionality in the UK: From welfare rights to conditional entitlements?' *The Canadian Journal of Sociology*, vol 29, no 2, p 265-87.

Ellison, N. (2011) 'The Conservative Party and the "Big Society"', in C. Holden, M. Kilkey and G. Ramia (eds) *Social Policy Review 23*, Bristol: Policy Press, pp 45-62.

England, R. (2006) 'The rise of private label', *Mortgage Banking* (www.Robertstoweengland.com/document/MBM.10-06EnglandPrivateLabel.pdf).

Froud, J., Haslam, C., Johal, S. and Williams, K. (2000) 'Shareholder value and financialisation: consultancy promises and management moves', *Economy and Society*, vol 29, pp 80-110.

Ferrari, E. (2014) 'The social value of housing in straitened times: the view from England', *Housing Studies*, pp 1-21.

Flint, J. (2006) *Housing, urban governance and anti-social behaviour: Perspectives, policy and practice*, Bristol: Policy Press.

Greenfield, C. and Williams, P. (2007) 'Financialization, finance rationality and the role of media in Australia', *Media, Culture & Society*, vol 29, no 3, pp 415-33.

Gurney, C. (1999) 'Lowering the drawbridge: a case study of analogy and metaphor in the social construction of home ownership', *Urban Studies*, vol 36, pp 1705-22.

Harrison, M. and Sanders, T. (2014) 'Setting the scene', in M. Harrison and T. Sanders (eds) *Social policies and social control: New perspectives on the 'not-so-big-society'*, Bristol: Policy Press, pp 3-22.

HM Treasury (2001) *Savings and assets for all: The modernisation of Britain's tax and benefits system*, Number Eight, London: HMSO.

Hodkinson, S. and Robbins, G. (2013) 'The return of class war conservatism? Housing under the UK coalition government', *Critical Social Policy*, vol 33, no 1, pp 57-77.

Ipsos MORI (2014) *Impact of welfare reforms on housing associations: Early effects and responses by landlords and tenants*, April, London: Ipsos MORI Social Research Institute.

Jacobs, K. and Manzi, T. (2012) 'New localism, old retrenchment: the "Big Society", housing policy and the politics of welfare reform', *Housing, Theory and Society*, vol 30, no 1, pp 29-45.

Jurgens, J., Naumann, K. and Rupp, J. (2000) 'Shareholder value in an adverse environment: the German case', *Economy and Society*, vol 29, pp 54-79.

Kear, M. (2013) 'Governing homo subprimicus: beyond financial citizenship, exclusion, and rights', *Antipode*, vol 45, no 4, pp 926-46.

Kim, K.-H. and Renaud, B. (2009) 'The global house price boom and its unwinding: an analysis and a commentary', *Housing Studies*, vol 24, no 1, pp 7-24.

Lindsay, C. and Houston, D. (2013) 'Fit for work? Representations and explanations of the disability benefits "crisis" in the UK and beyond', in C. Lindsay and D. Houston (eds) *Disability benefits, welfare reform and employment policy*, Basingstoke: Palgrave Macmillan, pp 1-14.

Lister, R. (2011) 'The age of responsibility: social policy and citizenship in the early 21st century', in C. Holdon, M. Kilkey and G. Ramia (eds) *Social Policy Review 23: Analysis and debate in social policy*, Bristol: Policy Press, pp 63-84.

Lister, M. (2014) 'Citizens, doing it for themselves? The Big Society and government through community', *Parliamentary Affairs*, 6 January.

Lowe, S. (1990) 'Capital accumulation in home ownership and family welfare', in N. Manning and C. Ungerson (eds) *Social Policy Review 1989-90*, Harlow: Longman.

Lowe, S. (2011) *The housing debate*, Bristol: Policy Press.

Lundström, R. (2013) 'Framing fraud: discourse on benefit cheating in Sweden and the UK', *European Journal of Communication*, vol 28, pp 630-45.

McNeill, J. (2014) 'Regulating social housing: expectations for behaviour of tenants', in M. Harrison and T. Sanders (eds) *Social policies and social control: New perspectives on the 'not-so-big society'*, Bristol: Policy Press, pp 181-95.

Mahmud, T. (2012) 'Debt and discipline', *American Quarterly*, vol 64, pp 469-94

Malpass, P. (2008) 'Housing and the new welfare state: wobbly pillar or cornerstone?', *Housing Studies*, vol 23, pp 1-19.

Meers, J. (2014) 'Challenging the "bedroom tax": disability, deference, and the evolving role of discretionary housing payments – R (MA) v Secretary of State for Work and Pensions', *Journal of Social Security Law*, vol 21, pp 97-102.

Mik-Meyer, N. and Villadsen, K. (2013) *Power and welfare: Understanding citizens' encounters with state welfare*, London: Routledge.

Moloney, N. (2012) 'The legacy effects of the financial crisis on regulatory design in the EU', in E. Ferran, N. Moloney, J. Hill and J. Coffee (eds) *The regulatory aftermath of the global financial crisis*, Cambridge: Cambridge University Press.

Patrick, R. (2012) 'All in it together? Disabled people, the Coalition and welfare to work', *Journal of Poverty and Social Justice*, vol 20, pp 307-22.

Renaud, B. and Kim, K.-H. (2007) 'The global housing price boom and its aftermath', *Housing Finance International*, vol XXII, no 2, pp 3-15.

Robinson, D. (2013) 'Social housing in England: testing the logics of reform', *Urban Studies*, vol 50, pp 1489-504.

Rolnik, R. (2013) 'Late neoliberalism: the financialization of homeownership and housing rights', *International Journal of Urban and Regional Research*, vol 37, pp 1058-66.

Rolnik, R. and Rabinovich, L. (2014) 'Late-neoliberalism: the financialisation of homeownership and the housing rights of the poor', in A. Nolan (ed) *Economic and social rights after the global financial crisis*, Cambridge: Cambridge University Press, pp 57-89.

Schneider, A. and Ingram, H. (2005) 'Public policy and the social construction of deservedness', in A. Schneider and H. Ingram (eds) *Deserving and entitled: Social constructions and public policy*, New York: New York University Press, pp 1-34.

Schwartz, H.M. and Seabrooke, L. (2008) 'Varieties of residential capitalism in the international political economy: old welfare states and the new politics of housing', *Comparative European Politics*, vol 6, pp 237-61.

Sherraden, M. (1991) *Assets and the poor: A new American welfare policy*, New York: M.E. Sharpe Inc.

Smith, S.J. and Searle, B.A. (2010) 'Housing wealth as insurance: insights from the UK', in S.J. Smith and B.A. Searle (eds) *The Blackwell companion to the economics of housing: The housing wealth of nations*, Chichester, Wiley-Blackwell.

Taylor-Gooby, P. (2013) 'Why do people stigmatise the poor at a time of rapidly increasing inequality, and what can de done about it?', *The Political Quarterly*, vol 84, no 1, pp 31-42.

Trnka, S. and Trundle, C. (2014) 'Competing responsibilities: moving beyond neoliberal responsibilisation', *Anthropological Forum*, vol 24, no 2, pp 136-53.

Valentine, G. and Harris, C. (2014) 'Strivers vs skivers: class prejudice and the demonisation of dependency in everyday life', *Geoforum*, vol 53, pp 84-92.

van der Zwan, N. (2014) 'Making sense of financialization', *Socio-Economic Review*, vol 12, pp 99-129.

Walker, B. and Niner, P. (2005) 'The use of discretion in a rule-bound service: Housing Benefit administration and the introduction of discretionary housing payments in Great Britain', *Public Administration*, vol 83, no 1, pp 47-66.

Walker, R. and Chase, E. (2014) 'Separating the sheep from the goats: tackling poverty in Britain for over four centuries', in E. Gubrium, S. Pellissery and I. Lodemel (eds) *The shame of it: Global perspectives on anti-poverty policies*, Bristol: Policy Press., pp 133-56.

Watson, M. (2009) 'Planning for a future of asset-based welfare? New Labour, financialized economic agency and the housing market', *Planning, Practice and Research*, vol 24, no 1, pp 41-56.

Whitworth, A. and Carter, E. (2014) 'Welfare-to-Work reform, power and inequality: from governance to governmentalities', *Journal of Contemporary European Studies*, vol 22, pp 104-17.

Wilcox, S. (2010) *Financial barriers to home ownership*, York: Genworth Financial and Centre for Housing Policy, University of York.

Wilson, W. (2014) *Housing Benefit: Discretionary Housing Payments (DHPs)*, House of Commons Library (SN/SP/6899).

FOUR

'The end of local government as we know it' – what next for adult social care?

Jon Glasby

Under the coalition government (2010–15), local authorities have suffered such massive funding cuts that one council leader has described the situation as "the end of local government as we know it". While councils have tried hard to protect their social care spending as best they can, this has inevitably led to significant financial challenges, and to social care leaders struggling to make ends meet. All this comes on the back of new responsibilities under the Care Act 2014, changing demographics and policy pressures to develop more personalised services and to integrate care more fully with the NHS. While both personalisation and joint working with partners might be part of a longer-term solution, pursuing both goals at a time of austerity is incredibly difficult – and both agendas are arguably being implemented in less than optimal ways. Taking stock of these developments, this chapter looks at recent changes in adult social care, and argues that even more fundamental reform will be necessary in future.

In 2014, the House of Commons Committee of Public Accounts published its review of adult social care in England. In a boxed summary at the start of the report, the Committee concluded that (p 3):

> The challenge posed to society by the changing and growing need for adult social care is considerable. The need for such care is increasing while public funding is falling. The Government's agenda to change and improve adult social care is rightly ambitious but achieving these ambitions will require unprecedented levels of coordinated working between government departments, between central and local government and across local authorities and health bodies. The Departments recognise the complexities and risks but we are not convinced that the responsible bodies will

deliver on these ambitions and are concerned that they are raising expectations too high.

The summary goes on to make recommendations around three main areas: 'collaboration across bodies involved in the care system'; 'better understanding of the capacity of the system to cope and for whether money really reaches the frontline services on which people depend'; and 'the Government's oversight arrangements to reflect the overriding importance of quality of care in a sector where up to 220,000 workers earn less than the minimum wage and around one third of the workforce are on zero-hour contracts' (p 3).

Building on the work of the Committee of Public Accounts, this chapter reviews selected recent developments in UK adult social care under the coalition government, focusing on three particularly prominent and challenging issues in current policy and practice: the financial and demographic pressures facing local councils; the implications of the Care Act 2014 (which could make such pressures worse); and the drive to integrate and personalise services (which are potentially important ways forward, but which are unlikely to prove to be a panacea). Without urgent (but also sustained, long-term) action, it is argued, the adult social care system could all but collapse – leaving only the most dependent and those on the very lowest incomes with any form of support at all. Indeed, one of the most unsung achievements of 2013–14 has arguably been the ability of frontline workers and social care leaders to keep the system going, seeking to maintain services as best they can in difficult circumstances. However, the current situation is not just the product of recent changes – pressures in adult social care have been building for several decades. Indeed, it could even be argued that previous funding increases prevented the need for a more fundamental rethink of current approaches, and that the financial challenges facing adult social care could, ironically, force a more genuine and long-term solution.

Pressures facing adult social care

Adult social care makes an important contribution to the quality of life of older people and of people with mental health problems, people with learning difficulties and people with physical impairments. However, it is a very targeted service (focused only on those with the highest needs) and is part of broader local government (thus enjoying less focus than more national and universal services such as education or health). It also involves a mix of care and state control, and has therefore tended to have a more ambiguous role and remit than some other welfare services (such as the NHS). For all these reasons, adult social care has therefore tended to be less popular, less well understood and therefore less well supported and funded than other public services.

When reviewing adult social care it is always easy to blame long-term and chronic under-funding. While tempting, this can sometimes seem a convenient excuse and does not give the full story. Lots of well-funded services can be poor and some dramatically under-funded services can deliver wonderful care – so funding alone is no guarantee of quality. However, even with this caveat, no review of current adult social care can begin without acknowledging and exploring the very difficult financial environment in which social care services are currently being delivered. In one sense, this is a longstanding issue, but it has also acquired even greater significance following the austerity measures pursued by the coalition government and the subsequent impact on local government finances.

In the run-up to the 2010 General Election, the New Labour government commissioned a review of the future costs of adult social care in order to inform a White Paper and Labour's future policy offer. Overseen by the Downing Street Policy Unit and the Department of Health, the review argued that the adult social care system was facing rising pressures from changing demography (with a rapidly ageing population), changes in family and social structures, the impact of new technology, rising public expectations and increased concern at national level about the dangers of a so-called 'postcode lottery' (Glasby et al, 2010). In response to these pressures, the review set out three different scenarios with three different spending implications:

- *Slow uptake:* under this approach, future policy and practice remain very much as they were then, with a rhetorical commitment to more radical reform, but with relatively little actual change in practice. On existing trends, the real costs of adult social care could double within two decades – and this would be the case for current services (which were already recognised by many policy-makers and practitioners as struggling to meet existing needs).
- *Solid progress:* while the stated aims of policy remain similar, there is a much more concerted effort to improve outcomes and to deliver savings through more radical change. In practice, the intended benefits are not fully realised, and thinking retreats back towards previous approaches. Under this scenario, the overall costs of the

system would continue to rise, albeit rather more slowly than for the 'slow uptake' scenario.

- *Fully engaged:* there is a sustained commitment to genuine change, motivated by a desire to realise in full the potential benefits for the health and social care system and for wider society. Although some of the evidence base is currently contested or unclear, the outcomes surpass expectations and the mechanisms of reform start to really deliver. If this scenario was to be fully achieved (and this requires a very demanding series of assumptions), we may see costs of adult social care contained at close to their current level.

Crucially, this review was undertaken at the end of a period of plenty, when public service expenditure had increased significantly under the New Labour governments of 1997–2010. Since 2010, local government as a whole has experienced massive cuts, with one prominent council leader describing the situation as the "end of local government as we know it" (quoted in Dudman, 2012). While many councils have tried to protect their spending on adult social care (and on children's services) as best they can, they still face very difficult decisions. According to the National Audit Office (2014a, p 7), adults' care needs are rising, but 'local authorities' total spending on adult social care fell 8 per cent in real terms between 2010–11 and 2012–13 and is projected to continue falling'. The same report also suggests that:

- Local authorities have reduced the total amount of state-funded care provided through individual packages of care every year since 2008–09.
- Rising needs, reducing local authority spending, and reductions in benefits may be putting unsustainable pressure on informal carers and acute health services.

Overall, it concludes that (p 11):

> Pressures on the care system are increasing. Providing adequate adult social care poses a significant public service challenge and there are no easy answers. People are living longer and some have long-term and complex health conditions that require managing through care. Need for care is rising while public spending is falling, and there is unmet need. Departments do not know if we are approaching the limits of the capacity of the system to continue to absorb these pressures.

Similar points are raised in the annual survey of the Association of Directors of Adult Social Services (ADASS, 2014, p 1), which suggests that:

> Since 2010, spending on Adult Social Care has fallen by 12% in real terms at a time when the population of those looking for support has increased by 14%. This is leading to fewer people receiving support, with councils over the last 4 years making savings to Adult Social Care budgets totalling £3.53 billion.

Perhaps unsurprisingly, Directors felt that this would lead to fewer people able to access support and to increasing legal challenges, financial difficulties for providers (with increased risk of provider failure) and increasing pressures on the NHS (p 3). To make such figures more concrete, one local authority has produced data suggesting that in 20 years' time, councils may be spending all of their budget on adult social care and children's services, with no funding at all for any other service (known colloquially as 'the Barnet graph of doom'; see Brindle, 2012). As if this situation wasn't already hard enough, these budget cuts and demographic changes have also been accompanied by new legislation and increasing ambitions – and it is to these that the next section of the chapter turns.

Implications of the Care Act 2014

As the pressures described above were becoming more apparent, the coalition government introduced and passed the Care Act 2014. While much of this legislation modernises and tidies up the underlying legal framework, these reforms may also bring significant new pressures. While the changes taking place are complex, some of the key features of the Act include:

- a duty to promote wellbeing;
- a greater emphasis on preventative services;
- a duty to provide information and advice (irrespective of whether people qualify for formal services);
- the creation of a national minimum threshold when determining whether someone has eligible needs;
- a stronger duty to meet the needs of carers.

To help local authorities understand the potential scale of different clauses, the Local Government Association (2014) has published an analysis that seeks to clarify which areas of the Act simply consolidate existing requirements, which are new in law but not really new in terms of existing practice, and which are entirely new in both law and practice. While it is too early to tell what implications these changes will have in practice, the fear is that there will be a growing mismatch between an under-funded system struggling even to provide basic care, and the vision of the Act around a system focused on broader wellbeing, prevention and the provision of information and advice. Although there remains significant support for the ethos of the Care Act, the danger is that the rhetoric simply does not match the reality, and that local authorities, frontline staff and people using services are set up to fail in a system that can do nothing else but over-promise and under-deliver.

Of all the changes, perhaps the most complex and controversial are those associated with the government's response to the Dilnot review (2011) on the future funding of long-term care. While these issues are discussed elsewhere (see Table 4.1 for a brief summary of the government's response to Dilnot; for a more detailed commentary, see also Humphries, 2013; Henwood, 2014), the new legislation could also generate a series of new tensions:

- There is a risk that people entering a care home hear media reports about 'free care' and do not realise that the proposed funding arrangements are complex – and indeed still potentially involve significant user charges for people's care (albeit with capped maximum costs) and ongoing living costs each year. Without sustained communication, this could create a major mismatch between what the new system offers and people's expectations of what is available, thereby further undermining trust and confidence in the social care system.
- The proposed cap may be set at a level that is too high to encourage people to prepare in advance for older age and potential future care costs. The Dilnot review modelled the impact of a cap of £35,000 – but the government's actual cap of £72,000 seems a very different proposition, and might benefit relatively few people in practice.
- An unknown number of people may seek sudden assessment of their needs as the new system is implemented because the costs they are paying for their care will not count towards the maximum contribution people can be asked to make until they have been assessed as having an eligible need. In some authorities (particularly

those with a large number of people funding their own care), this could dramatically increase assessment workloads and lead to significant delays, waiting lists and dissatisfaction.

• The new system might entail significant training and administrative costs that are yet unknown.

• While these changes represent a shift in the nature of the national 'offer', they do little to alter the overall funding available, and adult social care arguably remains dramatically under-funded (see the discussions earlier in this chapter about funding cuts and demographic changes). This could be exacerbated if the implications of the current changes are under-estimated or under-costed in any way.

So far this chapter has highlighted the challenges facing adult social care as it tries to respond to budgetary reductions, changing demographics

Table 4.1: (Very selected) Dilnot proposals and the subsequent government response

Proposal	Government response
To protect people from extreme care costs, there should be a cap on the lifetime contribution to adult social care costs that any individual needs to make at between £25,000 and £50,000. Where an individual's care costs exceed the cap, they would be eligible for full support from the state	Accepted – cap to be set at £72,000 from 2016, with a lower cap (to be decided) for working-age people
To extend protection to people falling just outside of the means test, the asset threshold for those in residential care beyond which no means-tested help is given should increase from £23,250 to £100,000	Accepted – the upper capital threshold for means-tested support will rise to £118,000 from 2016/17 (equivalent to £100,000 in 2010/11 prices) and the lower threshold to £17,000 (equivalent to £14,250 in 2010/11 prices)
Those who enter adulthood already having a care and support need should immediately be eligible for free state support to meet their care needs, rather than being subjected to a means test	Accepted – there will be a zero cap for people who turn 18 with eligible care and support needs
People should contribute a standard amount – £7,000 to £10,000 – yearly to cover their general living costs, such as food and accommodation, in residential care	Accepted – from 2016 people in residential care should pay a contribution of around £12,000 yearly towards general living expenses (£10,000 in 2010/11 prices)

Source: Humphries (2013, p 14)

and new legal duties. Two of the most prominent government policies that seek to address some of these issues are integrated care and personalisation – both of which are reviewed below.

Integrated care and personalisation

As adult social care grapples with rising need, reduced funding and new responsibilities, two potential solutions that have been offered take the form of greater integration with the NHS, and the creation of more personalised and tailored support. As suggested below, these are both potentially very positive developments – but may also have downsides, and certainly do not represent panaceas.

Integrated care

Under New Labour, there was significant emphasis on joint working between health and social care – memorably likened by the first New Labour Health Secretary, Frank Dobson, to 'bringing down the Berlin Wall between health and social services' (see, for example, *Hansard*, 1998). This was dramatic language, but the UK welfare state is based on an assumption that it is possible (and maybe even desirable) to distinguish between people who are 'sick' (who are seen as having 'health' needs met by the NHS free at the point of delivery), and people who are merely 'frail' or 'disabled' (who are seen as having 'social care' needs that are the responsibility of local authorities, and where people receiving support are means-tested and often charged for their care). This has then resulted in a series of barriers – different legal frameworks, budgets, accountability mechanisms, IT systems, geographical boundaries, cultures, and so on – which make joint working on the ground incredibly difficult (if not impossible) (see Glasby and Dickinson, 2014, for an overview). As the author of the 'five laws of integration' (Leutz, 1999) has suggested, you cannot 'integrate a square peg into a round hole' – and yet this is precisely what frontline workers in health and social care are asked to do on a daily basis. This has taken a number of forms over the years – whether a bathing service is a 'health' bath or a 'social bath', whether someone qualifies for free NHS continuing care, whether sufficient social care funds are available to enable people to be discharged from hospital in a timely fashion, and so on (see Glasby and Littlechild, 2004, for additional examples).

While New Labour was ultimately unable to resolve these problems, they deserve credit for identifying the issues at stake and for testing a series of different potential responses. According to a New Labour discussion paper (DH, 1998, p 3):

> All too often when people have complex needs spanning both health and social care good quality services are sacrificed for sterile arguments about boundaries. When this happens people, often the most vulnerable in our society … and those who care for them find themselves in the no man's land between health and social services. This is not what people want or need. It places the needs of the organisation above the needs of the people they are there to serve. It is poor organisation, poor practice, poor use of taxpayers' money – it is unacceptable.

Following on from this analysis, the late 1990s and the 2000s saw a series of policy initiatives in order to encourage more effective joint working between health and social services, including:

- The passage of the *Health Act 1999* to enable local partners to pool health and social care budgets, designate lead commissioners for particular user groups and create integrated provider arrangements.
- The creation of a small number of *care trusts* (fully integrated health and social care organisations).
- A national *Change Agent Team* and an *Integrated Care Network* to support joint working at local level.
- A new *statutory duty of partnership*.
- The introduction of *health scrutiny*, so that local authority scrutiny committees can hold the NHS to greater account locally.
- *Extra funding*, *new service models* and *new legislation* to reduce the number of people unable to leave hospital due to delays in arranging health and social care services in the community.

After the 2010 General Election, there were widespread fears that the coalition government's health reforms would lead to a greater emphasis on competition and would make joint working harder. The outcry with which these changes were greeted led to the creation of the NHS Future Forum to review the changes and, if necessary, propose amendments. From the beginning, the Future Forum emphasised the importance of what it called 'integrated care' – particularly for older people and people with multiple long-term conditions, who may need support from a range of different health and social care professionals and from primary care, community and hospital services within the NHS (NHS Future

Forum, 2012). While the language was different from the 'partnership' agenda of New Labour, there was significant continuity in practice, and the concept of 'integrated care' was picked up by government and used repeatedly in subsequent policy debates and announcements.

Despite this apparent continuity, it remains to be seen whether the commitment to 'integrated care' is real – or remains largely rhetorical. Often, the key terms are poorly defined (or not even defined at all), with different potential partners each believing they are committing to something slightly different. For Glasby and Dickinson (2014), 'integrated care' may be the latest in a long line of buzzwords that sound inherently positive and that can be used to mobilise key stakeholders; that refer to something important (almost as if we would need to invent the term if we didn't already have it); that are almost impossible to define (but you tend to know it when you see it); and yet which ultimately mean so many different things to different people that subsequent attempts to operationalise the concept become almost meaningless (other previous examples of such terms might be 'community', 'empowerment', 'involvement' and so on). It is also arguable that there is little clarity about the outcomes that 'integrated care' is meant to deliver – so much so, that Glasby and Dickinson (2014) have tried to re-frame the debate by asking: 'if integrated care is the answer, what was the question?'

Under the coalition, there have been a number of new policy developments, but the jury is still out as to whether these will be sufficient to bring about significant change. This includes:

- The creation of *Health and Wellbeing Boards* to provide strategic leadership at local level. While these could be an important forum for local debates about the future direction of services, such Boards have relatively little power in practice, and their impact could be mainly symbolic. There is also a suspicion that they were created at relatively short notice as the welding together of previous Conservative and Liberal Democrat policies led to the abolition of both primary care trusts (PCTs) and strategic health authorities (SHAs), thus leaving virtually no system leadership and the potential for significant fragmentation. Although Health and Wellbeing Boards are doing important work across the country and can be a significant force for good, there remains a danger that some could become 'talking shops', and that they will not prove sufficient to bind key partners to a joint vision.
- The identification of a series of *integrated care pioneers* (local areas working to generate innovative local solutions, to produce learning

about what works and to work with national partners to help spread key lessons and shape future policy). In many respects, this appears similar to a previous New Labour initiative (see RAND Europe/ Ernst & Young, 2012 for details of New Labour's integrated care organisation pilots), and – although some helpful learning may follow – seems insufficient to tackle the full extent of the problem.

• In many ways, the 'pioneer' process was upstaged by the announcement of a £3.8 billion *Better Care Fund* designed to support greater integration of health and social care in all local areas. While the need to submit proposed plans in response to the Fund prompted some helpful (and probably some not-so-helpful) discussions at local level, the sums involved (while significant) remain relatively small compared to the total NHS budget. From the author's personal experience, it also felt as if different stakeholders had different understandings of the underlying nature and purpose of the funding. Often, local government saw this as a means of the government preserving its commitment to ring-fence the NHS budget, but quietly transferring some of this money across to social care to stop it collapsing amidst the funding pressures described above. In contrast, the NHS tended to see the Fund as a way of investing jointly in shared priorities and encouraging mutual transformation. Of course, both interpretations are potentially legitimate in their own right – but they remain different. The policy also assumed that the £3.8 billion in question existed as a standalone chunk of money – perhaps in a bank account somewhere – that could simply be transferred. In practice, such funds are already invested in staff, buildings and services, and so extracting funds to subsequently transfer was always going to be a painful and controversial process. With hindsight, therefore, perhaps the local and national wrangling and acrimony that has followed (see, for example, Campbell, 2014) was inevitable with a policy that may have been well-intentioned but which was conceived and implemented badly (see also National Audit Office, 2014b).

Overall, the desire to more fully integrate the care provided to people with complex or multiple needs is a good one, and it may be that providing better care to people also ends up being most cost-effective in the long run. Certainly, this seems to be the aspiration – but the evidence to support such a belief is limited and patchy to say the least. Indeed, a second of the 'five laws of integration' cited above (Leutz, 1999) is that 'integration costs before it pays' – and many local leaders would doubtless add to this statement: 'integration costs before it pays (and we have never really stuck at anything for long enough to know whether it ever really pays).' While more integrated care for those who need it has to be part of a solution, the sloppy way in which such language is often used by policy-makers runs the risk of making things worse rather than better as everyone ends up frustrated with a concept that means too many different and potentially mutually incompatible things to different people. Certainly at ground level, frontline services seem no more integrated than before, and in some areas of the country, relationships are arguably more fragmented than under New Labour. Against this background some of the more recent policy mechanisms local areas have at their disposal might help a little, but are not sufficient to tackle a problem of this scale.

Personalisation

In addition to the coalition's emphasis on integrated care, a second potential solution to the challenges identified in this chapter comes in the form of the 'personalisation agenda' (often defined loosely as a desire to enable people receiving social care to have greater choice and control over their services). This has developed over many years (see Glasby and Littlechild, 2009; Needham and Glasby, 2014), beginning perhaps with the concept of direct payments invented by disabled people's organisations, and formalised in 1996 after longstanding campaigns by disabled people to gain greater control over the funds spent on their care. This was followed in the mid-2000s by the linked but separate concept of personal budgets, whereby people needing support are given an upfront indication of the possible amount of funding available to meet their needs, and can then plan more creatively and innovatively how best to use this money. The subsequent personal budget can be received as a direct payment as before, but can also be administered by others (whether a social worker, a trusted service provider, a family member, an independent trust, and so on) so that people in receipt of care know how much there is to spend, but can choose how much control they want over this funding.

Although direct payments were initially introduced under a Conservative government in 1996, they were championed by New Labour and the subsequent 'personalisation' agenda has continued to form the basis of the coalition's approach to adult social care. Previous policy had already committed to delivering all adult social care via personal budgets (except in an emergency), and this commitment has been retained. Indeed, the coalition has even gone one stage further, stressing its expectation that most personal budgets will be delivered by a direct payment (viewed as the strongest form of transferring control to the person using services). New Labour's attempts to test these concepts in other settings (such as children's services and parts of the NHS) have also been developed further, with personal health budgets to be rolled out for people with continuing healthcare needs in particular, and for people with other healthcare needs more generally (for a summary, see Alakeson, 2014).

Throughout, these changes have been contested and controversial (for the different viewpoints summarised below, see Glasby and Littlechild, 2009; Needham and Glasby, 2014). On the one hand, some see personalisation as a civil rights struggle, promoting greater citizenship for disabled people, and trying to ensure greater 'independent living' (that is, ensuring disabled people have the same choice and control over their lives as non-disabled people). At the same time, others see this as a neoliberal agenda designed to undermine traditional public sector services and values, transfer responsibility from the state to the individual and 'dress up' unfair and draconian cuts as a more positive policy reform. These issues are debated in much greater detail by Needham and Glasby (2014, p 5), who review a wide range of debates related to risk enablement versus risk aversion; the impact of personalisation on relationships with families, friends and local communities; the different experiences of different service user groups; issues of equity; the impact on the social care workforce; and so on.

Without rehearsing these debates, the key issue here is that personalisation can be both of these things (a campaign for citizenship or thinly disguised neoliberalism). Similar to the partnership/integrated care agenda above, perhaps one of the strengths of personalisation is that it is such an elastic concept that it brings different groups together and builds early momentum for change (see Needham, 2011). However, there is an equal danger that this initial consensus masks very different underlying value bases and motivations, and that the different stakeholders all arguing for greater 'personalisation' diverge quickly once such an approach is introduced. This is described in detail by Simon Duffy (2014, p 178), one of the key architects of the personalisation agenda, who sees the way in which personalisation is being implemented in practice as 'a mixture of the good, the bad and the ugly' – undoubtedly doing good in some areas and for some people, but at worst, representing a form of 'zombie personalisation' (where the language of citizenship and of community is used to bring about very different ends).

As with integrated care, therefore, the government's commitment to greater choice and control for people using adult social care (and potentially other services too) seems a good thing, with scope to be part of a broader solution. However, there is also a danger that lip-service is paid to some of the key values espoused by longstanding supporters of direct payments and personal budgets, and that warm and 'fuzzy' language is once again used to (at best) maintain the status quo and/or (at worst) justify something worse. Another similarity between integrated care and personalisation is that the current policy context creates space for local leaders (at all levels within local systems) to take such concepts and use them as best they can to improve services for local people. If no one is fully sure what 'integrated care' or 'personalisation' mean, then in one sense there is scope for key actors to create their own meaning at local level. Whether this will be a liberating and creative opportunity for good, or a recipe for chaos and inaction, remains to be seen.

Conclusion

This chapter has argued that adult social care faces a triple whammy of:

- massive financial challenges
- rapidly escalating need and demand
- possible new (and probably under-funded) responsibilities.

While policy responses such as integrated care and personalisation have the potential to be part of a solution, they are unlikely to be a panacea – and both agendas contain ambiguities and tensions.

Given the analysis above, one option would for adult social care to continue as it is and do its best to make the system work as well as possible, papering over the cracks and trying to be as inventive as possible in bridging the gap between demand and funding. However, this simply does not seem realistic in the long term, and the only other option is for something more profound. In one sense, this was attempted with the early advocates of personalisation – albeit the current system was arguably able to subvert these radical intentions and turn this passion for change into the 'zombie personalisation' so vividly described by Simon Duffy. However, one possible asset this time round may be the financial context (as strange as it sounds to try to turn such a negative into a positive). For a number of years now, major attempts at reform have taken place at a time of relative plenty, when there has always been enough money in the system to resist calls for more profound change and/or to afford the double-running costs of operating new approaches alongside the previous system. Faced with 'the end of local government as we know it', adult social care may have no choice but to reform itself more radically than ever before – because 'more of the same' simply won't be feasible. What such changes might look like is very much up for debate. Elsewhere, for example, it has been argued that social care needs to be re-framed from a basic safety net to a form of social and economic investment, and that previous deficit-focused approaches need to be replaced with a more asset-based emphasis on community development, community resources and social capital (see, for example, Glasby et al, 2010, 2013). However, what probably matters most for now is securing agreement around the nature and severity of the problems to be solved, resisting the temptation to leap straight into potential solutions. In one sense this seems to be the lessons of 'integrated care' (and possibly of 'personalisation' too), where there is a danger of the means becoming an end in itself. Without taking a step back and asking ourselves some more fundamental questions – what is adult social care for? What sort of life do we want to have together as a society? How much are we prepared to pay for this? and so on – there is a very real risk that the gap between rhetoric and reality, and between need and funding, could simply be too great for anyone to bridge.

Author's note

Please note a register of interest – Jon Glasby provides regular policy advice and works with a range of health and social care leaders around future service provision. As examples, he was an expert contributor to the NHS Future Forum on its work around integrated care, and was a panel member on the group choosing the coalition's 'integrated care pioneers'. He is also closely associated with the development of personal budgets/personal health budgets, and Dr Simon Duffy (quoted in this chapter) is an honorary member of staff at the Health Services Management Centre.

References

ADASS (Association of Directors of Adult Social Services) (2014) *ADASS budget survey report 2014: Final* (www.adass.org.uk/adass-budget-survey-2014/).

Alakeson, V. (2014) *Delivering personal health budgets: A guide to policy and practice*, Bristol: Policy Press.

Brindle, D. (2012) 'Graph of doom: a bleak future for social care services', *The Guardian Society*, 15 May (www.theguardian.com/society/2012/may/15/graph-doom-social-care-services-barnet).

Campbell, D. (2014) '£3.8bn NHS Better Care Fund policy delayed after damning Whitehall review', *The Guardian*, 7 May (www.theguardian.com/society/2014/may/06/nhs-better-care-fund-policy-halted-whitehall-review).

DH (Department of Health) (1998) *Partnership in action: New opportunities for joint working between health and social services – A discussion document*, London: DH.

Dilnot, A. (2011) *Fairer care funding: The report of the Commission on Funding of Care and Support* (The Dilnot Review), London: Commission on Funding of Care and Support.

Dudman, J. (2012) 'The end of local government?', *The Guardian Society*, 30 October (www.theguardian.com/society/2012/oct/30/end-of-local-government).

Duffy, S. (2014) 'After personalisation', in C. Needham and J. Glasby (eds) *Debates in personalisation*, Bristol: Policy Press, pp 167-84.

Glasby, J. and Dickinson, H. (2014) *Partnership working in health and social care: What is integrated care and how can we deliver it?* (2nd ed), Bristol: Policy Press.

Glasby, J. and Littlechild, R. (2004) *The health and social care divide: Understanding the experiences of older people*, Bristol: Policy Press.

Glasby, J. and Littlechild, R. (2009) *Direct payments and personal budgets: Putting personalisation into practice* (2nd edn), Bristol: Policy Press.

Glasby, J., Miller, R. and Lynch, J. (2013) *'Turning the welfare state upside down?' Developing a new adult social care offer*, Policy Paper 15, Birmingham: Health Services Management Centre in association with Birmingham City Council (www.birmingham.ac.uk/hsmc-policy-paper-fifteen).

Glasby, J., Ham, C., Littlechild, R. and McKay, S. (2010) *The case for social care reform – The wider economic and social benefits*, Birmingham: Health Services Management Centre/Institute of Applied Social Studies for the Department of Health/Downing Street.

Hansard (1998) 'Health and social services (co-operation)', HC Deb 02, June, vol 313 cc165-6.

Henwood, M. (2014) 'Self-funders: the road from perdition?', in C. Needham and J. Glasby (eds) *Debates in personalisation*, Bristol: Policy Press, pp 75-83.

House of Commons Committee of Public Accounts (2014) *Adult social care in England: Sixth report of session 2014-15*, London: The Stationery Office.

Humphries, R. (2013) *Paying for social care: Beyond Dilnot*, London: King's Fund.

Leutz, W. (1999) 'Five laws for integrating medical and social services: lessons from the United States and the United Kingdom', *The Milbank Quarterly*, vol 77, no 1, pp 77-110.

LGA (Local Government Association) (2014) *Care Act clause analysis* (www.local.gov.uk/care-support-reform/-/journal_content/56/10180/5761381/ARTICLE).

National Audit Office (2014a) *Adult social care in England: An overview*, London: National Audit Office.

National Audit Office (2014b) *Planning for the Better Care Fund*, London: National Audit Office.

Needham, C. (2011) *Personalising public services: Understanding the personalisation narrative*, Bristol: Policy Press.

Needham, C. and Glasby, J (eds) (2014) *Debates in personalisation*, Bristol: Policy Press.

NHS Future Forum (2012) *Integration – A report from the NHS Future Forum*, London: NHS Future Forum.

RAND Europe/Ernst & Young (2012) *National evaluation of the Department of Health's integrated care pilots*, Cambridge: RAND Europe.

Part Two

Contributions from the Social Policy Association Conference 2014

Towards the Welfare Commons: contestation, critique and criticality in social policy

Fiona Williams

Introduction

This chapter started life as a plenary paper for the 2014 Social Policy Association's Annual Conference on 'Resistance, Resilience and Radicalism', where I combined the themes of resistance and radicalism with work that sets out the development of a critical perspective in the discipline of social policy, past, present and future (Williams, 2016: forthcoming). Following a brief summary of the two sides of contemporary resistance, this chapter is divided into three parts. In the first part I suggest that it is helpful to go back to the 1970s and 1980s to identify the distinctive methods and concepts to have emerged from the critical perspectives of the welfare state at that time. By 'critical' I am referring to the sorts of critiques that place struggles and contestations over social justice at the heart of their theories, analyses and practices of welfare provision. This was defined succinctly by Marx as 'the self-clarification of the struggles and wishes of the age' (Marx, 1843, p 209).

The second part reviews how critical analyses responded to the political and intellectual challenges of the 1990s and the new century, particularly those of neoliberalism and post-structuralism, respectively. It argues that, in spite of a downturn in grass-roots activism, there were some important conceptual developments that lay the ground for a more nuanced understanding of the multiplicity of power and resistance in relation to social policy. In the third part I propose that, in considering how to develop a politically relevant critical perspective for the 21st century, we might take a cue from contemporary forms of resistance and, in the light of the 2008 crisis, from new thinking about the ethical, economic, social and ecological basis for future society. One of my arguments is that many of the recent critical analyses in social policy have been travelling along rather discrete paths, and that what is needed are 'conceptual alliances' that can connect these developments to transformative alternatives for the future. By way of example I use 'the Commons' (and, more specifically, the 'Welfare Commons') as a conceptual node that can point to new synergies and directions.

Over the past decade two pictures of resistance have been taking shape. On the one side there has been a revival at international, national and community scales of anti-capitalist mobilisations such as the Occupy movement and UK Uncut; there have been anti-poverty campaigns, especially, in the UK, by people with disabilities; and mobilisations in some parts of Europe against austerity. International support for environmentalist movements grows, along with local campaigns around food sovereignty, cultural diversity, indigenous people's and migrants' rights, against militarism, for territorial justice, as well as community pre-figurative experiments in generating zero growth, and ecologically sustainable local economies in transition towns. International campaigns for sexual citizenship have achieved remarkable cultural recognition that would not have seemed possible even a decade ago. In 2014, the newly formed Spanish anti-austerity party Podemos ('we can'), standing for social, economic, democratic and environmental justice, won electoral support to send four members to the European Parliament. The same year in Malmo, Sweden, 15,000 people attended a conference organised by the Nordic Women's Movement on 'New Action for Women's Rights', and the Swedish Feminist Initiative – a new party in Sweden with a commitment to feminism, anti-racism, ecological justice and a strong welfare state – polled sufficient votes to send one member to the European Parliament.

In other regions of the world pressures coming from what Hardt and Negri (2005) call this 'great multitude of movements' have been growing for longer. In Latin America since the 1980s and 1990s social movements have been a significant part of civil society politics characterised by attempts to create and reconceptualise democracy – building a democracy from the bottom up, creating horizontal alliances, with mobilisation often assisted through advances in social networking. These have involved movements significant for their plurality and multi-ethnicity, composed of landless peasants, workers, feminists, sexual rights activists, environmentalists, radical student movements, putting into practice in the here and now projects that reflect values of solidarity, harmony between nature, human development and meeting human needs as well as putting pressure on regional trade negotiators to break with old colonial forms of geo-political dependencies (Burbach et al, 2013; Yeates, 2013).

In all of this there is a sense that pressure for a more just world is building a head of steam. Guy Standing writes of the precariat that they 'are beginning to growl about the inequity and inequality in which they have to live. Their anger is justifiable, and it will not go away' (Standing, 2013, p xxii; see also Tyler, 2013). This connects to the view of many commentators that the time is ripe for new thinking. For example, Anna Coote suggests that the financial crisis, the 'fading lure' of consumerism, and the pressures of paid work and care have led to a 'gathering momentum behind the idea of moving to shorter hours' (Coote, 2013, p xix). Proposals such as these often involve fundamental challenges to the assumptions of economies built on growth and rising productivity, instead focusing on 'building an economy of care and culture' (Jackson, 2013, p 28). In many of these new areas of struggle and thinking is an invocation of 'the Commons' – the reclaiming of the world's resources – land, water, space, time, creativity, public services, care – from their increasing commodification and depletion, along with the envisioning of alternative democratic practices and communal and shared ownership.

However, these mobilisations stand on a knife edge. In her book, *End of equality*, Beatrix Campbell talks about a 'feminist renaissance': 'a neo-patriarchal and neo-capitalist matrix that assails – and provokes – feminism's renaissance' (Campbell, 2013, p 91). The other side shows the overwhelming power of neoliberalism spreading across the world. Deregulated labour markets, the commodification of natural resources, care, education and of health provision have intensified exploitation and eroded equality claims around gender, race, age and disability. In many countries neoliberal welfare reforms have widened inequalities and created a more stringent separation of deserving and undeserving based on the primacy of able-bodied labour market participation (Standing, 2011; Piketty, 2014). According to Campbell, new versions of patriarchal practices, particularly sexualised violence, ride on exploitation and on the increases in ethnic and religious conflict and militarism (Campbell, 2013). Alongside this there has been a shift from initial outrage at the corruption of both financiers and politicians after the financial crisis in 2008 towards a steady disaffection with parliamentary democratic politics (although the referendum politics in Scotland in 2014 was an exception), and a rise in support for far right anti-immigration political parties such as the UK Independence Party (UKIP), France's National Front and the Sweden Democrats (Anderson, 2013).

So what are the implications for social policy scholars of these complex and diverse political and cultural landscapes? As indicated above, I turn first to some important lessons for analysis from early critical perspectives in social policy.

Emergence of critical perspectives in social policy in the 1970s and 1980s

Although a critical perspective in social policy has a longer tradition, I begin with those ideas that started with a new Marxist *political economy of the welfare state* in the 1970s, that were refined by feminist understandings of gender inequalities and critiques around anti-racism, disability, sexuality, age and generation.

As mentioned, I focus on those critical approaches to understanding social policy that have placed *contestation* at the centre of their analysis. The political economy of the welfare state (Gough, 1979; Ginsburg, 1979) explained the development of the welfare state as the result of an uneasy truce between the interests of capitalism for a healthy, disciplined workforce, and the interests and struggles of the working class, on the other side, for protection from poverty, unemployment and ill health. Claus Offe (1984) summed this up as the *contradictions* of the welfare state: that capitalism couldn't live with a welfare state, but neither could it live without it.

By the 1980s in the UK and many European welfare societies, the women's movement, black people's organisations and anti-racist movements and, a little later, queer politics and the disability movements, all in similar and different ways extended and refined these concepts of contestation and contradiction. These movements' struggles were often about welfare provision, both in terms of its logics of redistribution – who got what benefits and services – and also in terms of the interconnected issues of the recognition of people's or groups' moral worth – their dignity, personhood and so on. They provided critiques of the way in which both post-war policy and practice of universalism (as well as mainstream and Marxist social policy) were grounded in a normativity that held white, able-bodied heterosexual male-breadwinning families as central welfare subjects.

The point I want to emphasise here is that these new critiques established some important insights. First, they *extended the notion of contestation* to the social relations of race, gender, class sexuality, disability and age. In addition, they developed an analysis of how these dimensions interact and change over time and place (Brah, 1996; Williams,

1989, 1992). This is now termed *intersectionality*. It was this method that permitted a deeper understanding of one of the central issues in social policy: the relationship between universalism (of provision) and diversity (of populations). Second, they *extended the notion of contradiction* to people's own experiences of the welfare state: while it provided people with resources and services they needed, it did so in ways that reinforced some of inequalities and hierarchies in which they already found themselves. Third, much of the activism highlighted a new form of struggle (or not-so-new) around the so-called *social relations of welfare* – that is, the relationship between providers and users of welfare provision. These developments gave rise to new self-help practices, but more than this, they involved attempts to *pre-figure new social relations*. Whether in women's health centres, Black Saturday schools, cooperatives, forms of early independent living, and support services for victims of rape and domestic violence, or lesbians and gay men, a new kind of relationship between provider and user began to take hold. This was one that was not discriminatory but was more democratic, equal and respectful, challenging in particular the constructed dependencies of women, older people, people with disabilities and those who are long-term unemployed.

The analyses associated with these moves marked out an important dimension of critical theory – sometimes referred to as *criticality* (Roseneil, 2011). This refers to the capacity of analysis not simply for normative thinking (what *ought* to be), which is so much part of the study of welfare states, but to ask how far the existing voices and practices of resistance allow us to prefigure and imagine a better world (see later). The activism that sought to change and prefigure an alternative approach to social policy also brought into analysis the importance of *representation* and *voice*, not only through formal parliamentary politics or through collective trade union or pressure group struggle, but at the local level, in the very delivery of welfare (Williams, 1989).

However, in the period that followed from the 1990s and into the first decade of this century, much of this activism declined, trade unions were weakened, welfare states were marketised, managerialised and modernised by neoliberalism, and, in the move to post-structuralist analysis, the meta-narratives and monoliths associated with capitalism, patriarchy and imperialism lost their intellectual purchase. Where, then, did this leave this newly established critical tradition in social policy?

Neoliberalism and social policy: political and intellectual challenges in the 1990s

In fact, although the profile of social movements dimmed, they did not go away. Movements around disability, around sexual citizenship, rights for migrants, for carers, older people, for children, all increased in activism and pressure group activity over this period, and that was reflected in social policy research. There were important struggles against racism in the police force, for example, in the battle for justice following the murder of Stephen Lawrence, although these were very hard fought and often on the back foot. There was the declaration of women's rights at the Beijing Conference in 1995; the beginning of important moves for gender equality and anti-racist policy in the European Union (EU); and preparation for the United Nations (UN) Convention on the Rights for Persons with Disabilities. This also reflects how these struggles were moving higher up the political hierarchy from their bases in the grass roots, as well as of social policy taking on a broader more cross-national and global reach. However, at the national level, there was also a sense, reflected in the policy documents of New Labour that came to power in the UK in 1997 (although less so in Scotland and Wales) that the politics of feminism, anti-racism and class were passé (Williams and Roseneil, 2004).

Intellectually, there was some mirroring of these shifts – in the disparateness of research areas and in some, but not all, of post-structuralism's turn to culture and subjectivity. However, I suggest that there were also important developments spearheaded by those who didn't reject materialism, contestation or contradiction, but attempted to work out ways of bringing them together with culture, subjectivity, identity and agency. These furthered understandings of the complexity and the multiplicity of power and of resistance in relation to social policy. Arguably, the turning point for this was *the structure–agency debate* (Deacon and Mann, 1999; Williams et al, 1999).

The background to this was that in the 1970s and 1980s, both the new social movements *and* neoliberals accused welfare state institutions of treating people as passive and of disempowering them. The neoliberals saw the solution in terms of creating 'welfare consumers' with 'individual choice', while social movements talked of 'welfare citizens' with 'voice', and new social democrats like New Labour focused on 'responsibilities with rights'. Common to all was a new emphasis on the welfare citizen/consumer as the agent of her/his welfare destiny and as articulating her/his differential welfare needs whether through the market (neoliberals), and/or through exercising social responsibilities (New Labour), or through local, democratic forms (social movements).

What this debate exposed was two things: the extent to which the political and philosophical right had dominated understandings and conceptualisations of the individual and individual agency in welfare debates; and second, how the welfare state had treated its subjects, especially those deemed to be in most need – people in poverty, frail older people and people with disabilities, single parents – as passive and voiceless, even if beneficently so. Agency, identity and personal experience were undeveloped concepts in social policy. Indeed, social policy research had often taken as given administrative welfare categories it studied, such as *the* poor, or *the* disabled. In this way, developing a more sophisticated analysis of the welfare subject became part of a new and critical paradigm for research by the end of the 1990s. While it reflected sociological debates of the time (Giddens, 1991), to some extent it also drew on the women's movement's mantra, 'the personal is political', which was an important linking of individual experience to political action, one not often reflected in mainstream social policy or in heavily structuralist Marxist accounts or in individualist liberal explanations. It was also strengthened by the disability movement, whose critique of welfare centred on the construction of the passive dependency of disabled people (Barnes, 2000).

The core of this new paradigm proposed that welfare subjects should be understood as creative and having agency through which they negotiate and develop their own strategies of welfare management, with the result that they help to reconstitute the forms of provision they use. This understanding was influenced by ideas about intersectionality, that is to say, that those who use welfare services and those who provide them (never entirely separate groups) inhabit multiple social categories (of gender, ethnicity, class, etc), and also categories of moral worth attached to provision and receipt of welfare provision (deserving/undeserving, 'scrounger' and so on), and that these, too, change over time and place. Furthermore, welfare subjects bring with them personal histories and experiences. The accounting of these contributes to the construction of self and social identities (Williams et al, 1999, chapter 9).

The importance of developing this new and critical paradigm was not just theoretical; it was about coming to grips with developing policies that could go with the grain of people's lives. It fundamentally influenced social policy research methodologies which became much more concerned to elicit the voices and experiences especially of those involved in poverty and at the sharp end of the social relations of welfare (see, for example, Ridge, 2002). More generally, it contributed to a more nuanced understanding of the social formation of groups, for example, how different ethnicities could be classed, gendered and racialised in different ways (Hughes and Lewis, 1998). This process set (at least) three other balls rolling, all of which furthered an understanding of the multiplicity of power. These are the *multivalent nature of resistance*, the *multi-layered nature of welfare settlements* and the *multileveled nature of policy-making*.

In relation to the multivalent nature of resistance, the development of ideas that struggles are about redistribution *and* recognition of personhood, dignity and moral worth, as well as claims for representation (Fraser, 1995; Honneth, 1995), had important implications for the analyses of social movements' struggles around the welfare state (Williams, 1999). These involved claims that were about the improvement of material conditions (say, benefits or housing) *and* the recognition of dignity and personhood (say, in the treatment of homeless people, victims of sexual violence, and mental health service users). Here was a formulation that broke through two dualisms that had dogged research on social movements and resistance. It pulled together the struggles around material issues with those of cultural issues, and connected the universal with the particular. In other words, the claims to have equal moral worth are not particular to, say, women or disabled people, but are universal and fundamental needs.

In a different way, the eliciting and analysis of voice and experience enabled an understanding of a different type of resistance, one I term 'aggregate resistance' (Williams, 2012a), in contrast to the conscious collective political action of social movements. This is where the overall effect of people interacting in the conditions of their everyday existence constitutes (or aggregates) significant social or cultural change. This may counter dominant social norms or represent quite radical change. For example, between 2000 and 2005, the Care, Values and the Future of Welfare Research project investigated changes in parenting and partnering.[1] This found that a number of areas of social and cultural change in the social relations of care and intimacy had been effected by an accumulation of 'quiet' shifts in subjectivities and interrelations that conveyed significant resistance to dominant discourses about family life. The dominant policy and legal discourses at that time prioritised the structure and convention of 'the family', whereas this research found that, on the whole, it was the *quality* of intimate and family relationships that mattered more to people. It was possible to see a growing acceptance of divorce, cohabitation, children born outside of marriage, working mothers and same-sex relationships which 15 years earlier would have been much more contested. In this way, family policy of the time, by holding to form and convention as the route to the quality of relationships, was out of step with people's own understandings and practices. In eliciting what mattered to people in their relationships of care and intimacy, the research also identified prevailing practices that came out of a grounded ethics based on the interdependence and reciprocity of close and intimate relationships (Williams, 2004). In many ways this was far removed from the neoliberal notion of a free possessive individualism, and also out of alignment with the dominant discourse of 'hard-working families' (in that the ethic of work was not the wellspring of people's raison d'être).[2]

The second multiplicity, relates to the *multilayered nature of welfare settlements*. What I mean by this is that many theoretical accounts of post-war welfare state change and crisis – whether the Keynesian crisis or the financial crisis today – privilege a *political-economic* settlement in the struggle for an equilibrium between the state, capital and labour. However, these newer ideas of welfare subjectivity, contestation and resistance emerging from a diversity of economic, political, social and cultural pressures point to an understanding of welfare change being, additionally, the outcome of struggles around both the *social* and the *organisational* (Clarke and Newman, 1997; Hughes and Lewis, 1998). The 'social' does not simply refer to the 'family' as distinct from 'the market' or 'the state' but to all those social, moral and cultural practices in which the social formation consolidates, fragments and reconstitutes itself – through conceptions of nationhood, citizenship, religion, moral worth, and so on. The *organisational settlement* refers to the modes, practices and discourses through which welfare provision is coordinated, delivered and received, referred to above as the social relations of welfare. The changing mode of the organisation of welfare, from a bureau-professional to a managerialist regime, has been the central site for the restructuring and modernising of welfare, as well, of course, one of constant struggle. This multilayered approach avoids depicting change in the post-war welfare state as serial in form – from one government to the next or 'from – to' dualisms of Fordism to post-Fordism or industrialism to post-industrialism. Instead changes are seen in terms of the formation, decline and reformation of 'unstable and multilayered equilibria', in which the state is not a monolith but constitutes an assemblage of policies, practices, people and objects in which governing is embodied (Newman and Clarke, 2009).

A third understanding of the multiplicity of power which emerged in analyses of this time referred to the *multiple levels* – local, national, regional, transnational and global – across which policy-making and resistance increasingly travelled. In relation to policy-making, from the mid-1990s one important development of a critical perspective was in the analysis of global social policy which identified the major influence of global social policy actors of The World Bank, International Monetary Fund (IMF), Organisation for Economic Co-operation and Development (OECD), United Nations (UN) and International Labour Office (ILO) in shaping welfare states and social policy (Deacon, 1997). At the same time, many of the new social movements referred to earlier became transnational movements, either because solidarities were forged through claims aimed at supranational governance of the EU, such as disability or feminism, or because the focus of mobilisation is itself global, or because specific struggles transcend national politics such as the anti-capitalist campaigns for global justice, migrant workers' rights, or ecology and climate change (della Porta and Tarrow, 2004).

Conceptual alliances, criticality and the Commons in the 21st century

What global social policy shows us is the indispensability of framing analyses within global political economy structures, institutions, discourses and struggles. Even cross-national comparison is not enough without this context. But I have two worries. In drawing attention to the global, does this recreate that very problem that faced critical analysis in the 1970s – of distancing global political and economic institutions and struggles away from the local, the social and the organisational struggles around participation and representation, as well as from other issues of contestation which conventionally stand outside of social policy's political economy – care, time or ecology? By the same token, how far are those rich micro-level studies on the complex intersectional logics of power operating in the enactment of welfare also floating free of some of the wider structures of inequality? It also concerns me that much of the excellent work on these different social issues is disparate, operating in its own silos.

If the point here is that research should attend to the vertical, multiscalar connections from micro-meso-macro, then there is also an argument for more conceptual connections horizontally across different areas of contestation. The priorities of contemporary civil society activism – whether for feminism, basic income, social protection, care, environment, human rights or against welfare cutbacks – are instructive here in highlighting the need for alliances across progressive groups. At a conference on 'Feminism, Then and Now' in London in 2013, Pragna Patel (of Southall Black Sisters) talked of the need for *intersectionality as a practice*, not just a theory. This refers to the importance of alliances and working alongside others, developing dialogue and deliberation across groups, sometimes called 'transversal politics' (Massey, 1999). This is also one of the themes in the social movements of Latin America, part and parcel of looking for new democratic ways of working across diverse groups. One way in which social policy scholarship can assist these processes is in developing integrated analyses that make connections across the struggles, crises and issues of our age. This involves the forging of *conceptual alliances* through vertical connections between scales and horizontal connections across forms of struggle and fields of analysis.

An example of conceptual alliance is Nancy Fraser's framing of the global financial crisis where she offers a critical reinterpretation of Polanyi's history of capitalist crisis in his 1944 classic *The great transformation* (Polanyi, 1944 [1957]; Fraser, 2013). Polanyi's argument is that capitalism's self-destructive impulse lies in its turning land, labour and money into 'fictitious commodities'. Fraser rewrites land, labour and money as the interlinked systemic crises of ecology, social reproduction and finance. Thus, in relation to social reproduction, integral to changes in labour today is 'reproductive labour as fictitious commodity'. The retrenchment of public services and the marketisation of care work have contributed to the commodification of women's previously unwaged labour, and the effect of employing migrant labour to do this work merely displaces those hidden reproductive processes. The affective and care processes, on which not only productive labour but also human solidarity depend, are jeopardised by a crisis of social reproduction. At the same time, the planet's sustainability is threatened by the crisis of ecology, and the capacity of money to store value for the future is undermined by the global financial crisis. Furthermore, each area of crisis is interlinked: the global financial crisis has generated austerity measures which themselves have intensified cutbacks in public services which support people's caring needs or activities, for example.

A framework such as this is important in linking the issues of social reproduction, ecology and the financial underpinning of neoliberalism, and making them central to an analysis of crisis. In other words, it takes us beyond an economistic frame of productivism and economic growth in which the global financial crisis, austerity measures and inequalities are taken as given and all other crises rendered secondary. It makes it more possible to think transversally about strategies and about the meaning of global social justice. It enables us to raise the ethical and material dimensions of sustainability and human flourishing, of how we are to ensure that people will be cared for, and how we care for the depleting resources of the world. This leads to a view of people not as atomised subjects of an inexorable neoliberal capitalism, but of people who are connected to each other and to their environment.

Let me develop these arguments with reference to the study of social policy, first, in terms of contestations and claims around policies to support people's care needs and caring responsibilities. Over the last two decades the care landscape has changed significantly with women's increased earning responsibilities throughout the world along with, in richer regions, an ageing population. In fact, as Fraser implies above, care is now a global issue, with Western welfare states increasingly solving their health and care social expenditure crises through employing migrant workers (Williams, 2012b). In researching the sorts of claims to emerge from groups mobilising around care provision – in this case, from those concerned with childcare, disability, caring for family members, trade unions representing care workers, and organisations representing migrant care workers – I found that claims clustered around three areas: recognition, rights and redistribution. Claims for *recognition* were about making care visible, giving greater voice and representation to those who provide care and receive support, and giving care greater social and economic value. Claims for *rights* centred around rights as carers, earners and citizens – to quality services, an enabling environment, social protection and flexible working, to decent wages, and human and civil rights. Claims for *redistribution* focused on redistributing care resources and responsibilities for care support – from women to men, from families to states, from poorer to richer regions, as well as democratic power to those who use services, and the reorganisation and redistribution of time and space (Williams, 2009). The meeting of such claims requires strategies for local, national, bi-lateral, transnational and global policy; they need to tackle a complexity of inequalities emanating from gender, class, poverty, insecurity, age, disability, race, nationality and geo-politics. And they need to be thought out temporarily in terms of immediate and longer-term strategies.

In the short term there are many strategies that could improve the rights of care providers and care receivers such as the regularisation of care and domestic work, improved training and person-centred care, formalising care career paths, rights to paid carer and parental leaves, improving migrants' rights to citizenship, and much more. Some of these are covered by the ILO's proposal for a comprehensive social protection floor under the global economy for all in need (Deacon, 2013) and the UN 2003 Covenant for the Protection of Migrant Workers. However, important as these are, they do not guarantee that the significance of care and the global care crisis is taken on board as a central issue for global (and national) social justice, that is to say, that the everyday relations of care carried out within a context of different forms of inequality are embedded conceptually and strategically in strategies for social justice. This would be necessary if the longer-term underlying issues, such as the limited advances of gender equality across the world, the commodification of care, or geo-political inequalities of care resources, are to be tackled. Fiona Robinson argues similarly that while social protection standards, employment rights and human rights through international organisations are essential, such standards are based on assumptions of the rights holder as an atomised individual rather than as an individual constituted through their relations of care and support for and from others (Robinson, 2006). As such, these rights do not really begin to challenge the thinking that places social questions of care as subordinate to economic issues of productivity, profit and performance. The dominant logic of policy-making in both developed and developing countries focuses on economic competitiveness, on the facilitation of markets, on the ethic of paid work, and now on austerity. Yet care is central to the global economy, its inequalities and its crises. Better to embed rights in an understanding of all people over their life course as having the need to care, and to be cared for by others. This is the perspective of care ethics that assert the social, economic and political value of care (Tronto, 1993; Williams, 2001).

However, greater leverage for the argument for recognising the centrality of care could be gained from developing synergies and conceptual alliances with critical approaches to climate change, the environment and the planet's resources (see, for example, Gough, 2013; Jackson, 2013; St Clair and Lawson, 2013; Unmüssig et al, 2013). Strategies for care and the environment have the potential to take us beyond profit and competition. They are both about crises in global sustainability whose effects are unequally spread and are rooted in historical processes of colonialism and colonisation. They remain marginalised in many areas of policy, both subsumed under market logics. In terms of their ethics, they both challenge free market individualism. They see citizenship as based on participatory democracy and presume interdependence and solidarity as a way of being. They invoke care for other and care for the world, and in turn, they both envision a society reorganised to create the conditions of time, security and space to enable the care of the individual and collective body, mind and soul and to 'restore the value of human labour' (Jackson, 2013, p 28).

In addition, both summon 'the Commons' as a way of reclaiming those resources that have been depleted (see Isaksen et al, 2008; Heinrich Böll Foundation, 2009). In support of developing conceptual alliances, the notion of the Commons represents an important node that can bring together different areas of critique and resistance. Its key demand focuses on re-embedding that which has been disembedded or commodified – public space, land, finance, time to care, people to care, climate, natural resources and public services, creativity. The Commons is a site for struggle (from the local to the global) as well as signifying a vision of something non-capitalistic in its form. In addition, it serves as a way of imagining possibilities of transformation. In this sense, it reignites an important beacon in the tradition of critical thinking in social policy.

I mentioned in the first part of this chapter that the new social movements of the 1970s and 1980s attempted to prefigure different forms of welfare provision, many of which subsequently became incorporated into state or third sector welfare. This practising in the present what might be hoped for in the future has a long tradition going back to the utopian socialists of the 19th century. Drawing on Rogoff's work in cultural theory, Sasha Roseneil (Rogoff, 2003; Roseneil, 2011) distinguishes between elements of a critical perspective: criticism, critique and *criticality*. While criticism is a mere descriptive identification of what an author disagrees with, critique attempts to deconstruct the underlying beliefs, claims and unexamined partiality in any given phenomenon, to point out omissions and injustices. Criticality, however, goes beyond this; it is forward-looking, it looks to political spaces for intimations of transformation. It is here, in the attempts by emergent voices to prefigure and to imagine a better future, that critical scholars in social policy can create a route from the analysis of the social movements of the past, through the realism of the contemporary forms of resistance to an alternative and perhaps to optimism for the future. Criticality, like the Commons, is not about what ought to be, not about imposing a blueprint, but about the ways in which those practices of resistance can be supported to articulate alternatives to the present.

The discussion has focused on care and the environment as two linked aspects of our Commons, but social policies (or 'eco-social policies') are about more than this; they are also about social security, healthcare, social services and housing – our 'Welfare Commons'. In their contribution to the *Kilburn Manifesto* – a series of essays on alternatives to neoliberalism

– John Clarke and Janet Newman argue that we cannot go back to a mythical golden age, nor to the idea that the state can simply be captured by progressive social forces. 'Rather,' they write, 'we propose an approach to the state that enhances notions of the commons, that reasserts collective (public) interests and enables collective (public) action' (Clarke and Newman, 2014, pp 7-8). In a similar vein but with a yet broader analysis, Francine Mestrum redraws social protection as the 'Social Commons' (Mestrum, 2013). She argues that proposals such as the ILO's for a global social protection floor represent a significant buffer against neoliberalism in elaborating rights to essential healthcare and income security across the globe for all in need, but they do not go far enough. They are based on rights and guarantees for individuals, but they do not address the collective dimension of the Commons – interdependence, solidarity – which also require support and protection. In contrast, her proposals for the Social Commons include universal contributions and benefits that are multileveled (from local to global, involving national and international redistribution), emphasising alliances of collective struggles and democratic participation, including not only contributory and non-contributory systems, education, health and social services, but also protection for the environment. The Social Commons would not be subsumed under the economy but would shape it by, for example, regulating agricultural prices, land affordability and accessibility, sanitation and communication.

Conclusion

These arguments for the Social Commons, along with those discussed above for combining the political ethics of care with the re-organisation of time and eco-social policy, have clear parallels and methods. They are based on concepts that have emerged over time from critical approaches in social policy which I described in the first and second parts of this chapter: of contestation, of the discursive and material contradictions of policy-making under capitalist neoliberalism and neo-imperialism, and of the political spaces these create. They speak to vertical and horizontal multivalenced, multileveled resistances within multilayered welfare settlements. And, as I argue above, they point to the importance of criticality. As social policy scholars, our role is to criticise and to critique, but it is also to create conceptual coalitions of grounded ethics and frames for forward thinking that can inspire the public imagination. This does not imply a return to the metanarrative but to place the studies we do – qualitative or quantitative – into bigger and more integrated frames, stretched in three dimensions – horizontally, vertically and futuristically – as I have described in relation to the Welfare/Social Commons. This is also the time for vigorous and passionate scholarship which, in addressing itself to the crises of the world, can create new terms – the precariat (Standing, 2011), social abjection (Tyler, 2013), social subjugation (Clarke, 2007), expulsion (Sassen, 2014) – terms that reflect the insecurity which motivates much of the activism and resistance of our times.

Notes

[1] Economic and Social Research Council-funded study of changes in parenting and partnering carried out at the University of Leeds from 2000–05.

[2] Of course, such ethics can also be mobilised in quite reactionary ways in support of an inward-looking protectionism of 'one's own'. This attempt to distinguish between different types of resistance and radicalism is not dissimilar to John Clarke's use of Raymond Williams' distinction between dominant, residual and emergent elements and tendencies within the social, and the way these collide and overlap. This reflects another important aspect of critical theory – conjunctural analysis (Clarke 2007; Williams, 1977).

References

Anderson, B. (2013) *Us and them? The dangerous politics of immigration controls*, Oxford: Oxford University Press.

Barnes, C. (2000) 'A working social model? Disability, work and disability politics in the 21st century', *Critical Social Policy*, vol 20, no 4, pp 441-58.

Brah, A. (1996) *Cartographies of diaspora*, London: Routledge

Burbach, R., Fox, M. and Fuentes, F. (2013) *Latin America's turbulent transitions: The future of twenty-first-century socialism*, London: Zed Books.

Campbell, B. (2013) *End of equality: The only way is women's liberation*, London: Seagull Books.

Clarke, J. (2007) 'Subordinating the social?', *Cultural Studies*, vol 21, no 6, pp 974-87.

Clarke, J. and Newman, J. (1997) *The managerial state: Power, politics and ideology in the making of social welfare*, London: Sage.

Coote, A. (2013) 'Introduction: a new economics of work and time', in A. Coote and J. Franklin (eds) *Time on our side: Why we all need a shorter working week*, London: New Economics Foundation, pp ix-xxii.

Deacon, A. and K. Mann (1999) 'Agency, modernity, and social policy', *Journal of Social Policy*, vol 28, no 3, pp 413-35.

Deacon, B. with P. Stubbs and M. Hulse (1997) *Global social policy: International organisations and the future of welfare*, London: Sage.

Deacon, B. (2013) *Global social policy in the making*, Bristol: Policy Press.

della Porta, D. and Tarrow, S. (2004) *Transnational protest and global activism*, Lanham, MD: Rowman & Littlefield.

Fraser, N. (1995) 'From redistribution to recognition? Dilemmas of justice in a "post-socialist" age', *New Left Review*, vol 212, pp 68-92.

Fraser, N. (2013) 'A triple movement? Parsing the politics of crisis after Polanyi', *New Left Review*, vol 81, pp 119-32.

Giddens, A. (1991) *Modernity and self-identity*, Cambridge: Polity Press.

Ginsburg, N. (1979) *Class, capital and social policy*, London: Macmillan.

Gough, I. (1979) *The political economy of the welfare state*, London: Macmillan.

Gough, I (2013) 'Climate change, social policy, and global governance', in A. Kaasch and P. Stubbs (eds) *Transformations in global and regional social policies*, Basingstoke: Palgrave Macmillan, pp 108-33.

Hardt, M. and A. Negri (2005) *The multitude: War and democracy in the age of empire*, London: Penguin Books.

Heinrich Böll Foundation (2009) *Strengthen the Commons – Now!* (www.boell.de/sites/default/files/assets/boell.de/images/download_de/Almmendemanifest_engl_screen.pdf).

Honneth, A. (1995) *The struggle for recognition: The moral grammar of social conflicts*, Cambridge: Polity Press.

Hughes, G. and Lewis, G. (1998) *Unsettling welfare. The reconstruction of social policy*, London: Psychology Press.

Isaksen, L.W., Devi, S.U. and Hochschild, A. (2008) 'Global care crisis: a problem of capital, care chain or commons?', *American Behavioural Scientist*, vol 52, pp 405-25.

Jackson, T. (2013) 'The trouble with productivity', in A. Coote and J. Franklin (eds) *Time on our side: Why we all need a shorter working week*, London: New Economics Foundation.

Marx, K. (1843) 'Letter to A, Ruge, September 1843', in R. Livingstone and G. Benton (translators) (1977) *Karl Marx: Early writings*, New York: Vintage.

Massey, D. (ed) (1999) *Soundings Special Issue: Transversal Politics*, issue 12, Summer.

Mestrum, F. (2013) *Human rights and the common good: Why social protection is a 'social commons'* (www.other-news.info/2013/10/human-rights-and-the-common-good-why-social-protection-is-a-social-commons).

Newman, J. and Clarke, J. (2009) *Publics, politics and power*, London: Sage Publications.

Newman, J. and Clarke, J. (2014) 'States of imagination', in S. Hall, D. Massey and M. Rustin (eds) *After neo-liberalism? The Kilburn Manifesto*, London: Soundings (www.lwbooks.co.uk/journals/soundings/pdfs/Manifesto_states_of_imagination.pdf).

Offe, C. (1984) *Contradictions of the welfare state*, Cambridge, MA: The MIT Press.

Polanyi, K. (1944 [1957]) *The great transformation: The political and economic origins of our time*, Boston, MA: Beacon Press.

Piketty, T. (2014) *Capital in the 21st century*, Cambridge, MA: Belknap Press.

Ridge, T. (2002) *Childhood and social exclusion: From a child's perspective*, Bristol: Policy Press.

Robinson, F. (2006) 'Beyond labour rights: the ethics of care and women's work in the global economy', *International Feminist Journal of Politics*, vol 8, pp 321-42.

Roseneil, S. (2011) 'Criticality, not paranoia: a generative register for feminist social research', *NORA – Nordic Journal of Feminist and Gender Research,* vol 19, no 2, pp 124-31.

Rogoff, I. (2003) *From criticism to critique to criticality*, European Institute for Progressive Cultural Policies (http://eipcp.net/transversal/0806/rogoff1/en).

Sassen, S. (2014) *Expulsions. Brutality and complexity in the global economy*, Cambridge, MA: Belknap Press.

St Clair, A.L. and Lawson, V. (2013) 'Poverty and climate change: the three tasks of transformative global social policy', in A. Kaasch and P. Stubbs (eds) *Transformations in global and regional social policies*, Basingstoke: Palgrave Macmillan, pp 134-52.

Standing, G. (2011) *The precariat: The new dangerous class*, London: Bloomsbury.

Standing, G. (2013) 'Foreword', in M. Torry, *Money for everyone: Why we need a citizen's income*, Bristol: Policy Press.

Tronto, J. (1993) *Moral boundaries: A political argument for an ethic of care*, London: Routledge.

Tyler, I. (2013) *Social abjection and resistance in neoliberal Britain. Revolting subjects*, London: Zed Books.

Unmüssig, B., Sachs, W. and Fatheuer, T. (2013) *Critique of the green economy – Toward social and environmental equity*, Berlin: Heinrich Böll Stiftung.

Williams, F. (1989) *Social policy: A critical introduction. Issues of 'race', gender and class*, Cambridge: Polity Press.

Williams, F. (1992) 'Somewhere over the rainbow: universality and diversity in social policy', in N. Manning and R. Page (eds) *Social Policy Review 4*, Canterbury: Social Policy Association, pp 200-19.

Williams, F. (1999) 'Good-enough principles for welfare', *Journal of Social Policy*, vol 28, no 4, pp 667-87.

Williams, F. (2001) 'In and beyond New Labour: towards a new political ethic of care', *Critical Social Policy*, vol 21, pp 467-93.

Williams, F. (2004) *Rethinking families*, London: Calouste Gulbenkian Foundation.

Williams, F. (2009) *The making and claiming of care policies: The recognition and redistribution of care*, Geneva: United Nations Research Institute for Social Development.

Williams, F. (2012a) 'Care relations and public policy: social justice claims and social investment frames', *Families, Relationships and Societies*, vol 1, no 1, pp 103-19.

Williams, F. (2012b) 'Converging variations in migrant care work in Europe', *Journal of European Social Policy*, vol 22, pp 363-75.

Williams, F. (2016: forthcoming) *Social policy: New critical perspectives*, Cambridge: Polity Press.

Williams, F. and S Roseneil (2004) 'Public values of parenting and partnering: voluntary organisations and welfare politics in New Labour's Britain', *Social Politics: International Studies in Gender, State and Society*, vol 11, no 2, pp 181-216.

Williams, F., Popay, J. and Oakley, A. (1999) *Welfare research: A critical review*, London: UCL Press.

Williams, R. (1977) *Marxism and literature*, Oxford: Oxford University Press.

Yeates, N. (2013) 'The socialization of regionalism and the regionalization of social policy: contexts, imperatives and challenges', in A. Kaasch, and P. Stubbs (eds) *Transformations in global and regional social policies*, Basingstoke: Palgrave Macmillan, pp 17-43.

SIX

New keys for old doors: breaking the vicious circle connecting homelessness and re-offending

Graham Bowpitt

Policy-makers concerned with preventing re-offending have long been aware of the relationship between crime and homelessness. Single homeless people are more likely to be victims of violent crime, to be drawn into criminal sub-cultures, and to receive custodial sentences when they offend. Likewise, offenders are more likely to re-offend in the absence of stable accommodation, while custodial sentences frequently put accommodation at risk, creating a vicious circle. This is especially true of offenders given short-term prison sentences of 3–12 months. This concern has been given a new imperative in the UK by the passing of the Offender Rehabilitation Act 2014, and the extension of statutory rehabilitation to short-term prisoners. Policy-makers concerned with effective offender management are therefore keen to explore ways in which securing stable accommodation might reduce re-offending.

This chapter seeks to provide evidence from an evaluation of a small-scale attempt to use the procurement of stable accommodation as a key element in a package of support designed to reduce the likelihood of re-offending among a particular group of offenders with short-term sentences for prolific acquisitive crime, 90 per cent of whom were homeless at the time they were sentenced. The evaluated project is managed by a partnership between a Category B community prison in the English Midlands and a voluntary sector day centre for homeless adults, to which service users frequently gravitate on release. The evaluation explores the effectiveness of the project in preparing participants for release and in preventing homelessness, re-offending and social isolation. Data were gathered from interviews with service users and key informants from housing and support services to whom referrals are made, in order to advance our understanding of what mediates the relationship between acquiring and maintaining secure accommodation and reductions in criminal activity, thereby informing wider debates around prisoner rehabilitation as a policy objective.

Enduring problem: homelessness and re-offending

Concerns about re-offending rates among ex-prisoners have long occupied the minds of policy-makers in the UK. The report by the Social Exclusion Unit, *Reducing re-offending by ex-prisoners* (SEU, 2002), is still regarded as something of a benchmark in tackling re-offending, partly because it was the first recognition of ex-prisoners as a multiply excluded group rather than merely a group of ex-offenders, but also because so little has changed in the intervening 12 years. Thus the 58 per cent reconviction rate within two years, rising to 61 per cent for offenders on sentences of less than 12 months, which the SEU found in 2002, was similarly recorded by the Ministry of Justice in 2011 (MoJ, 2013a).

Moreover, the SEU report showed a high degree of correlation between imprisonment and homelessness. Nearly 5 per cent of prisoners were sleeping rough at the time of their confinement, and 32 per cent had no secure accommodation. The longitudinal cohort study of short-term prisoners sentenced in 2005 and 2006, *Surveying Prisoner Crime Reduction* (MoJ, 2012a), implies things have, if anything, worsened in the intervening years: 9 per cent were sleeping rough, 7 per cent were otherwise homeless, and a further 34 per cent would be classed as vulnerably housed, having no security in the accommodation they occupied. The survey reported a 79 per cent reconviction rate for the homeless, compared with 47 per cent for the accommodated. The SEU further reported that stable accommodation can reduce reconviction rates by 20 per cent. At the time, a third of prisoners lost their housing directly as a result of imprisonment, and a third reported having nowhere to stay on release, amounting to around 30,000 people a year. Moreover, less than one in five had help with securing housing prior to release.

Prisoners lose accommodation on sentence, in the end, because terminating a tenancy is often the last thing on their mind when they have just been sent to prison. As we have seen (MoJ, 2012a), 16 per cent are homeless anyway, and the informal arrangements on which the 34 per cent vulnerably housed depended would in all probability end at sentence. A further 34 per cent have their own tenancies, but are mostly unemployed and dependent on Housing Benefit. Claims can continue for a maximum of 13 weeks in the tenant's absence, but prisoners may still be liable for rent thereafter if a notice period has to be served, or they simply fail to let their landlords know of their new situations. At discharge, prisoners are therefore likely to be both homeless and in debt, impeding future access to housing, especially if the landlord is a local authority or housing association.

Lack of accommodation on release increases the likelihood of re-offending for three reasons, enlightened by social capital theory (Halpern, 2005). First, offenders needing somewhere to live will revert to existing social capital, probably their former criminal fraternity. Second, housing itself is a source of social capital, giving offenders an interest in staying out of prison. And third, housing is a source of bridging capital, connecting them to services to address problems, and potential work opportunities.

A decade of failed policy responses

An appraisal of policy responses in England and Wales in the decade since the SEU report reveals a catalogue of ineffectiveness, but no shortage of good intentions, as the following highlights indicate. The Homelessness Act 2002 extended priority need groups to include adults vulnerable as a result of having been in detention or custody (DCLG, 2006). The 2003 Supporting People initiative, which established a fund for supported housing for people at risk of homelessness, has been highly relevant to short-term offenders with other 'vulnerabilities', for example, mental health and substance problems. Meanwhile, in the following year, the UK government published its response to the SEU report in its National Action Plan to reduce re-offending (Home Office, 2004). This set up the National Offender Management Service (NOMS) to take charge of resettlement, and to commit the prison service to increase the availability of housing advice in prisons, setting a target to increase the number of prisoners released with somewhere to live. As a result of this and other initiatives, the 2012 Prison Service Instruction (MoJ, 2012b) includes within its core offer a commitment to screen all new prisoners for housing need, to assist them in closing down tenancies and Housing Benefit claims, to provide a housing information and advice service and to operate partnerships with other key stakeholders to this end.

These measures designed to improve housing access for ex-prisoners have had limited effect for two main reasons (Bowpitt et al, 2011; Homeless Link, 2011). First, there are what can be termed support worker frustrations. These are felt by people often in voluntary sector homelessness organisations seeking to re-house ex-offenders who encounter exclusions arising from, for instance, landlords unwilling to accommodate people with a prison record, rent arrears or a record of anti-social behaviour, or Housing Benefit claimants more generally. This experience is then compounded by lack of integrated offender management (despite the widespread adoption of this model), lack of a coordinated approach to risk assessment or poor information sharing.

However, second, the frustrations experienced by support workers are compounded by those encountered by discharged prisoners. Thus, advice offered in prison is not followed up with action, leaving prisoners with just their £46 discharge grant and no one to meet them at the crucial point of discharge at the prison gate. Some complain of the narrow perspective of some services, such as probation officers facing continuous workload conflicts between their primary concern with offender management, and the more wide-ranging needs associated with prisoner rehabilitation.

Since 2010, we have seen the emergence of a new policy environment regarding prisoner rehabilitation. The 2010 Green Paper, *Breaking the cycle* (MoJ, 2010), promised a new approach to tackling re-offending. It included a commitment to tackle barriers to rehabilitation posed by inadequate access to housing. Following a more recent consultation, the UK government set out a more far-reaching strategy in *Transforming rehabilitation: A strategy for reform* (MoJ, 2013b), and accompanying legislation in the Offender Rehabilitation Act 2014. These measures set out more concrete commitments, including 'through the gate' support for short-term as well as long-term prisoners. Controversially, this will entail the sub-contracting of support services to Community Rehabilitation Companies, funded on a payment-by-results basis, rather than the traditional probation service.

Of considerable importance among agencies favoured to deliver rehabilitation support to discharged short-term prisoners are mentoring services, for which the Ministry of Justice has endorsed the 'justmentoring' website (Mentoring and Befriending Foundation, no date, a). A quick look at its directory of mentoring services reveals 208 mentoring schemes in England and Wales that currently work with offenders, 123 of which provide housing support. According to the Mentoring and Befriending Foundation (no date, b), mentoring schemes may be of two types: peer mentoring, which is undertaken by fellow prisoners prior to release; and volunteer mentoring, in which volunteers are trained to sustain a relationship 'through the gate', providing friendship and support both before and after release. The aims of mentoring schemes are to target problems (for example, lack of stable housing, social skills, etc), change behaviour (for example, offending), expand opportunities (for example, for work, training) and build support (for example, trust, resilience, relationships). Their effectiveness is claimed to derive from the provision of role models, the use of social equals (if not peers), the ability to identify with ex-prisoners (preferably through first-hand experience), continuity of support (through the gate), holistic support, bridging access to services, cost-effectiveness and the building of social capital.

What do we know about the effectiveness of mentoring schemes? A review of intermediate outcomes based on 23 studies (NOMS, 2013) showed that the effect on re-offending is inconclusive, but 'through the gate' mentoring is more effective than prison only. There are also indications linking mentoring to improved outcomes in, for example, employment, housing, addressing substance use and engagement with programmes to encourage desistance. A further study that specifically looked at peer mentoring (Fletcher and Batty, 2012) found that peer mentors may be better at engaging offenders, acting as role models, and sharing knowledge. However, the pool is small, the turnover is high, the role is ambiguous and the service needs a lot of support. Moreover, it is based on the current political assumption that all offenders need is a rehabilitative role model, forgetting the structural obstacles that earlier research found.

This brief policy review has sought to show UK prisoner rehabilitation to have reached a turning point. Decades of policy failure have left reoffending rates unchanged. The Offender Rehabilitation Act is at last attempting to put the rehabilitation of short-term prisoners on to a statutory footing by requiring them to engage with support services on release, or face the threat of recall to prison. Whether this will reduce re-offending or merely add to an ever-growing prison population will depend on the effectiveness of those support services in breaking the critical links between discharge and renewed criminality. What follows is a small-scale evaluation of a rehabilitation project that seeks to build on evidence that securing stable accommodation will break one of those links.

The rehabilitation project and the evaluation study

The subject of this evaluation is a prisoner rehabilitation project that combines planned post-release accommodation with the intensive personal support of a key worker and the underpinning social support of a homeless persons day centre. It is therefore designed to tackle one of the identified routes to re-offending, using a rehabilitative model with sufficiently distinct features to give it the potential for wider adoption and thus to warrant evaluation. After a brief description of the project, the methods used in the evaluation are outlined, including the characteristics of the service user and key informant samples.

The project employs an offender support officer (OSO) to meet with prisoners prior to release, to prepare them for release, and to support them for a period afterwards, with a particular focus on procuring stable accommodation and supporting independent living. The project is managed by a day centre in a city in the English Midlands in partnership with a local community prison, designated by the UK Ministry of Justice as one of six resettlement prisons to which prisoners are relocated prior to release. The project works with prolific repeat offenders on short-term sentences, 90 per cent of whom are homeless at the time they are sentenced. The OSO provides a wide range of highly flexible services that can include anything that will establish service users in a stable home. However, three aspects are crucial: consistency of involvement 'through the gate', attaching priority to housing, and a personal, holistic commitment that ensures that all barriers to resettlement – whether practical or relational – are removed, so that ex-prisoners have a genuinely alternative lifestyle into which they can walk. In total, the project had provided some assistance to 270 ex-prisoners in just over two years from the beginning of 2012 to the end of February 2014.

Evidence for the effectiveness of the project is drawn from a limited, small-scale study that explored its success in sustaining re-housing, preventing re-offending and overcoming social isolation, seeking to understand the processes by which the project achieves its goals to varying degrees according to the characteristics of different service users. Data were derived from semi-structured interviews with two small samples, the first of which was an opportunity sample of six ex-prisoner service users. Interviews explored their background in terms of family, crime, work, homelessness, substance use and mental health. Respondents were invited to offer their own explanation for their current circumstances and why the current system of offender management and rehabilitation had hitherto failed in their cases. Interviews then explored their understanding of resettlement and their aspirations for the future before inviting an account of their experiences of the project, the help it had provided and the likelihood of successes being sustainable. Access to the sample was facilitated by the OSO. Service users were drawn from her caseload of service users who were typical – in terms of their characteristics, background and current circumstances – of those for whom she was currently providing intensive support. The sample of six ex-prisoners were all male and exemplified a pattern of multiple exclusion that combines offending, homelessness, family breakdown, substance misuse and mental ill health (Bowpitt et al, 2011; Fitzpatrick et al, 2011; McDonagh, 2011). Table 6.1 provides introductory pen portraits, all names being fictitious.

Table 6.1: The service user sample

	Alan	Brian	Clive	Hanif	Eric	Garry
Age	36	40	36	36	35	39
Ethnicity	White British	White British	White British	Middle Eastern	White British	White British
Offending background	Shoplift-ing	Various prop-erty-related	Domestic and other violence	Contempt of court	Shop-lifting	Steal-ing
Current accommo-dation	Own tenancy	Hostel for ex-pris-oners	Hostel for ex-prisoners	Hostel for ex-prison-ers	Hostel for ex-pris-oners	Alco-hol reha-bilita-tion hostel
Homeless-ness back-ground	Slept rough	Slept rough	Slept rough	No, but at risk	Slept rough	Slept rough
Employ-ment back-ground	Manual unskilled	Some manual skills	Manual unskilled	Qualified teacher	Some manual skills	No work for 20 years
Engagement with project	2-3 months	3 months	Few weeks	Few weeks	3 months	2½ years inter-mit-tent

All six had been released from prison within the previous three months, and five of the six had worked with the project prior to release, mostly for just a few weeks, but intermittently for a period of two-and-a-half years, in Garry's case. Five were classed as prolific repeat offenders, having served a series of short-term sentences (less than 12 months) for property-related crimes in four cases and offences involving violence in Clive's case. All six were accommodated at the time they were interviewed, four in the hostel for ex-prisoners, while Garry was in another hostel that focused on alcohol problems, and Alan had his own tenancy. Apart from Alan, who had managed to retain his tenancy through his last brief sentence, all had been at risk of homelessness on release. Moreover, five of the six recounted a long history of homelessness, including long periods of sleeping rough, especially on release from previous sentences. All were unemployed at the time of the interviews, and with the exception of Hanif, none of the sample had experienced more than brief periods of largely unskilled employment; Garry had not worked for 20 years.

The other interview sample consisted of a purposive sample of five key informants, practitioners working for agencies that have been critical in providing move-on support. Access was once again facilitated by the OSO from among those with whom she collaborated in resettling service users. They included the OSO herself, a police officer working in offender management, the manager of the hostel for ex-prisoners, and support workers from two voluntary organisations providing mental health and employment support respectively. Interviews followed a similar pattern to those with service users, exploring the characteristics of the service user group that key informants typically encountered, their understanding of resettlement and what often impedes progress, and the key ingredients that make the rehabilitation project effective.

Service user background and the 'vicious circle'

The effectiveness of the project cannot be appreciated without first understanding the narratives that first drew the ex-prisoners into the vicious circle of homelessness and re-offending. In their interviews, key informants recounted a familiar story of how the effects of a damaging and traumatising childhood confront a service network ill-equipped to handle complex needs, setting people on a continually reinforcing and cumulatively destructive spiral of decline. The story begins with negative experiences of fathers who are chaotic, abusive, or die in traumatic circumstances, leaving an adolescent vulnerable to negative alternative male role models. The result is a disrupted education and an early introduction to drugs and a drug habit that needs to be sustained. In the absence of any regular income, acquisitive crime quickly follows. Homelessness may result from prison discharge, but more frequently it is the fall-out from inappropriate relationships formed with equally damaged young women that leave men the victims of eviction following relationship breakdown. Young men disabled by such life experiences then seek help from a welfare system almost designed to erect barriers in their faces, making re-offending the only logical survival strategy. They come out of prison with a £46 discharge grant that has to last 4-6 weeks until a benefit claim is processed. Problems associated with attending appointments for people who are homeless result in benefit sanctions, denial of medication and breach of license, making a return to prison inevitable. The struggle to secure housing encounters similar obstacles.

The six ex-prisoners confirmed much of this. Alan and Brian had substantial experience of the care system, while Clive, Eric and Garry had been essentially disowned by their original families mainly because of their substance misuse. Moreover, five of the six had had numerous long-term relationships that had produced children with whom they had lost contact. Five of the six had experienced serious problems with substance misuse, involving addiction to Class A drugs and alcohol. Furthermore, four had diagnosed mental health conditions for which they were receiving treatment, including Clive, who described himself as a long-term paranoid schizophrenic. Substance problems were an attempt to self-medicate to mask deeper issues arising from, for instance, child abuse, relationship breakdown or mental illness. Respondents recounted a continuous cycle of substance misuse funded by petty crime that incurred short-term prison sentences from which they were invariably discharged into homelessness and further substance misuse. Homelessness frequently intervened before imprisonment when rent money was spent sustaining a drug or alcohol dependency. Encounters with the criminal justice system had done nothing to break the cycle.

More worryingly, when liberty meant little more than sleeping rough, prison acquired a positive attraction. Respondents pointed to the inevitability of homelessness and a return to criminality once they got on to the treadmill of short-term sentences and unsupported discharge. Garry described his lack of priority for re-housing, and the delays he faced when submitting a benefits claim:

'When I came out ... they can't help with re-housing and that. Just go to [local authority] the day you get out. Sometimes you go to [local authority] and they say, come back tomorrow, come back tomorrow, you're not a priority. Because you are single male with no kids and stuff. When you're trying to set up a new claim you get released with only £46. Sometimes it can take 4 or 5 weeks for your new claim to be up and running. So I understand why people re-offend. I've re-offended quite a lot, coming out of jail.'

To this experience, Eric added the positive appeal of prison:

'To be honest with you, going to jail for me was a godsend. I got fed. I got a bed. I got people to sit and listen to me talk – inmates. I mattered. Out here I don't matter. In jail I mattered. I was in a bad point. No one wanted to know me when I was out here. When I was in jail I got people to talk to. I got warm. I'd got no concerns. I didn't matter out here.... I could have died and nobody would have bothered with me.'

Establishing the present

Findings from the evaluation are presented in the next two sections. The first explores the process of prison discharge and its immediate aftermath, seeking to identify the key ingredients that made a difference in establishing a new life away from drugs, crime and homelessness. Respondents could not over-emphasise the importance of the first ingredient, the establishment of a relationship inside prison, followed by the personal meeting at the prison gate on release. Eric described how he came across the project and its significance. "I spoke to another inmate and he said [name of project] from [day centre]. So I asked for a leaflet about services and whatever and [OSO] came to visit me in prison and she told me about all the services and all the help that can be provided for me. That was like a big door opened up for me. I'd never had this before." Moreover, "When I got out, she actually met me at the gate. If she'd not been there, I'd have ended up going back to [home town] and I'd be messed up on drugs again." This was confirmed by key informants. As the OSO explained, "I go and see prisoners on the wing and set up a care plan for their release and when appropriate I meet them at the gate and continue to support them afterwards." The hostel manager explained the enormous pressures on offenders with drug problems at the point of release, from which only a meeting at the gate can divert them.

The second ingredient was an attention to detail that turned the procurement of accommodation into the setting up of a home and the wherewithal to live in it. Alan was pleased that someone had kept his tenancy in order while he was in prison. For four of the others, the result of this attention to detail was a pre-arranged room in the hostel for ex-prisoners, which circumvented the standard local authority homelessness application that so often ends in failure (Dwyer et al, 2015). However, even a room in a hostel needs furnishing, and Brian described how "she took me to [recycled furniture store], you know to get all me furniture and that. She took us there and fetched us back."

Moreover, in recognition of likely delays in benefit, several respondents were glad that the project operated from a homeless person's day centre where they could get regular meals and food hampers to obviate the need to commit further offences just in order to survive. Furthermore, knowing that failure to attend appointments had frequently triggered a downward spiral in the past, the OSO would frequently accompany service users to meetings at the job centre or the Probation Service, not simply to ensure they got there on time, but to act as a mediator. For Clive, taking him to places in the car reduced the chances of further paranoid episodes on public transport, for which he had been arrested in the past. As the mental health support worker realised, prioritising housing for this group entails a lot more than just fixing up a tenancy. If "you take somebody who has been rough sleeping for 20 years and you put them in a flat, they are contained but that doesn't solve the problem". Housing is critical to accessing a range of other services, but "resettlement should be holistic. It's not just about housing.... It needs to be accessible for guys and it needs to be flexible and long term." This has important implications for debates around 'Housing First' (Johnsen and Teixeira, 2010; Pleace and Quilgars, 2013).

The underpinning support of the day centre from which the project operated provided an invaluable third ingredient in the early days following release. It provided an unobtrusive means by which the OSO could maintain contact. As Alan explained, "Even if I don't see her, she always phones me up to make sure I'm all right. Ask me, why haven't I been down [to the day centre]? Basically, checking up on me in the nicest possible way. She's like a second mum." Moreover, securing access to the day centre provided more than just a source of free food. It offered an alternative social network where Brian felt he would be accepted and understood and not lured back into his old lifestyle. This was "because they treat you as a human being, rather than some object ... or some criminal. They don't try and judge you. A lot of people, a lot of them who work down there who volunteer have gone through similar backgrounds as us."

What all this amounted to in the eyes of key informants was a fourth ingredient, a relationship of dependability, which is ironic in a society that frowns on services that are seen to promote dependency, but there is a difference. For the mental health support worker, dependability derives from trust, which has to be earned, "based on the fact that you've proven to them that the advice you've given them is accurate, that actually it's going to benefit them in some way". Crucial to earning this trust is showing that the relationship established in prison is affirmed at the prison gate and will continue afterwards. For the hostel manager, dependability is about being true to your word, but it is not about generating dependency. Quite the opposite: having someone who believes in you will promote a sense of self-belief in a population disabled by repeated failure and rejection. The OSO confirmed many of the views expressed by other key informants when she summarised the active ingredients in her work in terms of consistency combined with a practical flexibility that involved being there for service users when they needed her, and being willing to broker access to whatever it takes to make resettlement possible, using her vast knowledge of local community services.

Securing the future

Nevertheless, the key test of the project lay in its effectiveness in sustaining re-housing, preventing re-offending and overcoming social isolation. None of the sample had been charged with further offences since their most recent spell in prison. However, service users had three further aspirations which they associated with long-term resettlement: overcoming substance dependencies, finding an occupation, paid if possible, and restoring lost relationships often with children. If these were achieved, the more short-term goal of staying out of prison would follow naturally. There was a sense that these were not just aspirations in themselves; they were mutually reinforcing, and a means of ensuring an end to criminality. In this second section, we will see how far project and service user aspirations were realised.

How far had respondents succeeded in accessing long-term housing? With the exception of Alan, who had his own tenancy, the other five respondents were all in short-term supported accommodation, and recognised their need for somewhere more permanent. Initially, Brian was happy to have "got a roof over me head, that's not a night shelter", where he could feel some sense of ownership and could say, "this room is all mine. I've not had no possessions, not ever. It does feel good knowing you've got something." However, for Garry, resettlement entailed a much fuller community reintegration in which housing was central, and from which everything else followed. "Resettlement is getting my own tenancy, getting somewhere to live ... managing to keep on top of the bills and shopping, just doing normal things basically, but it doesn't involve drink or drugs. Integrating. Feeling of getting back into the community." Yet it was only for Clive that the OSO was making progress in securing permanent accommodation.

With regard to overcoming substance dependency, all six ex-prisoners were managing to abstain from drink and drugs, largely because of the regimes that operated in their current accommodation, making the choice of residence following release from prison particularly critical. Garry had "done detox and stuff in prison", but even the abstinent environment in his hostel still required a combination of willpower and some powerful chemical supports. "Yeah willpower. Or there's the other thing I can do, I can go on the Antabuse. If I even touch a drop of alcohol, I get violently ill." Yet he realised that willpower and Antabuse were much more likely to succeed with something to occupy his time and attention, and here again, the OSO was able to bring her fixing skills to bear. "I'm going to meet her next week for a coffee ... and see if there's anything else she can help me with. She'll be seeing me about some volunteering work and that, she knows there's a place ... a three-day painting and decorating course, so I'm going to have a look at that." The next stage would be paid work, using existing qualifications or gaining new ones. "I'd like to do some fork lift training, get my fork lift licence. I've done an industrial cleaning course; I've even been getting into that. I've got certificates for industrial cleaning."

For some respondents, a new network of relationships, usually involving restored contact with family members, was the best hope for permanent resettlement. Garry was in no doubt that healthier relationships and activities were two of the benefits of having your own accommodation. "I know people who don't drink, who don't do drugs.... They don't like seeing me when I'm drunk, they don't like seeing me when I'm on drugs. I can go and visit them and we can go to the football." Eric's real yearning was to have his children back. In the past, his criminal record and drug abuse were barriers. "Before, when I've come out of jail ... because of my drug use [and] something like 30 shop thefts, they've classed me as a risk. I can't blame them for thinking that." Now, the prospect of restored contact served as an incentive to work for the conditions that would make that happen, especially permanent accommodation and paid employment. "I'm fighting for contact, but really my children are my inspiration now. Obviously my children need me, but I need them more."

For the key informants, beyond the practicalities of brokering access to permanent accommodation and occupational opportunities, the project could activate other relational catalysts to sustainable resettlement. For instance, the hostel manager made good use of early successes as a learning tool in promoting a changed mind-set, restoring a sense of self-worth among people accustomed to failure. Another catalyst is the need for forbearance, of never giving up on people, recognising that effective rehabilitation needs to operate at its own pace, acknowledging the inevitability of reversals. For the hostel manager, this involves letting people return to her supported housing project to help with the practical problems of setting up home.

The possibility of the project providing a source of more lasting support raises the issue of mentoring discussed earlier. The OSO was aware that "there's only one of me so more to be able to do this will be really helpful, for the low-level support I think." It is in this role of continuous, low-level back-up for sustainable resettlement that the basing of the project at a day centre once again assumes particular significance. The employment support worker recognised in the day centre a potential source of informal mentors in providing unconditional welcome and support. "Somebody independent who can offer you the chance to meet and not judge where you are and not be so upset by the latest story that has happened to you.... And I think that is important to have that. Definitely [the day centre] provides that for people."

Discussion

The passing of the Offender Rehabilitation Act 2014 has generated a policy imperative to understand what works in the rehabilitation of short-term repeat offenders. This pilot evaluation of a small-scale rehabilitation project offers some contribution to this debate, especially with regard to the importance of preventing homelessness. The evaluation has shown four key elements to be effective in the short term. The first is consistency of support through the prison gate, including a personal meeting at the point of release. Not only does this serve a vital protective role, but it also testifies that promises made in prison will be kept. The second is the effective brokering of what might be called 'housing plus', that is, direct accompaniment both to pre-arranged accommodation and everything else needed to make it habitable. The third is the day centre base from which the project operated, which provided both emergency access to the means of survival and access to a new social support network through the team of volunteers that operates there. The fourth is the intrinsic value of the relationship with the OSO, over and above the services thereby procured.

However, to realise its long-term goals, the rehabilitation project has to give ex-prisoners an interest in avoiding re-offending, homelessness and social isolation. It can play some role through brokering access to permanent accommodation and meaningful activities, but the pilot also showed the importance of restored family relationships and a more positive mind-set. Also of great value are the project's forbearance in allowing people to develop at their own pace, always willing to give them another chance.

This small-scale study has given some indication of what the project has been able to achieve, some of which goes beyond what is claimed for mentoring schemes. The link with a day centre that serves the needs of homeless and multiply excluded adults means that, although the OSO does not herself provide a role model, act as a social equal, or identify with the backgrounds that offenders come from, she can put service users in contact with existing volunteers who have these characteristics. However, of far greater value to the overall effectiveness of the service was its continuity, not simply before and after release, but actually at the prison gate at the critical point of discharge, and thereafter, enabling relationships of trust to develop. Moreover, the OSO was able to act as an effective bridge to access a range of other services, of which housing and the practical wherewithal to sustain accommodation were particularly critical. In other words, effectiveness depended on her having an expertise in a crucial area. These characteristics are not always found together in mentoring schemes.

Findings from this brief evaluation inform debates around other approaches to working with people with a history of multiple exclusion, such as personalisation, 'psychologically informed environments' (PIEs) and 'Housing First'. When personalised approaches are used, for instance, with rough sleepers, service users are assigned to a single support worker with a designated budget that can be used with total flexibility for anything that would contribute to achieving agreed goals (Hough and Rice, 2010). Although the project did not assign a designated budget for each ex-offender, the flexible, holistic and personalised approach to resettlement very much mirrored the personalisation model, showing that it could work as well with other groups at risk of returning to a multiply excluded lifestyle. PIEs take this personalised approach one stage further by treating the relationship between service user and support worker as an essential ingredient in the process of change, over and above the services thereby procured (NMHDU, 2010; Keats et al, 2012). Adding further support to this approach was an unintended benefit of the project.

Although accommodation immediately on release was critical to success, its approach to housing fell well short of the 'Housing First' approach to working with chronically homeless people pioneered in New York in the early 1990s and widely adopted with considerable success in other developed countries including the UK (Johnsen and Teixeira, 2010; Pleace and Quilgars, 2013). Housing First is contrasted with 'staircase' models of resettlement in accommodating homeless people directly from the street into ordinary housing, all other support services being provided separately through mobile support workers or at designated sites. Success has been achieved not only in sustaining life away from the streets, but also in addressing problems associated with mental health and substance misuse. However, there is no evidence of its use with people who are homeless on discharge from prison. Apart from Alan, all the sample were in supported accommodation with staff on site, although they had their own rooms and a high degree of self-care was expected. There is no evidence that Alan was making more progress than the other five. While there are no obvious practical limitations to independent accommodation being arranged before release, there is evidence from the present study that service users valued hostel companionship, like Eric who insisted that "this is my family here … I've got like a mum or a big sister here every day."

Conclusion

The project would benefit from a more extensive evaluation with a more varied cohort who had engaged over a longer period. One of the limitations of the pilot study is that the sample had all been released from prison within the past three months, even Garry, despite his intermittent association over the past two-and-a-half years. However, we can conclude that at the time of their interview, all participants had sustained their accommodation since discharge, had not been arrested for any offences, had recorded virtually no lapses into problematic substance use, and were addressing mental health problems through engagement with specialised services. To that extent, the project was a success. Critical to that success was engagement with service users prior to release, meeting them at the prison gate on release, accompanying them to pre-arranged accommodation and appointments to secure essential resources and access to key services, the flexible, holistic and personalised approach of the OSO, and the accessible, convivial and largely unconditional support of the day centre that underpinned the project.

References

Bowpitt, G., Dwyer, P., Sundin, E. and Weinstein, M. (2011) *The HOME Study: Comparing the priorities of multiply excluded homeless people and support agencies*, Salford: University of Salford.

DCLG (Department for Communities and Local Government, 2006) *The homelessness Code of Guidance for local authorities*, London: DCLG.

Dwyer, P., Bowpitt, G., Sundin, E. and Weinstein, M. (2015) 'Rights, responsibilities and refusals: homelessness policy and the exclusion of single homeless people with complex needs', *Critical Social Policy*, vol 35, no 1, pp 3-23.

Fitzpatrick, S., Johnsen, S. and White, M. (2011) 'Multiple exclusion homelessness in the UK: key patterns and intersections', *Social Policy and Society*, vol 10, no 4, pp 501-12.

Fletcher, D.R. and Batty, E. (2012) *Offender peer interventions: What do we know?*, Sheffield: Centre for Economic and Social Research, Sheffield Hallam University.

Halpern, D. (2005) *Social capital*, Cambridge: Polity Press.

Home Office (2004) *Reducing reoffending: National action plan*, London: Home Office.

Homeless Link (2011) *Better together: Preventing reoffending and homelessness*, London: Homeless Link (www.homeless.org.uk/sites/default/files/Better%20Together%20Final%20Report_Sep11_prm.pdf).

Hough, J. and Rice, B. (2010) *Providing personalised support to rough sleepers: An evaluation of the City of London pilot*, York: Joseph Rowntree Foundation (www.broadwaylondon.org/ResearchInformation/Research/Personalisationforroughsleepers.html).

Johnsen, S. and Teixeira, L. (2010) 'Staircases, elevators and cycles of change: Housing First and other housing models for homeless people with complex support needs', Research Summary, York: University of York.

Keats, H., Cockersell, P., Haigh, R., Johnson, R. and Maguire, N. (2012) *Psychologically informed services for homeless people*, Southampton: University of Southampton College of Medicine.

McDonagh, T. (2011) *Tackling homelessness and exclusion: Understanding complex lives*, Round Up: Reviewing the evidence, York: Joseph Rowntree Foundation.

Mentoring and Befriending Foundation (no date, a) *Justmentoring hub* (www.justmentoring.org.uk/).

Mentoring and Befriending Foundation (no date, b) 'What is mentoring and befriending?' (www.mandbf.org/mbf-membership/what-is-mentoring-and-befriending).

MoJ (Ministry of Justice (2010) *Breaking the cycle: Effective punishment, sentencing and rehabilitation of offenders*, Cm 7972, London: Crown Copyright (http://webarchive.nationalarchives.gov.uk/20120119200607/http:/www.justice.gov.uk/consultations/docs/breaking-the-cycle.pdf).

MoJ (2012a) *Accommodation, homelessness and reoffending of prisoners: Results from the Surveying Prisoner Crime Reduction (SPCR) survey* (www.gov.uk/government/uploads/system/uploads/attachment_data/file/278806/homelessness-reoffending-prisoners.pdf).

MoJ (2012b) *Prison Service Instruction – Custody, PSI 12/2012*, p 14 (www.justice.gov.uk/offenders/psis/prison-service-instructions-2012)

MoJ (2013a) *Proven reoffending statistics*, Quarterly Bulletin: July 2010 to June 2011, England and Wales (www.gov.uk/government/uploads/system/uploads/attachment_data/file/192631/proven-reoffending-jul-10-jun-11.pdf).

MoJ (2013b) *Transforming rehabilitation: A strategy for reform*, Cm 8619, London: Crown Copyright (https://consult.justice.gov.uk/digital-communications/transforming-rehabilitation/results/transforming-rehabilitation-response.pdf).

NMHDU (National Mental Health Development Unit (2010) *Meeting the psychological and emotional needs of homeless people*, London: NMHDU.

NOMS (National Offender Management Service (2013) *Intermediate outcomes of mentoring interventions: A rapid evidence assessment* (www.mandbf.org.uk/wp-content/uploads/2014/01/Intermediate-outcomes-of-mentoring-interventions.pdf).

Pleace, N. and Quilgars, D. (2013) *Improving health and social integration through Housing First: A review*, York: Centre for Housing Policy, University of York.

SEU (Social Exclusion Unit) (2002) *Reducing reoffending by ex-prisoners*, London: Office of the Deputy Prime Minister.

SEVEN

Embedded neglect, entrenched abuse: market failure and mistreatment in elderly residential care

Joe Greener

Since the Community Care Act reforms of the 1990s, social care in the UK has been transformed into a multibillion-pound industry where a range of providers now compete in a market (Fotaki et al, 2013). The effects of the privatisation and marketisation of social care systems on the day-to-day realities of giving and receiving care, however, have been the subject of much critical scholarly attention (MacDonald and Merrill, 2002; Lynch, 2007). Concerns have been raised about whether the introduction of profit motives gives priority to commercial agendas to the detriment of service quality. At the same time, social care services in general are under threat from the impact of fiscal austerity. Local authority budgets in many parts of the UK have been heavily reduced, having an impact on the ability for care providers to meet service user needs. Evidence would suggest that services for older people have experienced worsening quality, the introduction of new or higher charges as well as declining accessibility (Age UK, 2014, p 2).

Speaking to these wider concerns, this chapter uses covert ethnographic data collected in an elderly residential home to show how forms of abuse and neglect can become embedded within the routines and practices of care work. It has been argued that marketisation and privatisation have both had a negative impact on the way in which care is performed. It seems that workers' rights have been affected by a drive across the sector to maintain and sustain low pay. When care is done for profit, services can become subject to a process of extreme rationalisation as providers strive to decrease costs in order to increase profits. Many aspects of the service can be affected, including staffing levels, funding for medical supplies or extras such as entertainment and social budgets, and a generalised pressure is exerted on the quality of care (Lopez, 1998; Folbre, 2006). A growing theme in this literature is the existence of a rift between the expectations of care workers held by employers and state regulatory frameworks, and the actual ability for frontline workers to deliver the sort of care that is being asked of them. A recent article by Bolton and Wibberley (2014), for example, shows how the formal management of domiciliary care work through rotas and care plans fails to capture the complex and demanding requirements of those relying on the service to meet their needs.

This chapter speaks to these themes in order to explore how forms of abuse and neglect became unavoidable for the care assistants employed in one home. As the primary contribution of the chapter is the empirical data relating to the frontline realities of care work, a methodological overview of the covert ethnographic approach is the point of departure. The subsequent section provides a brief overview of the company that owned the home where the research took place, in order to highlight the links between the micro-level practice and the macro-level processes with which the chapter is theoretically concerned.

The more directly data-driven sections then show how degrading, inhumane and negligent practices were embedded in the social and temporal organisation of care in the home. Due to the relatively limited space for discussion of the qualitative data, four significant aspects of care are considered in greater depth: feeding and hydration, continence care, moving and handling, and the failure to provide care that was sensitive to individual needs. Finally, the discussion then provides a broader assessment of how we might theorise the empirical findings, focusing attention on how social care labour processes are influenced and shaped by external corporate-level and state-level processes. Before going on, however, the chapter offers an explanation of the use of covert methods, which were at the heart of uncovering the ritualised forms of abuse prevalent in the home.

In defence of covert methods for researching for-profit residential care

The data presented in the following section were collected between 2008 and 2009 during a covert ethnographic observational study undertaken through employment in an elderly residential care home, owned and managed by the company Southern Cross. The need to adopt a covert stance to the research emerged from two issues: (1) the desire to acquire a particular form of data; and (2) the inability to acquire this sort of data through any other means (BSA, 2002). Ethical considerations were a consistent priority throughout the research.[1]

Crucial to the approach used here is its participatory element. It allowed the researcher to get 'inside' caring as an everyday physical and emotional activity. The findings show that 'doing' care work, rather than asking about care work, builds a picture of the kinds of pressures which face staff in these facilities that may not have emerged using a more mainstream methodological approach.

Second, there was also a political basis to the covert participatory stance used. Southern Cross was a powerful corporation responsible for providing care to a large number of elderly UK citizens. Uncovering the financial pressures facing the company at that time, and the effect of these difficulties on the care provided, would have been impossible if research strategies had followed the conventional ethical procedure of acquiring informed consent from gatekeepers. Opening up this hidden world of corporate, for-profit care to academic scrutiny can be viewed as in the public interest. In order to contextualise the firm-level processes that are significant to an analysis of the empirical data presented shortly, it is also necessary to describe the problems that were encountered by Southern Cross during the period the research took place.

Demise of Southern Cross

When Southern Cross announced its collapse on 11 July 2011 it was the largest provider of elderly residential care services in the UK, with 800 facilities and the physical capacity to provide care for 37,000 people. It employed in the region of 42,000 staff and had homes in almost every region of the UK (Southern Cross Healthcare, 2009). Southern Cross grew substantially and made large profits up until 2007. While there was a management buy-out of the company in 2002, many of Southern Cross' problems seemed to have begun in 2004 when it was purchased by New York equity firm, Blackstone Group (*The Scotsman*, 2004). Blackstone subsequently bought the property company Nursing Home Properties (NHP), and shortly after, imposed a sale-and-leaseback strategy. Private equity firms commonly use this tactic to realise quick returns from restructuring ventures (Clark, 2009; Appelbaum et al, 2012). By stripping companies of some of their assets and leasing these back through newly created property arms, businesses are left with new costs. Blackstone turned Southern Cross into an operating company, which leased its homes from a variety of other property firms (*Sunday Telegraph*, 2011).

Blackstone then floated Southern Cross on the stock market, withdrawing their involvement in the care provider (*The Times*, 2008), at which point the company's problems began to become clear. In the years following its flotation, Southern Cross struggled to realise profit even as its share of the market and its revenue both started to rise. Revenue in 2008 was £889.4 million and jumped up to £937.1 million in 2009, largely due to increasing average fees, according to the 2009 annual report (Southern Cross Healthcare, 2009, p 16). However, the company continued to experience rising rents, which increased from £221.6 to £239.1 million from 2008 to 2009 (Southern Cross Healthcare, 2009, p 17), and in spite of increasing revenue, in 2008 the operating loss was £5.2 million, increasing to £12.7 million in 2009. The company continued to buy up further homes and appeared committed to increasing the capacity of care provision, adding 1,147 beds in 2009 (Southern Cross Healthcare, 2009, p 16) and 3,121 in 2008 (Southern Cross Healthcare, 2008, p 7) through various acquisitions and developments.

What occurred at Southern Cross was clearly complex and involved other enterprises which, arguably at least, had shorter-term motivations for being involved with the care provider. The academic literature would suggest that the involvement of financialised interests often results in more fleeting profit goals displacing longer-term commitment to the securing of commercial stability (Clark, 2009; Thompson, 2013). The losses incurred through increasing rent charges are arguably a direct result of the sale-and-leaseback model instigated by Blackstone. Blackstone stripped Southern Cross of homes that it had previously owned and sold them to a number of other parties (such as NHP), removing the ability of Southern Cross to control fixed costs. Rising rental costs may have been avoided had property been retained within the company's assets.

Since Southern Cross's bankruptcy, a growing amount of evidence has emerged indicating that the quality of care that was being provided in many of their homes was inadequate (Sussex County Council, 2014). The remainder of this chapter investigates care in one Southern Cross home, and suggests that there is a clear association between the problems being experienced at the corporate level and delivery of care on the front line.

Embedded abuse, entrenched neglect

This article employs labour process theory as the conceptual lens by which to analyse the embedded forms of malpractice. Labour process theory seeks to conceptualise the nature of work in contemporary capitalist society with special attention paid to how capitalism organises purposive human activity into a spatial and temporal process with the intention of creating surplus value (Braverman, 1974). Human labour, technology and systems of managerial control and surveillance are arranged by capitalist enterprises in an attempt to transform labour power (or the potential for work) into actual directed and meaningful labour aimed at producing commodities.

The theoretical approach has been picked up in various ways by scholars seeking to understand the nature of care work. Part of this literature has emphasised the way in which care suffers when it becomes a rationalised and bureaucratically driven process, done with the intention of maximising profit or minimising expenditure (Lopez, 1998; Folbre, 2006; Bolton and Wibberley, 2014). The basic idea is that care is a particular form of relational and affective activity that cannot easily be standardised, routinised or rationalised without affecting its central intention – that of meeting the needs of others in a responsive, compassionate and empathetic manner (MacDonald and Merrill, 2002). This body of research demonstrates how the potential relations between cared-for and carer are predisposed by the social and political climate that surrounds the activity of caring.

The empirical data for this analysis was gathered in a residential home referred to as 'Meadowvale'. The capacity of the home was 36 residents. As is normal for residential service users, the needs of the home's residents were complex, including those related to a host of cognitive difficulties, limited mobility and a range of mental and physical health problems or disabilities (see Shah et al, 2010; Darton et al, 2012). Dementia was, however, the most prevalent diagnosis.

The following discussion focuses on how the arrangement of work practices at Meadowvale continually created a context where mistreatment was part and parcel of completing the work. The description of care in this Southern Cross care home exposes how minimal staffing levels and failing managerial control resulted in specific forms of mistreatment. The forms of malpractice considered in more depth are moving and handling, nutrition and hydration, continence care and personalisation. Moving and handling is central to many care tasks, and often involves the use of various aids that help manoeuvre care recipients to and from toilets, baths, beds and chairs while also reducing the risk of injury to workers and those being cared for. Again, nutrition and hydration is a central component of care work – ensuring that people's dietary requirements are met, and that appropriate assistance is given in feeding and drinking is essential for the quality of people's lives and health. Continence care is discussed as the management of toileting habits is one of the main areas of work with which elderly residential workers are engaged, and critical for service users to maintain dignity. Lastly, the home's ability to deliver personalised care is discussed. While personalisation is a policy-driven concept, arguably driven by an ideology of individualism, it does also reflect concerns about the tendency of social care services to deliver institutionalised forms of care, which fail to be responsive to the needs and wishes of users. It is discussed here in order to bring to light the way the labour process denied people autonomous decision-making over their own lives.

Low input labour process

At Meadowvale, the one care assistant to five residents ratio, which was the minimum standard set at the time, was often breached. Managers generally attempted to follow this, but if the number of residents in the home was over a multiple of five, then the staff ratio was always rounded down. For example, if there were 29 residents in the home then five, rather than six, carers would be on duty. Second, at times, staffing levels fell seriously below this – for example, if a number of workers were off sick, there was no use of agency staff (see also Sussex County Council, 2014, p 76). When individual residents needed assistance to attend medical appointments off site, one of the care assistants would be required to accompany them, again meaning that staffing 'on the floor' fell below the one-to-five ratio. It does need to be emphasised, and will be elaborated in the next section, that even when staffing met minimum standards, this was not sufficient to achieve the specified workload. The company also engaged in other cost-reducing strategies during the period of research. The entertainment budget (used for events such as birthdays or New Year's Eve parties) had been withdrawn, and a 'dealing with dementia' course, which had previously been available for staff to attend in order to help them develop dementia-specific communication and care skills, had also been halted. At the time of research, the food budget was also under threat, and management proposed a cutback of 10 per cent, despite the budget being a meagre £2.75 per resident, per day.

Pay and entitlements were already at the legal minimum for care assistants and therefore could not be further reduced. Even after promotion to senior care assistant, pay only increased by 23p per hour. The workforce in Meadowvale also included a significant number of migrant workers. The use of migrant labour brought with it a number of advantages for the employers, as these foreign workers were less likely to leave for alternative work and tended to commit themselves to a greater number of hours every week due to conditions imposed through immigration regulations (Cangiano et al, 2009; Shutes, 2012).[2]

The low staff to service user ratios, the extensive use of highly exploitable foreign workers and the attempt by management to make further savings in food and entertainment budgets all indicate an inadequately resourced working environment. Problems that emerged from the supervision of care activities in the home were also a reflection of the minimal staffing.

Managerial control: if it's written down, did it actually happen?

The major tool for measuring and manipulating work was through various documents that were filled in by care workers daily, and recorded which care tasks had taken place with which residents. Workers were expected to measure almost all aspects of the work, and to record various care processes for each resident in the home. Every resident had their own file, and in it handwritten records were kept which noted, for example, how many litres of fluid and what weight of foodstuffs had been consumed, whether the resident had been washed (and whether this was in the form of a bath, shower or bed-bath), and the frequency and nature of toileting habits for that day. As Timmermans and Almeling (2009) rightly argue, this kind of bureaucratisation is not necessarily a problem in itself: standardising practices within health and social care institutions are often at the heart of improvements in outcomes. Ensuring that the appropriate personal care tasks had been completed would be largely impossible without some system that measured the tasks taking place.

The temporal configuration of each 12-hour shift was highly restricted with the expectation that sets of tasks were to be completed at specific times. Between 8 am and 11 am, for example, all residents had to be assisted in getting out of bed, washed and provided with breakfast. At 11 am tea and biscuits were provided, and so on. Even in spite of this highly ordered and regimented day, many important tasks were left uncompleted. Many residents rarely received showers or baths and were provided only with bed-baths that were much speedier to undertake. As discussed below, care in relation to moving and handling, feeding, continence and following policy guidance on personalisation all fell short of what would be deemed humane, with many tasks being hurried or left undone altogether.

What resulted was consistent fabrication of the care records. Towards the end of each shift workers would simply fill in the records so that it appeared as if each resident had been toileted the appropriate number of times, had eaten and drunk the correct amount and had been bathed in the correct manner. Managers only reprimanded workers when forms were not filled in. The home's mantra, consistently repeated by managers and written on the wall next to the location of the residents' files, was 'if it's not written down it didn't happen'. Managers were actually rarely present on the 'shop floor' and seldom engaged in any direct supervision over the work. Training courses at Meadowvale, such as the control of hazardous substances, moving and handling, care practices relating to feeding and drinking and how to deliver care based on personalisation and dignity, all emphasised the importance of each worker assuming responsibility over care delivery. As well as providing the necessary information, these courses always asserted the potential criminal culpability of the workers if someone were to be harmed as a result of not following the formal procedures.

Lopez's research, also looking at elderly residential care, detailed how the formal rules of managers, and the informal practices of workers, can depart into 'parallel universes' (2007, p 225). He applied the concept of 'mock-routinisation' to his account of elderly residential care where workers behaved in ways that contradicted formal procedures, but that can also be seen as aligned with managerial objectives. Taking short-cuts and general rule-breaking can allow the workers to attend to more residents and meet demands around the quantity of work. The account given here would depart from Lopez's explanation to a degree, as he emphasises how this routine contradiction of formal rules can be in the interests of all three groups involved (that is, managers, workers and residents). For instance, he describes how residents accept workers' informal methods (and may, in some cases, even insist upon them) because they have their own interests in ensuring that the care schedule itself is maintained (Lopez, 2007, p 229). The methods used by an employee may contravene health and safety regulations, but may allow the resident to be attended to, quickly and respectfully, without the use of hoists and stand-aids, for example.

The lack of direct supervision by the managers at Meadowvale is best understood as an attempt to distance themselves from culpability and responsibility of any potential legal ramifications if a mishap were to occur. It would then be possible to argue that records were checked, appropriate training regimens were followed and managerial bureaucratic instruments were in place. If an accident did happen, then care assistants and nurses could be constructed as responsible, either by fraudulently completing records or failing to follow appropriate guidelines on how care should be performed.

The following four sections analyse aspects of care in the home that are significant in revealing how staff consistently broke the formal rules on appropriate care, but the dialogue suggests that mistreatment of residents was largely unavoidable given the organisation of the work. The divergence between formal managerial prescriptions and actual practice of care was particularly stark in the context of the use of moving and handling machinery.

Moving and handling

While in certain forms of social care communication technologies have been used as a tool to increase efficiency (Brown and Korcynski, 2010), equipment that gets aggregated into the care labour process is often a manifestation of health and safety concerns, and not intended to increase the exploitation of labour or intensify the work. Much of this equipment is designed to help care workers move residents to/from beds, toilets, baths and armchairs without the risk of injury to themselves and those for whom they are providing care. Use of machinery involved in care work is more time-consuming and requires greater labour power than if the same task was done without it.

When it came to carrying out care tasks with residents who had limited mobility, the staff were presented with a number of different methods for moving residents to/from beds, toilets and chairs. The 'hoist and sling' was the method of moving intended for the most immobile residents, but was also the most labour and time-intensive. Hoisting requires manoeuvring the sling underneath the resident and then securing it to the crane-like hoist. Procedures on using hoists in the home required that two workers should always be present: one carer should hold the patient steady and another worker should operate and reposition the whole machine. Injuries on hoists are relatively common, and can even result in death. The Health and Safety Executive (2013a), for example, recently prosecuted a care homeowner after a resident died in hospital due to an injury incurred from being hoisted. Also, 'nursing auxiliaries and assistants', 'care worker and home carers' and 'nurses' were the third, fourth and fifth highest occupational categories in 2012/13 for numbers of handling injuries, according the Health and Safety Executive (2013b, p 4).

Despite the dangers, workers in the home consistently engaged in moving and handling practices that put themselves (and the residents) at threat of potential injury, and by consequence, also criminal conviction. Staff frequently used the strap in favour of the hoist or the stand-aid, which was considered more dangerous for the carer and cared-for – the strap is a small canvas belt with handles on either side that allows two people to quickly move another by fixing the device around their middle and lifting them. This was, however, used only for moving lighter residents. Management consistently informed staff, both in formal training sessions and in day-to-day supervision, that they should not use the strap, but they never removed the item from the home. This underlines the duplicitous form of managerial command which demanded that work be completed in a certain manner but within a labour process context where this was not feasible.

Nutrition and hydration

As well as the widespread malpractice in moving and handling at Meadowvale, there were also considerable problems around feeding and intake of fluids. First, records rarely reflected what tasks had taken place. This meant that during many shifts, the team were unaware of how much food and drink each resident had actually consumed. The practical demands of the day meant that care files were not completed until the evening, and employees were not necessarily able to recall exactly what foodstuffs and drinks each resident had consumed.

The more serious problem with ensuring good nutrition and hydration was that there was inadequate time to assist the frailest residents. Many of the home's inhabitants required one-on-one feeding. Due to either biological impairment, such as oesophageal peristalsis, or cognitive difficulty, certain residents needed facilitation to eat over a long period of time (an hour-and-a-half for one meal, in some cases). There was often insufficient time to ensure every single resident consumed a full meal. A number of studies have identified the importance of providing elderly care home residents with lengthy, one-on-one assistance to ensure appropriate food intake (Ruigrok and Sheridan, 2006; Barnes et al, 2013). Perhaps less significant for the survival of residents than the intake of foodstuffs, but certainly no less important for them maintaining dignity, was the issue of continence care, which is where this chapter now turns.

Continence care

The use of incontinence pads in care homes is recognised in the medical literature as a last resort for continence management. Dignity in continence care essentially orientates around the practice of 'voiding'

(Schnelle and Leung, 2004), where people with difficulties in maintaining continence are assisted to the toilet frequently and at established times, which has been shown to greatly reduce levels of incontinence. In a mandatory training session for all staff in Meadowvale, the NHS district continence nurse offered guidance on how to follow voiding, and the home's management endorsed the practice.

In reality, workers had very little scope to employ voiding approaches to dealing with incontinence through the day, due to the extra labour time it would have required. Residents can be categorised into two distinct groups in terms of the continence care practices they were subject to. First, those who suffered from regular instances of incontinence but who spent their daytimes in the more public area of the residents' lounge were fitted with a fresh incontinence pad at the start of the day. These residents were sometimes toileted, but this, once again, was dependent on what other stresses on time the staff experienced during that shift. Because a rigorous schedule of voiding was not followed, instances of incontinence were frequent every day, and when they occurred, residents were escorted to the nearest toilet to be cleansed and have a new pad fastened. The second group of residents were those who remained in their bedrooms. These residents were subjected to an even more undignified form of forced incontinence. Pads were fitted on to these residents at four-hour intervals. This inevitably meant that they frequently lay in their own faeces and urine for significant periods of time.

Care practices revolving around moving and handling, nutrition and hydration and continence care were all clearly neglectful. The last empirical area discussed relates more to the level of control that the residents had over their own lives.

Personalisation

Much of the advertising material produced by Southern Cross publicised the company's commitment to providing an individually tailored service, where the preferences, needs and wishes of each individual were at the heart of what they did. As stated in the 2009 annual accounts, the aim was to 'champion the dignity of our residents at all times' by 'respecting their right to as much independence as possible, to privacy and to choice' (Southern Cross Healthcare, 2009, p 9). This also reflected the wider political project of personalisation that promotes the notion that welfare models based on consumer choice are the most appropriate (Beresford, 2009; Lloyd, 2010). Mandatory courses on personalisation were set for the employees and delivered by regional managers. Care assistants were instructed to ensure that residents should have control over their own destinies in terms of what they ate and what they did with their time.

Once again, the rift between the ideal practice that formal managerial agendas endorsed and the actual capabilities of staff to provide this level of choice was colossal. The ability of residents to realise self-determination is reliant on the material, emotional and social context within which care takes place. In real terms, the routine at Meadowvale was rigid and unyielding as far as it could accommodate particular individuals' choices. At times residents requested to do things with their day that sat outside of the normal routine, but were mostly refused. So, for example, residents might have wished to stay in bed for longer in the morning or, if they were feeling unwell, they might ask carers if they could stay in bed all day. Residents might have wanted to stay up later or go to bed early. All of these requests were generally refused by the staff as they tended to increase workloads and threatened the routine. More labour effort was required if residents were spatially dispersed across the home. In addition, residents who wished to stay in bed or went to bed early could then ring buzzers for assistance, requiring the care assistants to leave the floor to go and attend to their needs. The more residents that could be spatially centralised in the lounge area, the greater the number of tasks the staff could accomplish.

The discussion of the last four aspects of care has revealed the neglectful and abusive practices that were enmeshed into routines. The last section suggests that the nature of this labour process can be linked to the market failure of Southern Cross.

Discussion

The data presented in the previous sections provides a clear indication of how various forms of mistreatment experienced by residents in one elderly residential care home can be understood with reference to the configuration of work processes. It is clear that caring practices fell short of the formal regulatory guidance on moving and handling, nutrition and hydration, management of incontinence and delivery of de-institutionalised care. Workers had little choice in the face of extremely low staffing but to leave out many of the tasks necessary for ensuring the comfort, dignity and wellbeing of the residents.

The care plans documenting the tasks represented the control imperative – it was these that turned the capacity for work into actual labour. Yet these rules were constantly breached. Managerial agendas intended to maintain and further cuts in costs simultaneously attempted to place responsibility for negligent practices in the hands of the workers. Workers were unable to complete the workload, but direct supervision by managers was only rarely exercised. This allowed the appropriate records to be shown to the relevant inspection authorities while also transferring responsibility for faking the records on to the frontline care staff. The impossibility of putting into practice the expectations of managerial systems and regulatory codes, due to informal aspects of the work, is an emerging theme in the literature on care. Lopez's (2007) study showed how breaking official rules which guided the conduct of care became like a 'fix' for the incongruity between the formal expectations of how the work should be completed, and the inability for frontline staff to actually deliver this style of care. Research looking at domiciliary care has also shown that the time provided in rotas for carers failed to match the care needs of those using the service (Bolton and Wibberley, 2014).

Explaining this abuse and neglect through a labour process approach then links this malpractice to both proceedings further up the company hierarchy and in the wider political economy within which production is embedded (Thompson and Smith, 2009). The following discussion argues that mistreatment emerges here in the context of a particular firm-wide strategy attempting to maintain low costs in service delivery. This strategy is historically situated by the previous restructuring engineered by the involvement of multinational finance interest, and the market conditions that shape social care in the UK.

The original restructuring of the company undertaken by Blackstone left Southern Cross with rising rental commitments, while a number of profit-constraining factors inherent to elderly social care meant that the company became focused on a cost-reduction strategy. In the 2007/08 annual statement the Southern Cross chair, Philip Scott, argued that the huge decrease in share price was not only the result of rising rents, but also inadequate fee rates paid by local councils, staff costs and problems with filling beds. However, Blackstone's financial engineering had left Southern Cross with little manoeuvrability to establish a reliable, long-term business plan. As the earlier discussion highlighted, Blackstone orchestrated a disaggregation of the company, leading to reconstructed rent obligations to a range of property companies. In the short term this generated huge returns for Blackstone (*The Times*, 2008), but over a longer period, seriously affected the viability of Southern Cross. Disaggregation is a well-recognised strategy of financialised capital, which is seen to place emphasis on more immediate wealth-creation strategies (Clarke, 2009; Fine, 2010), often at the expense of longer-term sustainable growth. What benefited some of the stakeholders involved with Southern Cross in the immediate timeframe did not necessarily align with maximising profit through production over the longer term (Thompson, 2013).

After 2007, when the share price began to drop significantly, Southern Cross was left in a vulnerable situation which, it is argued here, resulted in two distinct business strategies: attempting to create dominance in the market and rationalising production costs. Scourfield (2007, 2012) argues that securing ascendency in certain areas, a process he labels 'care-telisation', has become increasingly important among elderly residential care providers. He argues that the formation and maintenance of monopolies has become critical because local authorities remain a key force in determining the rates that are paid. Locally based market dominance allows these large players to strengthen their bargaining position for increased payments, because councils have access to few competitor options in provision for the care of vulnerable people. Second, through the formation of pressure groups, the largest care providers have been able to more successfully lobby for rising rates of payment. This strategy may not guarantee profits, as the Southern Cross experience showed, but it does give an indication as to why the company continued to expand even when losses were being made. This process of centralising power in markets, it needs to be highlighted, is not abnormal, and capital will often attempt to do away with competition. As David Harvey describes, 'most capitalists, given the choice, prefer to be monopolists' (2014, p 138) because it can 'stabilise the business environment to allow for rational calculation and long-term planning, the reduction of risk and uncertainty' (Harvey, 2014, p 141).

Debatably, however, the need to accomplish market dominance became more significant for Southern Cross due to the limited capability that all providers of care have for innovating the labour process. Industries that revolve around bodies, such as care work, it has been contended, cannot easily reconfigure their labour process in order to achieve efficiency gains, at least not without threatening the standard of care. Care work, when it is done with compassion at least, is supposed to attentively meet the needs and desires of those being cared for. The problem for managerial attempts to standardise work into a predictable labour process is that people's needs are inherently impulsive and driven biological processes (Cohen, 2011).

Conclusion

Since the ethnography took place, there is considerable evidence that care delivery across Southern Cross homes had degraded to an extremely low level in the period before its collapse. The data presented here is indicative of the kinds of practices in other care homes. A recently published serious case review investigating the mistreatment of residents in another Southern Cross-owned elderly care home, Orchid View, confirmed that 19 residents whose deaths were unexplained had experienced 'suboptimal' care, and that five of these deaths had resulted directly from neglect (Sussex County Council, 2014). A range of reports from newspapers identified similar situations in other Southern Cross-owned care homes, giving weight to the idea that the practices described here may have been more widespread (for some instances, see *The Times*, 2008; Mail Online, 2009; *Express*, 2011; *Daily Record*, 2012). Accordingly, it is convincing to suggest that mistreatment emerged from company-wide strategies, rather than from the irregular mismanagement of individual establishments.

When Southern Cross became overburdened with debt, it is difficult to see exactly how the company could reconcile the needs of residents with long-term profits. Improving care required greater commitment to staffing and resources, but increasing margins depended on the exact opposite – finding savings in production. The attempt to make reductions in production costs resulted in minimising staffing levels, often to below legal levels, even though this put the company (and its employees) at risk of criminal culpability. The involvement of the state through regulation and inspection represented a limitation on how far the company could make savings, although the form of regulation seemed largely ineffectual.

Of course, many of the pressures facing Southern Cross are the same pressures that many care-providing firms experience. Inadequate council budgets, ageist distribution of resources in society and the gendered status of care work are all social processes that set the scene for the story that has been told here. Additionally, at the company layer of analysis, the drive to extract profit out of the already meagre state funding helped to structure a labour process that was neglecting even the basic requirements of residents. Mistreatment was therefore embedded in the overall technical, spatial and human organisation of the labour.

Notes
[1] A full ethical discussion of the research can be found in Greener (2011).
[2] See Greener (2014) for an extended discussion of how immigration status shaped the experiences of the foreign workers in the home.

References

Age UK (2014) *Care in crisis: What next for social care?*, London: Age UK Campaigns.

Appelbaum, E., Batt, R. and Clark, I. (2012) *Implications of financial capitalism for employment relations research: Evidence from breach of trust and implicit contracts in private equity buyouts*, Washington, DC: Center of Economic and Policy Research.

Barnes, S., Wasielewska, A., Raiswell, C. and Drumond, B. (2013) 'Exploring the mealtime experience in residential care settings for older people: an observational study', *Health and Social Care in the Community*, vol 21, no 4, pp 442-50.

Beresford, P. (2009) 'Social care, personalisation and service users: addressing the ambiguities', *Research, Policy and Planning*, vol 27, no 2, pp 73-84.

Bolton, S.C. and Wibberley, G. (2014) 'Domiciliary care: the formal and informal labour process', *Sociology*, vol 48, no 4, pp 682-97.

Braverman, H. (1974) *Labor and monopoly capital: The degradation of work in the twentieth century*, New York: Monthly Review Press.

Brown, K. and Korcynski, M. (2010) 'When caring and surveillance technology meet: organisational commitment and discretionary effort in home care work', *Work and Occupations*, vol 37, no 3, pp 404-32.

BSA (British Sociological Association) (2002) 'Statement of ethical practice for the British Sociological Association', Durham: BSA.

Cangiano, A., Shutes, I., Spencer, S. and Leeson, G. (2009) *Migrant care workers in ageing societies: Research findings in the United Kingdom*, Oxford: COMPAS.

Clark, I. (2009) 'Owners and managers: disconnecting managerial capitalism? Understanding the private-equity business model', *Work, Employment and Society*, vol 24, no 4, pp 775-86.

Cohen, R.L. (2011) 'Time, space and touch at work: body work and labour process (re)organisation', *Sociology of Health and Illness*, vol 33, no 2, pp 189-285.

Daily Record (2012) 'Shocking care standards at Southern Cross's Scottish old folks home exposed' (www.dailyrecord.co.uk/news/scottish-news/shocking-care-standards-at-southern-crosss-1115848).

Darton, R., Bäumker, T., Callaghan, L., Holder, J., Netten, A. and Towers, A. (2012) 'The characteristics of residents in extra care housing and care homes in England', *Health and Social Care in the Community*, vol 20, no 1, pp 87-96.

Express (2011) 'The abuse shame past of crisis-hit Southern Cross' (www.express.co.uk/news/uk/250895/The-abuse-shame-past-of-crisis-hit-Southern-Cross).

Fine, B. (2010) 'Locating financialisation', *Historical Materialism*, vol 18, pp 97-116.

Folbre, N. (2006) 'Nursebots to the rescue: Immigration, automation, and care', *Globalizations*, vol 3, no 3, pp 349-60.

Fotaki, M., Ruane, S. and Leys, C. (2013) *The future of the NHS? Lessons from the market in social care in England*, London: Centre for Health and the Public Interest.

Greener, J. (2011) 'The bottom line: an ethnography of for-profit elderly residential care', E-thesis, University of Nottingham.

Greener, J. (2014) 'The role of immigration policy in the exploitation of migrant care workers: an ethnographic exploration', in M. Lavalette and L. Penketh (eds) *Race, racism and social work*, Bristol: Policy Press, pp 243-56.

Harvey, D. (2014) *Seventeen contradictions and the end of capitalism*, London: Profile Books.

Health and Safety Executive (2013a) 'Former care home owner prosecuted after resident death', 26 March (www.hse.gov.uk/press/2013/rnn-e-01313.htm).

Health and Safety Executive (2013b) 'Handling injuries in Great Britain, 2013', London: National Statistics.

Lloyd, L. (2010) 'The individual in social care: the ethics of care and the 'personalisation agenda' in services for older people in England', *Ethics and Social Welfare*, vol 4, no 2, pp 188-200.

Lopez, S.H. (1998) *Nursing home privatization: What is the human cost?*, Harrisburg, PA: Keystone Research Center.

Lopez, S.H. (2007) 'Efficiency and the fix revisited: informal relations and mock routinization in a nonprofit nursing home', *Qualitative Sociology*, vol 30, pp 225-47.

Lynch, K. (2007) 'Love labour as a distinct and non-commodifiable form of care labour', *The Sociological Review*, vol 55, no 3, pp 550-70.

MacDonald, C.L. and Merrill, D.A. (2002) '"It shouldn't have to be a trade": recognition and redistribution in care work advocacy', *Hypatia*, vol 17, no 2, pp 67-83.

Mail Online (2009) 'Heating was off for TEN days at the care home where eight residents died' (www.dailymail.co.uk/news/article-1154972/Heating-TEN-days-care-home-residents-died.html).

Ruigrok, J., and Sheridan, L. (2006) 'Life enrichment programme; enhanced dining experience, a pilot project', *International Journal of Health Care Quality Assurance*, vol 19, no 5, pp 420-9.

Schnelle, J.F. and Leung, F.W. (2004) 'Urinary and fecal incontinence in nursing homes', *Gastroenterology*, vol 126, no 1, pp 41-7.

Scotsman, The (2004) 'NHP agrees £564m sale', 29 November (www.scotsman.com/business/transport-industry/nhp-agrees-163-564m-sale-1-563961).

Scourfield, P. (2007) 'Are there reasons to be worried about the "caretelization" of adult residential care services?', *Critical Social Policy*, vol 27, no 2, pp 155-80.

Scourfield, P. (2012) 'Caretelization revisited and the lessons of Southern Cross', *Critical Social Policy*, vol 32, no 1, pp 137-48.

Shah, S.M., Carey, I.M., Harris, T., DeWilde, S., Hubbard, R., Lewis, S. and Cook, D.G. (2010) 'Identifying the clinical characteristics of older people living in care homes using a novel approach in a primary care database', *Age and Ageing*, vol 20, no 5, pp 617-23.

Shutes, I. (2012) 'The employment of migrant workers in long-term care: dynamics of choice and control', *Journal of Social Policy*, vol 41, no 1, pp 43-59.

Southern Cross Healthcare (2008) *Annual report and accounts, 2007/2008*, Darlington: Southern Cross Healthcare.

Southern Cross Healthcare (2009) *Annual report and accounts, 2008/2009*, Darlington: Southern Cross Healthcare.

Sunday Telegraph (2011) 'Old, sick – and homeless?', 5 June (www.telegraph.co.uk/news/8557086/Old-sick-and-homeless.html).

Sussex County Council (2014) *Orchid View serious case review*, Sussex : West Sussex Adults Safeguarding Board.

Times, The (2008) 'Rising death rate hits Southern Cross profit' (http://business.timesonline.co.uk/tol/business/industry_sectors/health/article4240660.ece).

Thompson, P. (2013) 'Financialization and the workplace: extending and applying the disconnected capitalism thesis', *Work, Employment and Society*, vol 27, no 3, pp 472-88.

Thompson, P. and Smith, C. (2009) 'Labour process theory and critical realism', in P. Thompson and C. Smith (eds) *Working life: Renewing labour process analysis*, Critical Perspectives on Work and Employment, Basingstoke: Palgrave Macmillan.

Timmermans, S. and Almeling, R. (2009) 'Objectification, standardization, and commodification in health care: a conceptual readjustment', *Social Science & Medicine*, vol 69, pp 21-7.

EIGHT

What variety of employment service quasi-market? Ireland's JobPath as a private power market

Jay Wiggan

Introduction

Since the late 1990s, social protection and labour market policies among Organisation for Economic Co-operation and Development (OECD) member states have been recalibrated so as to make the promotion of entry to the labour market for working-age individuals the priority of state intervention. Traditional concerns with income replacement in times of unemployment or income assistance to help meet the costs of life contingencies (disability, parenting) continue, but the emphasis has shifted to enacting reforms that 'activate' people into paid work (Bonoli, 2013). Accompanying changes to benefit eligibility, value and conditionality, and job placement and assistance schemes have been changes to the institutional arrangements for the delivery of benefit administration and public employment services. One of the most striking reforms has been the introduction of quasi-markets, through which various functions, previously performed by the public employment service or designated social partners, have been contracted out to for-profit and not-for-profit organisations through competitive tendering. Employment service marketisation has become commonplace across OECD states, but there is considerable diversity in how states configure market regulation, choice and competition, which effects how service users, service providers and the state act within the market, and their capacity to influence its evolution (van Berkel et al, 2012; Struyven, 2014; Zimmerman et al, 2014; Wiggan, 2015).

This chapter provides a case study of a new employment service quasi-market introduced in 2015 by the Irish government. Ireland is an interesting case as, while it may seem an ostensibly liberal welfare regime, its levels of expenditure on labour market programmes have been somewhat higher than other Anglo-Liberal welfare states such as the UK (Immervoll and Scarpetta, 2012, p 12). Until recently it was also a laggard in its embrace of the types of activation recalibration and employment service marketisation reforms embraced elsewhere (Murphy, 2012). In the aftermath of the financial crisis of 2008-09 and the Irish bank bailout of 2010 (see below), this has changed, and a programme of rapid 'modernisation' has taken place. Reforms to social security benefits have strengthened work-related conditionality, a new 'one-stop shop' integrating benefits and employment service support has been introduced and, from 2015, employment services for the long-term unemployed have been outsourced under the new JobPath programme. The focus here is an examination of JobPath to identify what kind of quasi-market it is, and what this implies for the role and influence of service users, the state or service providers. To facilitate this I draw on the typology of quasi-markets developed by Gingrich (2011). Based on analysis of institutional arrangements, socioeconomic context *and* partisan political preferences, this is a sophisticated conceptual tool for categorising quasi-markets and identifying which market interests (service users, providers and the state) and political party preferences are privileged by different market arrangements.

The chapter proceeds as follows. The first section is an account of the political-economic context in Ireland within which JobPath has developed. The second provides an elaboration of Gingrich's (2011) typology of quasi-markets. The third section applies this analytical approach to unpack Ireland's JobPath. The investigation indicates the new employment service quasi-market has few instruments available to empower service users, and instead privileges new service provider interests, while retaining a role for the state in shaping service standards. The fourth section discusses the potential partisan political logic underpinning both the embrace of provider interests and retention of a role for the state. What is particularly interesting about the configuration of the JobPath market is that it is similar in policy direction and content to the provider-directed market in employment services that Wiggan (2015) argues has developed in Britain under the Conservative–Liberal Democrat coalition government. A full comparison of the systems in Ireland and Britain would make a useful contribution to the literature on diversity in activation markets (van Berkel et al, 2012; Struyven, 2014; Wiggan, 2015), but is beyond the scope of this chapter. However, as an initial, if limited, contribution to sketching out the diversity in activation markets, the fourth section also provides a brief comparison of outcome-based funding, provider competition and service quality regulation in Ireland's JobPath and Britain's Work Programme. The fifth section concludes.

Context: developing activation, service integration and marketisation in Ireland

The global financial crisis that erupted in 2008 left Irish banks particularly at risk of collapse given their lending practices during the boom. The decision of the Irish state to guarantee the liabilities of all its banks initially stabilised the situation, but by 2010, the unprecedented scale of the losses facing the banks led Ireland to seek financial support from the International Monetary Fund (IMF) and European Union (EU) (Dukelow, 2011, p 408). In exchange for a package of loans, the Irish government agreed to a programme of welfare state reforms and public expenditure cuts, outlined in a 'Memorandum of Understanding' with the IMF, the European Central Bank and European Commission (hereafter the 'Troika') (European Commission, 2011, p 42; Hick, 2014, p 398).

Prior to the economic crisis, propitious economic growth meant successive centrist Fianna Fáil-led governments had been able to deliver notable improvements to existing social security benefits, and had shown little interest in the development of a comprehensive active labour market strategy. Since 2008, however, the value of key working-age benefits has been cut, and/or changes to eligibility and work-related conditions have been introduced. While this began with the Fianna Fáil-Green Party coalition government, it has continued under the Fine Gael-Labour Party coalition government of the centre right and Social Democratic left that took office following the February 2011 General Election (Little, 2011, p 1309; Dukelow, 2015; Murphy, 2014, p 138).

Responsibility for delivering social security and employment and training services, meanwhile, had long been fragmented between multiple government departments and agencies.[1] The resulting divergent institutional interests made gaining a consensus on activation reforms difficult, and this contributed to the slow and limited adoption of active labour market policies (Murphy, 2012, p 36). The agreement with the Troika gave impetus to domestic policy-makers to 'modernise' social protection and labour market policy and governance to seek a seemingly more cost-effective and 'work first' orientated active labour market regime (Murphy, 2012, 2014; Dukelow, 2015). Reviews by the OECD and the Irish government of Ireland's activation regime portrayed it as comparably high cost, poorly targeted and ineffective (DPER,

2011, pp 12-14; Grubb et al, 2009, pp 128-38; DSP, 2012b; see also McGuinness et al, 2011). The dominant unemployment policies were public sector job creation schemes and vocational training, criticised by the OECD as among the least effective tools for securing rapid labour market reintegration (OECD, 2000, p 98; DSP, 2012b). In 2011, for example, €348 million of the €770 million that Ireland's Department of Social Protection (DSP) spent on working-age employment schemes was spent on a single job subsidy scheme – the Community Employment Programme (CEP) (DSP, 2012b, p 11). The Fine Gael-Labour coalition government has not discontinued CEP, and has, in fact, introduced additional job creation and wage subsidy schemes (DSP, 2012a, p 13), but it has also embarked on a programme of rapid organisational restructuring. As a result, Ireland has belatedly adopted the types of service integration and marketisation that has become commonplace among the social security administration and employment service delivery of other OECD states (Askim et al, 2011; van Berkel et al, 2012; Minas, 2014; Struyven, 2014).

In line with the Fine Gael-Labour coalition's *Programme for government 2011-16* (Department of the Taoiseach, no date, p 8), various social protection and public employment service organisations have been merged into a single government department – the Department of Social Protection (DSP) – and delivery rationalised. For example, job assistance, placement and benefit administration for short-term unemployed claimants have been integrated, creating a new 'one-stop shop', known as 'Intreo' (Martin, 2014, p 15). Employment support for the long-term unemployed provided under the Fine Gael-Labour coalition government's new JobPath programme (see below) has, however, been contracted out to private and third sector providers. Policy-makers have suggested this is a practical means to secure additional staffing capacity and to gain access to previously untapped private and third sector 'expertise' in client advice, job placement and employer engagement activity (DSP, 2011, p 36; DSP, 2012c, p 20, 2013a, p 35, 2014a, 2014b, pp 20-1). Whether or not this was necessary or will provide the access to expertise that results in higher job entry and sustainability is beyond the focus of this particular chapter. Our interest here is in understanding the type of quasi-market emerging, and what this implies in terms of whose preferences and interests are being prioritised/marginalised. The following section sets out the theoretical and analytical framework used to facilitate this.

Unpacking and explaining variation in public service quasi-markets

The marketisation of public employment services has typically retained some role for the state as purchaser and/or regulator of service provision, while introducing instruments to foster competition and/or choice into the organisation of a public service on the grounds that market rationality induces improvements in efficiency, economy, innovation, responsiveness and effectiveness (Wiggan, 2015). The marketisation of public employment services is, therefore, a form of quasi-market, but this on its own tells us little about how the market shapes and is shaped by those involved in the market – the state, service providers and service users. We know, for example, that quasi-market arrangements vary substantially, both within and between policy sectors and countries, and over time. Scholars have unpacked the instruments used in such markets as a means to identify and classify markets, often according to some notion of more or less competition/consumer choice (Anttonen and Meagher, 2013, p 16; Powell, 2015, p 114) The approach developed by Gingrich (2011, p 212) encompasses choice and competition, but also includes the financing and regulation of markets by the state. The former relates to how public services are produced in the market, while the latter relates to how access to services is allocated in the market (Wiggan, 2015, p 4). Different combinations of competition/choice indicate how the production of services within the market is configured around the needs and (dis)empowerment of either the state, service users or providers. Examination of allocation mechanisms in turn gives some indication of whether equity among service users and broader implications for social solidarity is prioritised or not. For example, services may be free at the point of use because they are financed by the state, or access may depend on payment by the individual user, potentially curbing use of services by those on low incomes. Extensive regulation of provider activity by the state ostensibly promotes equitable access to services and underpins quality, whereas weak regulation empowers providers, giving them greater freedom to vary service access and/or quality offered to different users (Gingrich, 2011, p 12; Wiggan, 2015, p 4). How markets are configured effects how services are managed, regulated and accessed, and consequently, different markets are more or less orientated to the state, service user or service provider. This, in turn, works to construct, support or undermine particular class coalitions and socioeconomic and political objectives. Establishing what types of market exist and what political actors and preferences they may support

155

is, therefore, central to understanding variation in public service markets (Gingrich, 2011, p 217).

Based on assessment of production/allocation instruments, Gingrich identifies three broad categories of state, user or provider-driven markets that disaggregate into six quasi-market ideal types (Gingrich, 2011, p 12; see also Powell, 2015, p 111):

- consumer-controlled market (CCM) or two-tiered market (TTM) (service user-driven)
- state-managed market (SMM) or austerity market (AM) (state-driven)
- pork barrel market (PBM) or private power market (PPM) (provider-driven).

The two service user-driven ideal types are based on strong regulation of service user rights to choose between providers, and are either financed collectively (CCM) or individually (TTM). In CCM the perception is that introduction of user choice and funding attached to the user creates an incentive for providers to drive up service quality and to respond to the expressed preferences of users. The potential trade-off is that this may imply lower profits (provider) or higher public spending (state). In contrast, TTM is premised on the individualisation of service provision cost, either through direct charging or giving providers scope to offer differential quality provision. Those with the most resources and the fewest needs gain, but conversely, those with the greatest need and limited incomes lose (Gingrich, 2011, p 16).

Achieving service efficiency and economy through the retention of state capacity to direct public service markets is the hallmark of SMM and AM. SMM relies on regulation, monitoring of state-specified performance as a means to free providers to pursue cost-containment goals as they see fit, while the state retains arm's-length oversight and control to promote service quality and equity. Collective financing of provision is retained to prevent the direct costs of accessing services falling on the individual. AM involves the state setting standards, but pursues efficiency and cost control through (partially) reallocating the cost of provision to reduce demand and encourage individual users to ration their use of provision (Gingrich, 2011, p 14).

Where the state has withdrawn from extensive regulation or indicated its intention to exercise limited oversight, and users have few opportunities to exercise market choice or exit, then provider influence increases. According to Gingrich, this manifests in either PBM or PPM. PBM is a state-financed market with services purchased via limited market competition, resembling a private oligopoly able to use its strong negotiating position and influence to gain greater access to public resources in a relatively benign public spending climate. PPM is similarly dominated by providers, but emerges in the context of public expenditure constraint with providers given freedom to bear down on service costs, either through user charges or market structures that permit selective provision/under-provision which transfers the burden of adjustment under austerity to individual users (Gingrich, 2011, p 17).

Actual public service markets may, of course, differ in how close they adhere to these ideal types, but they provide a means for understanding how particular combinations of production and allocation favour different market interests and partisan preferences, and why such combinations merge in particular contexts (Gingrich, 2011, p 34). For Gingrich (2011, p 5), political parties of the left and right systematically favour different market types and seek reforms that best accord with their long-term ideological preferences and electoral calculations. In short, parties and governments of the right favour markets that constrain public spending and state provision, fragment social solidarity and make more comprehensive welfare retrenchment and privatisation more feasible in the long run. Conversely, the left seek to use markets that retain state involvement in financing and/or oversight of welfare provision, while protecting social solidarity and helping construct/secure a less hostile environment for future state welfare expansion (Gingrich, 2011, p 38). The broader financial context, and whether the existing service and supporting welfare institutions (for example, social security, training policy) are uniform/fragmented and/or provided on a universal/residual basis (Gingrich, 2011, p 33), in turn mediates whether the environment is more or less hostile to reforms preferred by left or right political parties. The left might favour market structures that empower service users (CCM ideal type), but is unlikely to champion such reforms when services are residual and public support for greater spending is weak, as this risks exacerbating existing socioeconomic inequalities (Gingrich, 2011, p 5). In such contexts, SMM may be the preferred compromise as it avoids empowerment of service providers that could further undermine the role of the state, and enables the left through the state to mitigate the potential for public service markets to lead to inequity in service access/quality. The right, in contrast, will enact provider-driven market reforms where possible, most likely in services that have limited public support, as the political and electoral opposition is weaker, enabling the right to advance market structures that both reduce existing state activity and create new constituencies for additional market reform. In the 'Discussion' section later we return to this issue and offer some tentative reflections on the potential connection between the JobPath quasi-market type and the partisan politics of market reform in Ireland. First, however, our attention turns to the JobPath market structure itself.

JobPath: a private power quasi-market?

Production

In 2013, the procurement of JobPath commenced, with organisations invited to submit bids to manage service delivery as a single prime provider in one of four geographic contract area 'lots' (1-4). The DSP also offered potential providers the opportunity to bid for a combined 'lot' (5 and 6), with each bundling together two separate contract areas (DSP, 2013a; INOU, 2014). Contracts are awarded for four years in the first instance, with the possibility of two one-year extensions. To bid for a contract each organisation (or partnership/consortia) was required to have an annual turnover of €20 million for each of the previous three years. Ostensibly this is to ensure that only organisations with a healthy financial track record could secure a contract, mitigating the risk inherent to a 'payment by results' system that an organisation is unable to manage the demands of resourcing investment in service provision upfront, and prior to receipt of outcome payments (DSP, 2013a, p 17). In October 2014 the winning bids were announced as two combined 'lots', meaning that two prime providers were contracted to manage four contract areas, with each provider responsible for service provision solely in their own two contract areas. The combined 'lot' for provision in the north of the country was awarded to the private for-profit organisation Seetec (a prime contractor in the British Work Programme), and the second combined 'lot' for provision in the south went to a new third sector organisation, Turas Nua Ltd (DSP, 2014a), a partnership between (another Work Programme prime contractor) Working Links (Working Links, 2014) and FRS Recruitment (part of an Irish cooperative network).

The decision to specify a high and consistent level of turnover as a requirement means the structuring of procurement curtails the number and type of organisations that are well placed to tender for JobPath. Larger organisations or consortia capable of satisfying the €20 million requirement and willing to take on (and perhaps have experience of) the degree of risk inherent to an outcome-based system are privileged by this market structure. The losers are smaller, more specialist and/or local organisations less able and/or willing to compete on these terms, whose options are now to participate as sub-contractors within the supply chain of one of the two prime contractors. The decision to have each contract area managed by a single prime means there is no scope for post-procurement competition. There can be no intra-contract area peer pressure between competing providers, and the DSP has no mechanism for reallocation of a portion of client caseload from poor to better performing providers. Consequently there is no scope for service users to directly exercise any choice of provider in the JobPath quasi-market. The direction of the market is very much about the relationship between the state and the contracted provider(s), with service users at best enjoying a mediated influence on service provision. With no post-procurement competition or prescription of service content beyond the stipulation of a common service guarantee detailed below, the JobPath primes are relatively free to innovate in service provision. The state seeks to direct providers towards its policy objectives primarily via the financial incentives built into JobPath by a 'payment by results' system.

The payment model is divided between a registration fee and a job sustainment fee, which, depending on job sustainment performance, means up to five payments to providers during a participant's return to work journey. The registration fee is paid once a participant has completed a personal progression plan with the provider, with sustainment payments commencing for sustained employment at 13 weeks, 26 weeks, 39 weeks and 52 weeks (DSP, 2013a, p 133). At the time of writing the JobPath market is limited to the long-term unemployed and those at risk of long-term unemployment, but DSP has left open the possibility of expanding coverage to claimants of benefits paid on grounds of lone parenthood or sickness or disability (DSP, 2013a, p 39). The ratio of process fees to outcome fees in the JobPath quasi-market is 35:65 (DSP, 2013a). The retention of a substantial registration fee implies concern that relying solely on outcome payments could undermine the financial stability of providers and increase the incentives to 'game' the payment-by-results system. The caseload of programme participants is divided into six referral groups (RG 1-6), with four groups relating to the duration of a client's receipt of a jobseeking benefit or assessment as having characteristics that place them at high risk of progressing into long-term unemployment (see Table 8.1). The income a provider receives for registration and job sustainment for each referral group has not been disclosed. DSP did indicate during procurement that fees should vary according to distance from the labour market (DSP,

2013b) as a means to encourage providers to serve both the job-ready and harder-to-place service users.

The instruments of market production in JobPath show an interesting tension between DSP seeking to use contracted providers to create freedom to innovate, and the fear that this will undermine service quality. Rather than build a market where the service user is empowered to choose between different providers or is able to exit the market

Table 8.1: High-level overview of key features of the JobPath quasi-market

Contract areas	Four contract areas (six 'lots' invited for tender as DSP allowed bidding on bundled 'lots') Lot 1 (West, Midlands North, North East, North West) Lot 2 (Cork Central, South East, Mid-Leinster) Lot 3 (Mid West, South West, Midlands South) Lot 4 (Dublin Central; Dublin North, Dublin South) Lot 5 (Lots 1 and 4 together) Lot 6 (Lots 2 and 3 together)
Providers	Seetec Turas Nua Ltd
Contract duration	Phase one: four years Phase two: one-year extensions for maximum of two years
Service quality	Grey box approach. Common set of minimum service requirements apply to each provider Annual service user satisfaction survey which can influence DSP to withhold a portion of provider fees
Client referral groups	RG 1: Unemployed receiving jobseeker benefit passing 12 months RG 2: Unemployed receiving jobseeker benefit 12-24 months RG 3: Unemployed receiving jobseeker benefit 24-36 months RG 4: Unemployed receiving jobseeker benefit 36 months + RG 5: Unemployed jobseeker benefit less than 12 months but high risk of long-term unemployment RG 6: Part time and in receiving jobseeker benefit, looking for full-time paid work Future referrals may expand to other groups, for example, recipients of one-parent family benefit and sickness/disability payments
Differential pricing Payment model	Yes Registration fee paid on completion of personal progression plan Job sustainment fee paid at 13 weeks, 26 weeks, 39 weeks, 52 weeks
Service user choice	No

Source: DSP (2013a, p 57); INOU (2014)

completely without financial penalty in the form of loss of benefits, the state has instead constructed a market where it acts as both the purchaser and the collective proxy customer. The private power market emerging in Ireland is then notable for the state's attempt to retain some collective influence over how services are allocated through a measure of public regulation and monitoring.

Allocation

Long-term unemployed clients are not required to purchase employment services in a private market or to make a co-payment in order to access public provision. This is not surprising as there are good social and economic reasons why employment services are collectively financed. Given the concentration of unemployment among low-skilled, low-income individuals, it would be difficult to insure against this life risk and/or bear the cost of paying to access services. The collective financing of employment services ensures access is relatively equitable, and this improves the state's capacity to 'activate' and match jobseekers to labour market vacancies. This does not, of course, eliminate the risk that allocation of services will be affected by the judgement providers make about the relative costs/benefits associated with moving clients with multiple or seemingly intractable constraints on employment into the labour market. JobPath attempts to mitigate this risk through its 'payment by results' contracting model. Research into 'payment by results' systems in employment service quasi-markets, however, shows that providers always seek to maximise their income from job-ready clients and minimise their expenditure on the less job-ready (Bredgaard and Larsen, 2008; Finn, 2010). Policy-makers in Ireland are aware that market reforms that enhance provider freedom can also negatively affect service equity (DSP, 2013b, p 16), and the DSP has settled on a combination of state-mediated user 'voice' and state-mandated minimum service standards to promote equitable allocation of services.

User voice is exercised 'by proxy', with the DSP collating service user views through surveys of participant satisfaction with service quality. Should a prime provider fail to achieve satisfactory ratings in the annual survey, the DSP may withhold up to 15 per cent of fees payable (DSP, 2014b, p 1). The prescription of common minimum service provision is set out in the JobPath Service Guarantee (SG). This stipulates that providers must hold one-to-one meetings within 20 days of referral, and agree a personal progression plan with all clients. The plan must contain basic contact information and a detailed record of the client's employment experience, skills and barriers to employment, and a plan setting out the return to work trajectory. The provider must hold a further one-to-one meeting with the client every 20 working days until they gain employment, and a full review of the plan must take place periodically (at 13 weeks, 26 weeks, 39 weeks) if the client remains unemployed. Where a programme participant has entered employment, the provider is responsible for delivering 'in-work' assistance during the first 13 weeks, which includes contact with a personal adviser within five days, and contact every subsequent 20 working days. A programme exit interview must also be held when a client reaches the end of their period of programme participation (12 months) (DSP, 2013a , pp 32-4). How effective the SG proves to be in promoting equity is necessarily an empirical question that must wait for programme evaluations.

Discussion

The contemporary political, economic and institutional arrangements in Ireland appear to favour the emergence of a provider-directed employment service market that seeks to expand private sector involvement in delivery, but also attempt to moderate the scope for providers to redirect the costs of serving all clients to the state or service users. Politically the coalition government in Ireland, for example, is dominated by the centre right Fine Gael Party, whose 2011 election manifesto indicated support for introducing some form of voucher system into employment service provision, while Labour made no mention of employment service marketisation at all (Fine Gael, 2011; Labour, 2011). The Troika's monitoring and reporting on the progress of the public service reforms and its encouragement of orthodox economic policy which has been embraced by the government (Dukelow, 2015) has meanwhile diminished the scope for state provision to be expanded to deliver an intensified activation service for the long-term unemployed. Moreover, as a service concentrated on a small and stigmatised portion of the working-age population (the long-term unemployed), the ability of service users or left political actors to draw on wider public solidarity to promote either a state monopoly or development of a client-centric market is likely limited. Working within these policy and political parameters it is plausible that PPM would emerge, albeit a variant that offered some compromise to the Labour Party's (they hold the social protection portfolio) core preference for protecting equity and retaining state involvement in welfare provision.

A brief comparison of key market instruments (outcome-based funding and service quality regulation) in Ireland's JobPath with those found in Britain's similar activation scheme – the Work Programme – draws out the degree to which Ireland has embraced a PPM variant that places slightly less emphasis on provider empowerment and the primacy of market rationality. The Work Programme was introduced in Britain in 2011 under the centre right-dominated Conservative–Liberal Democrat coalition government that was committed to reducing state delivery of public services through market expansion (HM Government, 2011), and built on an established pattern of contracting out employment services (Gash et al, 2013).

The commitment to market rationality and provider direction is built into the structure of the outcome-based funding system and model of service delivery. The British Work Programme's payment by results system, for example, makes a higher proportion of provider funding dependent on them securing job outcomes than in Ireland's JobPath. In the Work Programme, total funding available to providers over the course of the contract is intended to split 20·80, meaning that four-fifths of total payments to providers should be paid on the basis of job outcomes secured. Conversely, providers in Britain have been given greater freedom over service content through what is termed a 'black box' model of delivery. The British state has withdrawn from prescribing content in order to maximise provider freedom to innovate and shape the market. Instead, Work Programme prime providers each propose their own minimum set of services that are then agreed individually with British policy-makers (Wiggan, 2015). In contrast, Ireland's JobPath suggests a more cautious embrace of market rationality and the empowerment of providers, and a greater role for state regulation and state-mediated user influence. The service to outcome fee payment ratio is lower, at 35:65, and rather than a 'black box', a 'grey box' approach to service delivery is taken through state stipulation of common minimum provision through the JobPath SG. The service user survey also gives the state some means to 'check' the experience of users themselves, which, given the lack of post-contract award market competition, is a useful tool for policy-makers seeking to shape provider behaviour. In Britain there is no scope for the collective expression of services users to direct provider behaviour. Instead, policy-makers rely more on financial incentives and state-mediated competition between providers that is possible due to the two to three providers operating in each contract area (Wiggan, 2015).

The earlier unpacking of JobPath indicates it is a form of PPM, and comparison within another PPM (the British Work Programme) suggests that policy-makers in Ireland sought to create a PPM that reduces the scope and incentives for providers to game the system by retaining a comparably greater level of state intervention in the market. Further empirical investigation would be necessary, however, to establish whether, and how, this was influenced by organisations such as the Troika and/or the Centre for Economic and Social Inclusion,[2] and the specific preferences of Labour and Fine Gael.

Conclusion

The economic crisis and ensuing implementation of austerity in Ireland has enabled successive Irish governments to reframe the social contract to emphasise responsibilities rather than entitlements, and to radically overhaul the organisation of social security and labour market policy to promote labour activation and the commodification of public employment services, through marketisation of provision for the long-term unemployed (Dukelow, 2015; Murphy, 2014). The investigation and unpacking of the new JobPath employment programme shows that the market reforms enacted have introduced a form of PPM in employment service provision for the long-term unemployed. The state has relinquished direct control of service provision, but has chosen not to introduce service user-centric market reforms that empower programme participants through offering a choice of provider. Nor has the state directed public resources to existing local providers of employment services in Ireland, which would indicate market reforms more akin to those of a PBM (Gingrich, 2011). Instead, through setting a €20 million threshold for market entry, policy-makers in Ireland have deliberately constructed a market to appeal to new market entrants with the size and capability to advance and embed new provider-orientated market reforms. Yet policy-makers have also sought to protect equity in access to services through prescription and oversight of a common set of standards for all clients that each prime provider must adhere to. Policy-makers have seemingly determined that if service quality and reductions in benefit expenditure through job entry is to be maximised, retention of some state regulation is necessary to mitigate the tendency for providers to selectively invest resources in some (more job-ready) clients and not others (Shutes and Taylor, 2014, p 213). The JobPath market in this sense differs from the similar provider-directed employment service quasi-market introduced in 2010 in Britain, where policy-makers sought to maximise provider freedom and to minimise the direct influence of the state (and service users) (see Wiggan, 2015).

Notes

[1] Prior to the reorganisation, FAS (under the Department of Enterprise, Trade and Employment) was the training and employment agency. An additional Local Employment Service (LES) provided job search assistance in a number of locations. Together FAS/LES formed Ireland's Public Employment Service (Grubb et al, 2009, p 30). Mainstream social security was administered by the then Department for Social and Family Affairs with the Community Welfare Service (CWS) of the Health Services Executive administering Supplementary Welfare Allowance. From 2010 the employment and social security functions of FAS/CWS were moved to the new Department for Social Protection and work began on creating a new customer-facing one-stop shop (Intreo). Intreo and LES now deliver social security and short-term employment support while from 2015, activation of the long-term unemployed is with contracted JobPath providers.

[2] The Centre for Economic and Social Inclusion is a British research and policy organisation brought in by the DSP to advise on employment service marketisation.

References

Anttonen, A. and Meagher, G. (2013) 'Mapping marketisation: concepts and goals', in G. Meagher and M. Szebehely (eds) *Marketisation in Nordic eldercare: A research report on legislation, oversight, extent and consequences*, Stockholm Studies in Social Work 30, pp 13-22, Stockholm: Stockholm University (www.normacare.net/wp-content/uploads/2013/09/Marketisation-in-nordic-eldercare-webbversion-med-omslag1.pdf).

Askim, J., Fimreite, A.L., Mosely, A. and Pedersen, L.H. (2011) 'One-stop shops for social welfare: the adaptation of an organisational form in three countries', *Public Administration*, vol 89, no 4, pp 1451-68.

Bonoli, G. (2013) *The origins of active labour market policy: Labour market and childcare policies in a comparative perspective*, Oxford: Oxford University Press.

Bredgaard, T. and Larsen, F. (2008) 'Quasi-markets in employment policy – do they deliver on their promises?', *Social Policy and Society*, vol 7, no 3, pp 341-52.

Department of the Taoiseach (no date) *Programme for government 2011-16* (www.taoiseach.gov.ie/eng/Work_Of_The_Department/Programme_for_Government/Programme_for_Government_2011-2016.pdf).

DPER (Department of Public Expenditure and Reform) (2011) *Labour Market Activation and Training*, Comprehensive Review of Expenditure Thematic Evaluation Series, (http://igees.gov.ie/wp-content/uploads/2014/02/Comprehensive-Review-of-Expenditure-Labour-Market-Activation-and-Training.pdf).

DSP (Department for Social Protection) (2011) *Project plan for the development and implementation of the National Employment and Entitlements Service*, August (www.welfare.ie/en/downloads/nees.pdf).

DSP (2012a) *Community employment financial review of schemes* (www.welfare.ie/en/Pages/Community-Employment-Financial-Review-of-Schemes.aspx).

DSP (2012b) High-level issues paper emanating from a review of Department for Social Protection Employment Support Schemes, November (www.welfare.ie/en/pressoffice/pdf/High%20Level%20Issues%20Paper%20-%20Employment%20Support%20Schemes.pdf).

DSP (2012c) *Pathways to work: Government statement on labour market activation*, Government of Ireland (www.welfare.ie/en/downloads/pathwaystowork.pdf).

DSP (2013a) Request for tenders by the Department of Social Protection for the provision of Employment Services ('JobPath') (www.welfare.ie/en/downloads/JobPath-RFT.pdf).

DSP (2013b) 'JobPath proposed contracting of third party providers of employment services', Information Session, Friday 26 July, Chartered Accountants House, Dublin (www.welfare.ie/en/downloads/jobpath-info-session-260713.pdf).

DSP (2014a) 'Tánaiste: new JobPath employment programme will help 115,000 jobseekers return to work', Press release, Monday 13 October (www.welfare.ie/en/pressoffice/pdf/pr131014.pdf).

DSP (2014b) JobPath RFT – Clarification questions & answers [cont.], 21 January, p 1 (www.welfare.ie/en/downloads/Clarification-Q-A.pdf).

Dukelow, F. (2011) 'Economic crisis and welfare state retrenchment: comparing Irish policy response in the 1970s and 1980s with the present', *Social Policy & Administration*, vol 45, no 4, pp 408-29.

Dukelow, F. (2015) '"Pushing against an open door": reinforcing the neo-liberal policy paradigm in Ireland and the impact of EU intrusion', *Comparative European Politics*, vol 13, no 1, pp 93-111.

European Commission (2011) *Economic Adjustment Programme for Ireland – Winter 2011 review*, Occasional Papers 93, March, Director General Economic and Financial Affairs (http://ec.europa.eu/economy_finance/publications/occasional_paper/2012/pdf/ocp93_en.pdf).

Fine Gael (2011) *Fine Gael Manifesto* (http://michaelpidgeon.com/manifestos/byelection.htm).

Finn, D. (2010) 'Outsourcing employment programmes: contract design and differential prices', *European Journal of Social Security*, vol 12, no 4, pp 289-302.

Gash, T., Panchamia, N., Sims, S. and Hotson, L. (2013) *Making public service markets work*, London: Institute for Government (www.instituteforgovernment.org.uk/sites/default/files/publications/Making_public_service_markets_work_final_0.pdf).

Gingrich, J. (2011) *Making markets in the welfare state: The politics of varying market reforms*, Cambridge: Cambridge University Press.

Grubb, D., Singh, S. and Tergeist, P. (2009) *Activation policies in Ireland*, OECD Social, Employment and Migration Working Papers, No 75, Paris: OECD (http://dx.doi.org/10.1787/227626803333).

Hick, R. (2014) 'From Celtic tiger to crisis: progress, problems and prospects for social security in Ireland', *Social Policy & Administration*, vol 48, no 4, pp 394-412.

HM Government (2011) *Open public services White Paper*, Cm 8145, London: The Stationery Office (http://files.openpublicservices.cabinetoffice.gov.uk/OpenPublicServices-WhitePaper.pdf).

Immervoll, H. and Scarpetta, S. (2012) 'Activation and employment support policies in OECD countries. An overview of current approaches', *IZA Journal of Labour Policy*, vol 1, no 9, pp 1-20.

INOU (Irish National Organisation of the Unemployed) (2014) 'JobPath explained' (www.inou.ie/download/pdf/20140821105619.pdf).

Labour (2011) *One Ireland: Jobs, reform, fairness, Manifesto 2011*, (http://michaelpidgeon.com/manifestos/byelection.htm).

Little, C. (2011) 'The General Election of 2011 in the Republic of Ireland: all changed utterly?', *West European Politics*, vol 34, no 6, pp 1304-13.

McGuinness, S., O'Connell, P.J., Kelly, E. and Walsh, J.R. (2011) *Activation in Ireland: An evaluation of the National Employment Action Plan*, Research Series No 20, Dublin: Economic and Social Research Institute (www.esri.ie/UserFiles/publications/RS20.pdf).

Martin, J. (2014) *Activation and active labour market policies in OECD countries: Stylized facts and evidence on their effectiveness*, IZA Policy Paper No 84 (http://ftp.iza.org/pp84.pdf).

Minas, R. (2014) 'One-stop shops: Increasing employability and overcoming welfare state fragmentation?', *International Journal of Social Welfare*, vol 23, pp 40-53.

Murphy, M. (2012) 'The politics of Irish labour activation: 1980 to 2010', *Administration*, vol 60, no 2, pp 27-49.

Murphy, M. (2014) 'Ireland: Celtic tiger in austerity – explaining Irish path dependency', *Journal of Contemporary European Studies*, vol 22, no 2, pp 132-42.

OECD (Organisation for Economic Co-operation and Development) (2000) *What works among active labour market policies? Evidence from OECD countries' experiences*, Paris: OECD (www.oecd.org/social/labour/2732343.pdf).

Powell, M. (2015) 'Making markets in the English National Health Service', *Social Policy & Administration*, vol 49, no 1, pp. 109-27.

Shutes, I. and Taylor, R. (2014) 'Conditionality and the financing of employment services – implications for the social divisions of work and welfare', *Social Policy & Administration*, vol 48, no 2, pp 204-20.

Struyven, L. (2014) 'Varieties of market competition in public employment services – a comparison of the emergence of the new system in Australia, the Netherlands and Belgium', *Social Policy & Administration*, vol 48, no 2, pp 149-68.

van Berkel, R., de Graaf, W. and Sirovatka, T. (2012) 'Governance of the activation policies in Europe', *International Journal of Sociology & Social Policy*, vol 32, no 5/6, pp 260-72.

Wiggan, J. (2015) 'Varieties of marketisation in the UK: examining divergence in activation markets between Great Britain and Northern Ireland 2008-2014', *Policy Studies*, pp 1-18.

Working Links (2014) 'Who we are' (www.workinglinks.co.uk/specialist_divisions/welfare_to_work/who_we_are.aspx).

Zimmerman, K., Aurich, P., Graziano, P. and Fuertes, V. (2014) 'Local worlds of marketisation – employment policies in Germany, Italy and the UK compared', *Social Policy & Administration*, vol 8, no 2, pp 127-48.

Part Three

25 years after *The three worlds of welfare capitalism*: a retrospective

NINE

Applying welfare regime ideal types in empirical analysis: the example of activation

Deborah Rice

Introduction

Twenty-five years of welfare state research after the publication of Esping-Andersen's seminal *The three worlds of welfare capitalism* (1990) have shown that the welfare regime approach is here to stay, in spite of the manifold criticism that has been raised against Esping-Andersen's regime typology, not only on methodological but also on conceptual grounds. More specifically, neither dissatisfaction with Esping-Andersen's classification of liberal, corporatist-conservative and social-democratic welfare states, nor the objection that important social policy dimensions such as gender or activation are lacking from Esping-Andersen's framework, and not even the shortcoming that Esping-Andersen's regime conception is too monolithic and static, have led to a discarding of the basic insight that welfare cultures and welfare institutions display a limited number of internal 'logics' (cf Arts and Gelissen, 2002; Kasza, 2002; Scruggs and Allan, 2006; Danforth, 2014). In order to mitigate these shortcomings while ransoming the idea that welfare states decommodify social risks and structure the life chances of their citizens to different degrees and in different ways, a growing body of literature has proposed that Esping-Andersen's empirics-based regime typology should be replaced by purely analytical ideal types. A major advantage of welfare regime ideal types is that they can be applied not only to welfare states, but also to regional and local welfare systems as well as to particular welfare programmes such as healthcare, family policy or unemployment protection (see, for example, Bambra, 2007; Aspalter, 2011; Ferragina and Seeleib-Kaiser, 2011; Powell and Barrientos, 2011; Rice, 2013).

Interestingly, and despite a growing consensus that welfare regimes should be understood not as fixed entities but as heuristic tools for mapping and analysing differences between welfare systems and programmes, systematic applications of regime ideal types in empirical analysis are still rare (some exceptions include Bolderson and Mabbett, 1995; Bannink and Hoogenboom, 2007; Aurich, 2011; Hudson, 2012). Instead, most comparative welfare regime analyses continue to rely on state-centric and inductive methods of regime classification, building or probing welfare regime typologies based on empirical differences within small samples of welfare states. In order to advance the use of welfare regime ideal types in social policy research, this chapter offers some reflections on the practical applicability of regime ideal types. More particularly, the following sections address the questions of how welfare regime ideal types can be adapted to a broad array of research objects other than just welfare states, and how regime ideal types can be applied in empirical research. The ideal-typical welfare regime framework proposed in Rice (2013), described briefly in the next section, provides an adequate starting point for answering these questions. In the later sections, the example of active labour market policies in 11 European countries is used to illustrate the methodological arguments made. The countries were deliberately selected from all of Esping-Andersen's postulated three worlds of welfare capitalism (including some hybrid cases) plus an additional Mediterranean-residual world of welfare and one post-Communist country in order to ensure a sufficient analytical generalisability of the presented arguments (cf Leibfried, 1992; Ferrera, 1996; Fenger, 2007).

Welfare regime ideal types: a general framework

Before delving into the question of how welfare regime ideal types can be applied in empirical analysis, let us briefly recount how Esping-Andersen's empirical regime typology can be transformed into a purely ideal-typical classification. As mentioned in the introduction to this chapter, the main idea behind using theoretically derived welfare regime ideal types rather than empirics-based welfare state typologies is that welfare systems and cultures exist not only at the state level, but also at the sub-state, supra-state and programmatic level. Furthermore, welfare regime ideal types transcend historical peculiarities whereas empirics-based typologies can be skewed by the 'distribution' of welfare-institutional or welfare-cultural characteristics at certain moments in time. Therefore, a comprehensive ideal-typical regime framework is needed that justifies theoretically on which dimensions welfare systems or programmes may differ, and why. The ideal-typical welfare regime framework proposed in Rice (2013) departs from the assumption that welfare systems and programmes can be aligned along two analytical axes that are implicit in Esping-Andersen's welfare regime typology: a conservatism-liberalism axis that distinguishes welfare entities by whether they see individuals as autonomous or embedded in primordial collectives such as families or nations; and a residualism-solidarism axis that reflects preferences for limited or extensive income redistribution by the welfare state.

Besides the two analytical axes of conservatism-liberalism and residualism-solidarism, three ideal-typical regime dimensions can be derived from Esping-Andersen's empirical framework: culture, institutions and stratification effects (see Rice, 2013). These ideal-typical regime dimensions run across both analytical axes. Thus, on the conservatism-liberalism axis, one finds conservative welfare *cultures* that regard status differentials between primordial groups such as men/women or natives/foreigners as natural, therefore favouring two-tier *institutional* systems of social protection that insure mainly dominant primordial groups such as majority-ethnic male breadwinners against social risks, leaving others to means-tested minimum income provisions. This effectuates a strong division between societal insiders and outsiders on the *stratification* dimension. Contrariwise, liberal welfare *cultures* are marked by a civic universalism, seeking to free individuals from any restrictions imposed on them by primordial markers of identity such as gender, ethnicity or sexual orientation. For this reason, liberalism tends to be associated with universally accessible and state-funded social protection *institutions* that transform pre-existing differentials in social status on the *stratification* dimension.

On the second ideal-typical regime axis – residualism versus solidarism – one finds residualistic welfare *cultures* that are wary of any state intervention in society, whereas solidaristic welfare cultures accredit the state with high redistributive legitimacy, grounded in the logic that society as a whole will benefit from a structural resolution of class conflicts (cf Korpi, 1983; Donzelot, 1991). By implication, solidaristic welfare *institutions* are characterised by generous benefits and services, administered by large public sectors whose employment opportunities provide stable income and employment to a large segment of the population and especially women, thereby levelling out income differences on the *stratification* dimension. Contrariwise, the restricted benefit/service budgets and small public sectors characterising residualistic welfare *institutions* leave a large share of welfare provision to the private market or charity, thereby establishing a dualism between poorer and more affluent strata of society on the *stratification* dimension.

Figure 9.1 gives a graphical illustration of the ideal-typical welfare regime framework sketched out above, incorporating the two regime axes of conservatism-liberalism and residualism-solidarism beside the three regime dimensions of welfare culture, welfare institutions and the socioeconomic stratification effects of welfare policies. The result is four encompassing regime ideal types: a conservative and a liberal pure type alongside a socio-conservative and a socio-liberal variant.

Adapting general ideal types to specific research topics: the example of activation

When seeking to apply welfare regime ideal types to entities other than only welfare states, as in Esping-Andersen's welfare state regime typology,[1] the first analytical step consists in adapting the general regime framework explicated above (or any other ideal-typical regime framework) to a specific kind of welfare system, policy or programme. In this chapter, the example of active labour market policies (ALMPs) is used to illustrate how this can be done. ALMPs first emerged in the Nordic countries and especially Sweden, originally under the premise that labour supply and labour demand should be brought in balance via systematic training measures for the unemployed (Sihto, 2001). Since the 1990s, however, activation policies have been both extended and ideologically reframed, now extending to new policy areas such as disability or pension policy, while also focusing on individual responsibility for work, meaning that the former training focus has been amended – if not replaced – by so-called 'demanding' activation measures such as stricter entitlement criteria, shorter benefit durations and sanctions for non-compliance with job search duties (see Clasen and Clegg, 2006; Dingeldey, 2007).

Figure 9.2 shows an ideal-typical regime framework that has been adapted to the particular policy area of activation. In order to create this framework of 'activation regime' ideal types, the literature has been searched for clues on how conservative, liberal, residualistic and solidaristic regime characteristics might play out on the three regime dimensions of activation culture, activation institutions and the socioeconomic effects of ALMPs. On the *activation-cultural* dimension, one can assume that the conservative-liberal division between paternalistic and individualistic notions of responsibility for welfare will translate into a division between holistic versus purely labour market-

Figure 9.1: Four welfare regime ideal types: a general framework

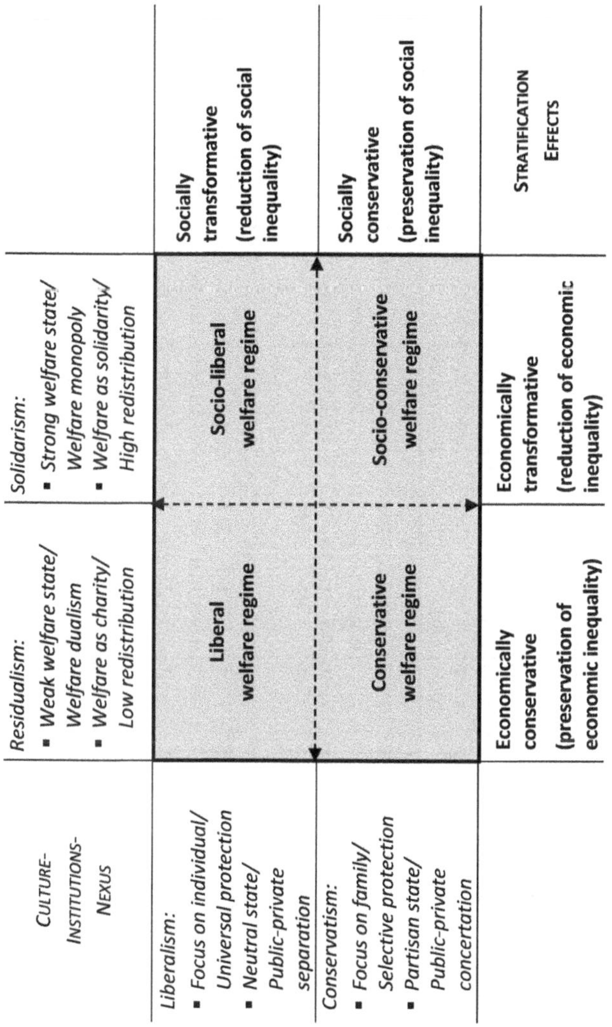

Source: Rice (2013)

Figure 9.2: An ideal-typical activation regime framework

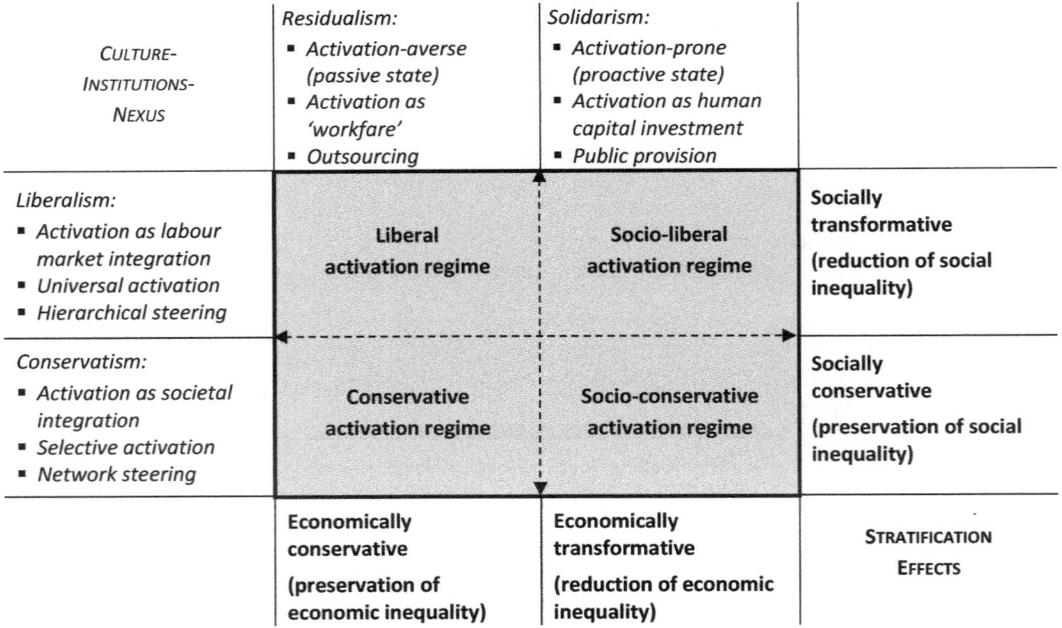

CULTURE-INSTITUTIONS-NEXUS	Residualism: ■ Activation-averse (passive state) ■ Activation as 'workfare' ■ Outsourcing	Solidarism: ■ Activation-prone (proactive state) ■ Activation as human capital investment ■ Public provision	
Liberalism: ■ Activation as labour market integration ■ Universal activation ■ Hierarchical steering	Liberal activation regime	Socio-liberal activation regime	Socially transformative (reduction of social inequality)
Conservatism: ■ Activation as societal integration ■ Selective activation ■ Network steering	Conservative activation regime	Socio-conservative activation regime	Socially conservative (preservation of social inequality)
	Economically conservative (preservation of economic inequality)	Economically transformative (reduction of economic inequality)	STRATIFICATION EFFECTS

Adapted from Rice (2015).

oriented notions of activation, grounded in the logic that volunteer work, care work and so on will be regarded as equally legitimate as paid work in conservative environments, whereas in liberal environments, more emphasis will be placed on making each citizen independent and self-sufficient via an income from work. In residualistic versus solidaristic terms, the general welfare-cultural distinction between 'nightwatchman-like' and redistributive state traditions that see welfare provision as a task of either private charity or public solidarity can be adapted to activation by assuming that solidarism is more likely to embrace the activation agenda than residualism, because the very concept of activation presupposes a proactive state. In addition, residualistic activation cultures are likely to frame unemployment primarily as a problem of 'dependency' on state help, whereas solidarism will tend to frame unemployment primarily as a problem of 'social exclusion' (Lødemel and Trickey, 2000, p 15; see also Aurich, 2011).

On the *institutional* dimension, the conservative/liberal principles of selective versus universal social protection may translate into target groups of activation that differentiate clients either by social problem categories (such as lone parenthood, migrant background and so on) or by mere distance from the labour market. Furthermore, conservatively designed activation systems are more likely to feature local variation in policy objectives and instrument portfolios than liberal activation systems, where national standards are likely to be introduced based on the principle of equal citizen treatment. A final distinction between conservative and liberal activation systems may lie in the steering mechanisms used for providing active labour market services to citizens, with relational and partly informal provider networks predominating in conservative activation systems and hierarchical principal agent relations predominating in liberal activation systems (cf Considine and Lewis, 2003). Ideal-typical differences between activation-averse residualistic and activation-prone solidaristic activation systems can be enumerated more quickly, ranging from limited activation budgets, a focus on workfarist activation measures and rampant outsourcing to private providers in residualistic activation systems to generous activation budgets, an emphasis on human capital-enhancing activation measures such as training, and a strong state engagement in activation in solidaristic activation systems.

Taken together, the nexus between ideal-typical activation cultures and associated activation institutions can be expected to produce socially conservative versus socially transformative *stratification* effects on the conservatism-liberalism axis, with conservative activation systems reinforcing patterns of social exclusion rooted in primordial identity markers, and liberal activation systems offering more equal chances of labour market (re-)entry to all citizens. On the residualism-solidarism axis, economically conservative versus transformative stratification effects can be expected to ensue from activation, with individuals being helped to find quality employment in solidaristic activation systems, whereas a push towards quick labour market entry – often at the cost of low-quality employment – is likely to prevail in residualistic activation systems (to the disadvantage especially of those with low skills and little labour market experience). However, it is important to keep in mind that the causal relationship between the culture-institutions nexus and stratification effects is more complex in the case of activation than in the case of passive income replacement. For instance, whereas the liberal principle of equal citizen treatment fosters equal life chances in the area of passive benefits, a narrow interpretation of the same principle in the area of activation could lead to a reproduction of existing socioeconomic cleavages because skilled people are likely to benefit more from one-size-fits-all activation offers than unskilled people or people with multiple placement barriers. Hence, if activation is to transform pre-existing structures of socioeconomic inequality, the liberal tenet of equal citizen treatment must be stretched to include selective human capital and/or 'good' employment-promoting measures for structurally disadvantaged groups (cf Betzelt, 2008, p 14). Moreover, employment services must be complemented with social services such as affordable childcare if activation is really to empower women, people with disabilities, and other outsider groups on the labour market, as O'Connor and Robinson (2008, p 39) point out.

Applying regime ideal types in empirical research

In the former two sections, the example of ALMPs was used to show how general welfare regime ideal types can be adapted to specific policy areas and welfare systems at the supra-national, national or sub-national level. This section explores how welfare regime ideal types can be operationalised in empirical research. Staying with the example of ALMPs, descriptive statistics are used to illustrate how comparative social policy research can benefit from the application of regime ideal types in three main analytical areas: the mapping of similarities or differences between welfare entities, the tracing of regime changes over time, and the identification of frictions between regime dimensions.

Mapping of similarities or differences between welfare entities

The main heuristic function of welfare regime ideal types is the mapping of similarities or differences between welfare entities as a basis for systemic comparisons. For such a purpose, the regime characteristics in one's general or specific ideal-typical regime framework must be operationalised using suitable quantitative or qualitative indicators that can be numerically or semantically associated with the two ideal-typical regime axes. Subsequently, a variety of methods, such as correlation analysis, cluster analysis, qualitative comparative analysis (QCA) or even simple tables and graphs can be used to make visible how empirical welfare entities are distributed along the two ideal-typical regime axes at one or several moment(s) in time. Ideal-typical regime mapping exercises are advantageous over the Cartesian mappings of welfare regime differences that are already a familiar sight in the comparative social policy literature, because, as Ferragina, Seeleib-Kaiser and Tomlinson (2013) remark, traditional Cartesian regime maps are generally inductively derived rather than theoretically substantiated, which makes them difficult to compare – a shortcoming that an ideal-typical welfare regime framework can remedy. When looking at existing mappings of welfare regime differences through the lens of an ideal-typical regime approach, it becomes apparent that many inductive regime maps already implicitly cover two ideal-typical regime dimensions, such as the relationship between welfare institutions (for example, social security budgets, low-income targeting, family-friendly social policies) or cultural attitudes (for example, towards social inequality or redistribution) on stratification patterns (for example, in the realm of labour force participation, income redistribution, gender pay differences, or gender/ class/sector cleavages; see, respectively, Goodin, 2001; Korpi and Palme, 1998; Siaroff, 1994; Koster and Kaminska, 2012; Svallfors, 1997). Other regime maps observably stay on a single regime dimension, such as Pfau-Effinger's (2004) qualitative analysis of housewife cultures and urban bourgeois traditions or, on the institutional dimension, Bonoli's (1997) investigation of the relative weight of contribution-based social expenditure, as well as Sellers and Lidström's (2007) juxtaposition of supra-local and local political authority. Besides thus calling by name the regime dimensions on which existing Cartesian regime graphs operate, an ideal-typical welfare regime framework can also foster the comparability of regime maps across regime axes. Interestingly, of the eight examples from the literature cited above, five implicitly cover both the residualism-solidarism axis and the conservatism-liberalism axis, which underlines the suitability of the ideal-typical regime framework underlying this chapter for application in comparative social policy research.

Besides adding more theoretical robustness and systematic comparability to the mapping of differences between welfare entities, a further advantage of an ideal-typical welfare regime framework is that it solves the methodological problem afflicting Esping-Andersen-based regime mappings of 'the creation in every case of a threefold/fourfold typology' (Ferragina et al, 2013, p 786). To explain why this is so, the example of activation culture will be used below, operationalised by relevant survey items from the European Values Study (EVS).[2] The conservatism-liberalism axis of activation culture, which contains two ideal-typical regime characteristics according to Figure 9.2 – namely, the goals of societal integration versus labour market integration, and a selective versus universal activation logic – is operationalised by EVS items

c024 (Important in job: useful for society)
c001 (Jobs are scarce: giving men priority)
c002 (Jobs are scarce: giving [nation] priority)

with high support for those items reflecting a conservative-holistic notion of work or else the conservative ideal of role-differentiated employment promotion, and low support pointing towards the liberal ideal of self-sufficiency through paid work or else universal employment promotion. In juxtaposition, the residualism-solidarism axis of activation culture is operationalised by EVS items

e037 (Individual versus state responsibility for providing for oneself)
e038 (Take any job versus right to refuse a job)

with a high rate of positive answers indicating strong support for solidaristic state engagement in activation or else the promotion of quality employment, and low support reflecting activation-adversity or else support for workfarism. Responses to all five survey items are given in Table 9.1 for an exemplary sample of 11 European welfare states: Switzerland (CH), Germany (DE), Denmark (DK), Spain (ES), France (FR), Great Britain (GB), Ireland (IE), Italy (IT), the Netherlands (NL), Poland (PL), and Sweden (SE). For each item, the figures in the top rows correspond ideal-typically with conservative/residualistic cultural attitudes, whereas the figures in the bottom rows refer ideal-typically to

Table 9.1: EVS items connected with two ideal-typical regime axes (%), 2008-10

		CH	DE	DK	ES	FR	GB	IE	IT	NL	PL	SE
c001	**Jobs are scarce: giving men priority**											
	(1=agree)	20.0	14.4	2.3	16.3	13.3	13.3	15.6	20.1	12.4	20.3	2.4
	(2=disagree)	73.8	62.9	95.4	69.7	84.4	77.2	68.6	65.0	84.7	62.8	92.1
c002	**Jobs are scarce: giving [nation] priority**											
	(1=agree)	43.1	49.7	24.3	55.5	40.2	66.4	66.2	58.5	36.3	70.9	20.6
	(2=disagree)	44.7	28.1	63.8	28.9	54.8	23.2	21.9	26.8	57.5	20.0	70.2
c024	**Important in job: useful for society**											
	(1=mentioned)	27.0	27.6	18.4	20.0	29.2	35.8	42.3	50.2	60.4	36.8	13.6
	(0=not mentioned + -2=no answer)	72.6	71.9	80.5	79.5	70.4	64.0	57.3	48.7	38.9	61.0	86.4
	Sum conservatism:	90	92	45	92	83	116	124	129	109	128	37
	Sum liberalism:	191	163	240	178	210	164	148	141	181	144	249
	Residue liberalism minus conservatism:	101	71	195	86	127	49	24	12	72	16	212
	Ideal-typical regime category:	lib	lib	lib	lib	lib	lib	lib	lib	lib	lib	lib
e037	**Individual vs state responsibility for providing for oneself**											
	(1=individual + 2 + 3)	46.2	44.4	11.1	17.6	38.3	9.1	43.3	27.2	10.8	25.9	10.2
	(8 + 9 + 10=state)	7.6	14.4	30.3	21.6	15.9	52.6	12.6	21.8	31.0	20.7	42.0

		CH	DE	DK	ES	FR	GB	IE	IT	NL	PL	SE
e038	Take any job vs right to refuse a job											
	(1=take any job + 2 + 3)	37.1	48.3	33.8	25.7	25.6	47.0	32.6	54.6	35.1	34.3	41.5
	(8 + 9 + 10=right to refuse a job)	12.8	12.0	19.0	18.2	31.5	12.2	17.3	8.5	9.2	15.0	15.3
	Sum residualism:	83	93	45	43	64	56	76	82	46	60	52
	Sum solidarism:	20	26	49	40	47	65	30	30	40	36	57
	Residue solidarism minus residualism:	−63	−66	4	−4	−17	9	−46	−52	−6	−25	6
	Ideal-typical regime category:	res	res	sol	res	res	sol	res	res	res	res	sol

liberal/solidaristic activation-related attitudes. As a quick eyeball analysis of Table 9.1 reveals, 10 out of 11 activation cultures are not internally monolithic because the EVS items cover at least three out of four possible cultural orientations (that is, conservative, liberal, residualistic, solidaristic) in all countries but Switzerland. Nevertheless, when adding up the item scores associated with each ideal-typical orientation and then weighing the conservative sum against the liberal sum and the residualistic sum against the solidaristic sum, clear overall regime orientations emerge in most cases, as the respective residue values in Table 9.1 show (with positive residues signifying liberalism/solidarism, and negative residues signifying conservatism/residualism).

The residue values that result for each country from subtracting the conservative sum from the liberal sum and the residualistic sum from the solidaristic sum can be mapped in an ideal-typical Cartesian space (see Figure 9.3). As Figure 9.3 illustrates, using an ideal-typical rather than an inductively derived regime map has the advantage that both a negative (conservative/residualistic) and positive (liberal/solidaristic) regime spectrum will emerge in the regime map, even if some quadrants remain empty. By contrast, the inductive method of using low indicator values as signifying conservatism/residualism and high indicator values

Figure 9.3: Eleven European activation cultures, ideal-typical mapping

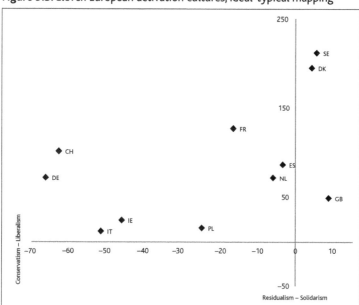

as signifying liberalism/solidarism (or vice versa) runs the risk that some welfare entities will be classified as conservative or residualistic even if, in reality, they are merely the least liberal or least solidaristic entities in a given sample (see Figure 9.4 for an illustration). Although only crude descriptive statistics have been used here for a rough illustration of this general argument, the same methodological criticism applies to inductive correlation or cluster analyses of welfare regimes, whereas multiple correspondence analysis and the fuzzy set method seem more apt for classifying welfare entities on the basis of conceptual ideal types (cf Kvist, 2007; Ferragina et al, 2013; Hudson and Kühner, 2013; see also Da Roit and Weicht, 2013).

In analytical terms, an ideal type-guided mapping of activation cultures yields important new insights that cannot be gained from a purely inductive mapping of activation cultures (or any other selection of welfare entities). Thus, in contrast to established regime typologies that postulate a high dispersion of European welfare (and activation) cultures across the spectrum of conservatism-liberalism and residualism-solidarism, the ideal-typical mapping of 11 European activation cultures in Figure 9.3 yields the surprising result that all 11 activation cultures are

Figure 9.4: Eleven European activation cultures, inductive mapping

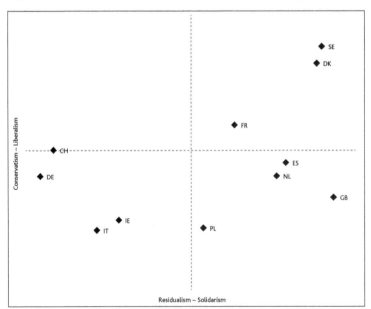

to be classified as liberal (albeit to different degrees) and most of them as residualistic – with the exception of the solidaristic Danish, Swedish and British activation cultures. In contrast, the inductive mapping of activation cultures in Figure 9.4 is more in line with existing regime classifications, displaying four rather than two activation-cultural regimes: a socio-liberal type (Sweden, Denmark, France), a socio-conservative type (Spain, Netherlands, Poland, Great Britain), a conservative pure type (Germany, Italy, Ireland), and a liberal-conservative hybrid type (Switzerland). Only the British case diverges from established views in the literature, which might be explained by a solidaristic cultural backlash against a strong institutional residualism in terms of low activation budgets and minimalistic employment support (for a similar argument, see Arts and Gelissen, 2001).

To summarise the main methodological argument of this section, regime ideal types have the advantage that because they are theory-based rather than inductively derived, they allow robust insights into similarities and differences between welfare entities, irrespective of the composition of the sample. This differs from traditional inductive welfare regime comparisons, in which the number and selection of the compared entities has a high influence on the resulting regime maps – which, by definition, always display three or four main types of regimes, whereas ideal-typical maps may contain more than one empty quadrant. In the next section, a second advantage of regime ideal types in applied analysis is discussed: the possibility of tracing regime shifts and regime changes over time.

Tracing of regime changes over time

As Scruggs and Allan (2006) and others have argued, many existing welfare regime classifications disregard the temporal dimension and hence the possibility that welfare regimes may undergo relative regime shifts or even type-crossing changes over time. A recent exception includes Danforth's sophisticated cluster analysis of welfare regimes in the period 1950–2000, but given the inductive nature of his longitudinal study, Danforth cannot prove whether the identified regime shifts occurred within or across ideal-typical regime axes. This can be remedied by an ideal-typical regime conceptualisation that provides clear cut-off points between conservative versus liberal and residualistic versus solidaristic welfare entities. Especially the fuzzy set method seems well-suited for such ideal type-based regime comparisons over time, as illustrated by Kvist's (2007) analysis of 'old' and 'new' social-democratic, labour, conservative and liberal welfare regimes in the period 1990 to 1999, and Aurich's (2011) tracing of the evolution of three activation regimes between 1990 and 2010. Also, the multiple correspondence analysis of welfare regime changes between 1971 and 1999 conducted by Ferragina et al (2013) provides an innovative example of the inter-temporal applicability of welfare regime ideal types.

In order to justify analytically why welfare regime ideal types are better able to distinguish between relative regime shifts and absolute regime changes than inductive approaches, let us expand the above illustrative mapping of 11 European activation cultures to the 19-year period 1991–2010. Since no data for Switzerland are available in the second EVS wave, Switzerland must be eliminated from this illustrative analysis of activation-cultural stability and change over time. Table 9.2 contains the same survey items as Table 9.1, yet for only 10 countries and for the period 1991–93. As in the previous table, upper-row values pertain to conservatism/residualism, whereas bottom-row values pertain to liberalism/solidarism. As a first look at Table 9.2 reveals, no ideal-typically solidaristic activation cultures were contained in our sample in 1991–93, contrary to 2008–10, when three solidaristic activation cultures were identified: Denmark, Sweden and Great Britain. This supports the earlier supposition that the British activation-cultural solidarism may be a new trend in reaction to an increasing residualism in the institutional domain. In addition, two conservative activation cultures (Italy, Poland) and a conservative-liberal hybrid (Spain) can be detected in the 1991–93 wave of the EVS, whereas only liberal activation cultures remain 19 years later, as discussed above. Hence, based on an ideal-typical analysis, one can make a clear distinction between activation-cultural regime shifts within ideal-typical regime categories, and border-crossing regime changes from conservatism to liberalism or from residualism to solidarism over time.

Figure 9.5 gives a graphical illustration of activation-cultural regime shifts/changes in the 10 countries between 1991 and 2010. Dashed arrows signify relative regime shifts within one and the same regime category, while full arrows depict regime changes across regime ideal types. Furthermore, period '1' refers to the timeframe 1991–93, whereas period '2' refers to the timeframe 2008–10. As mentioned above, six out of 10 activation cultures made a border-crossing movement over the course of 19 years, with three activation cultures having moved from residualism to solidarism (Sweden, Denmark and Great Britain), two activation cultures having moved from conservatism to liberalism (Italy,

Table 9.2: EVS items connected with two ideal-typical regime axes (%), 1991-93

		DE	DK	ES	FR	GB	IE	IT	NL	PL	SE
c001	Jobs are scarce: giving men priority										
	(1=agree)	28.9	10.5	27.6	32.4	34.6	35.2	39.1	24.5	53.7	7.5
	(2=disagree)	55.5	85.5	63.7	58.2	58.0	58.5	46.9	69.1	31.7	86.2
c002	Jobs are scarce: giving [nation] priority										
	(1=agree)	59.7	51.5	75.7	60.8	51.6	67.8	69.5	32.4	56.9	33.0
	(2=disagree)	25.8	37.0	14.9	30.0	40.1	28.1	17.4	60.3	29.4	54.1
c024	Important in job: useful for society										
	(1=mentioned)	39.6	21.1	38.4	28.1	28.7	29.8	47.8	48.4	33.5	41.8
	(0=not mentioned + -2=no answer)	60.4	78.9	61.6	71.9	71.3	70.2	52.2	51.6	66.5	58.2
	Sum conservatism:	128	83	142	121	115	133	156	105	144	82
	Sum liberalism:	142	201	140	160	169	157	117	181	128	199
	Residue liberalism minus conservatism:	14	118	-2	39	55	24	-40	76	-17	116
	Ideal-typical regime category:	lib	lib	con	lib	lib	lib	con	lib	con	lib
e037	Individual vs state responsibility for providing for oneself										
	(1=individual + 2 + 3)	48.9	41.2	19.8	44.5	28.9	37.1	28.4	32.4	23.3	62.1
	(8 + 9 + 10=state)	16.4	10.4	30.0	12.8	24.9	22.6	30.5	12.4	28.8	6.2

		DE	DK	ES	FR	GB	IE	IT	NL	PL	SE
e038	Take any job vs right to refuse a job										
	(1=take any job + 2 + 3)	35.2	41.3	37.8	42.2	28.1	32.2	53.9	27.1	39.2	52.8
	(8 + 9 + 10=right to refuse a job)	22.0	19.0	18.1	16.2	28.6	27.8	12.1	14.9	25.1	13.3
	Sum residualism:	84	83	58	87	57	69	82	60	63	115
	Sum solidarism:	38	29	48	29	54	50	43	27	54	20
	Sum solidarism minus residualism:	–46	–53	–9	–58	–4	–19	–40	–32	–9	–95
	Ideal-typical regime category:	res	res	res	res	res	res	res	res	res	res

Figure 9.5: Ten European activation cultures, ideal-typical mapping over two time periods (1 = 1991-93, 2 = 2008-10)

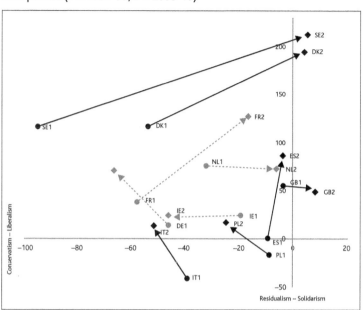

Poland), and one activation culture having moved from conservative-liberal hybridity to full-fledged liberalism (Spain).

It should be noted that tracing ideal-typical regime transitions over time can only serve as a starting point for empirical analysis, because in isolation, it explains nothing. However, studying regime shifts and changes from an ideal-typical perspective can help to identify important questions to be asked and answered about the evolution of welfare systems or programmes. For example, a key question emerging from Figure 9.5 is why some activation cultures cross regime types after the introduction of more individualised forms of activation since the 1990s. In addition, it would be interesting to investigate using more sophisticated methods of analysis why a move in the direction of more activation-cultural residualism can be observed in four countries (Ireland, Poland, Italy and Germany) whereas a shift towards more solidaristic attitudes dominates elsewhere and especially in Sweden, Denmark and France. As a final example, the question arises from Figure 9.5 how activation-cultural transitions relate to the institutional dimension of activation – for instance, do they precede or follow changes in ALMP budgets or regulations (and if so, through which mechanisms) or are they completely decoupled from the institutional environment? Such questions on the relationship between different ideal-typical regime dimensions are the topic of the next section.

Identification of frictions between regime dimensions

Above, we saw that many comparative studies implicitly compare welfare entities across two regime dimensions, for instance, by juxtaposing cultural attitudes with institutional configurations or institutional aspects with socioeconomic stratification effects. This chapter argues that an ideal-typical welfare regime approach not only adds theoretical backing to such multidimensional regime comparisons, but also provides clues as to regime-inherent structural ambiguities or tensions that can serve as potential explanations of why some regimes change over time, while others do not. After all, as Seo and Creed (2002) have argued, structural contradictions may prompt policy agents to consciously or unconsciously re-appropriate regulations and worldviews in daily application, thereby causing more official regime recalibrations over time. Also Thelen (2003) has posited that 'institutions evolve' once regulations, worldviews and/or life course patterns are no longer fully congruent with each other, leading to an adaptation of formal social policy to new cultural, institutional or social realities in the course of time.

In the following, the example of activation culture juxtaposed with the institutional characteristics of 10 European activation systems is used to illustrate how multidimensional regime comparisons can be used to detect internal regime frictions as a signpost of ongoing or potential regime change. The conservative versus liberal institutional characteristics of activation systems are captured by the availability of formal childcare as a vital precondition for the labour market participation of parents, and especially mothers. In order to avoid the inductive trap of simply taking low childcare coverage rates as indicative of conservatism and high childcare coverage rates as indicative of liberalism, it was decided to look more specifically at the ratio between part-time and full-time childcare, defining as conservative countries where part-time childcare predominates and as liberal countries where full-time childcare is the norm.[3] As Table 9.3 shows, the majority of the analysed countries lean towards the liberal side of the ideal-typical spectrum, yet with Spain, the Netherlands, Ireland and the UK following a more conservative institutional model – suggesting that Lewis' (1992) analysis of Ireland and the UK being 'historically "strong" male breadwinner states' continues to hold in the activation age.[4]

Table. 9.3: Institutional characteristics of ten European activation systems, 2010

	DE	DK	ES	FR	UK	IE	IT	NL	PL	SE
Children aged 0-3 in formal childcare (%)										
0-29 hours weekly	7	10	20	17	31	21	6	44	0	18
30+ hours weekly	13	68	18	26	4	8	16	6	2	33
Total	20	78	38	43	35	29	22	50	2	51
Relative weight of full-time childcare	0.65	0.87	0.47	0.60	0.11	0.28	0.73	0.12	1.00	0.65
Ideal-typical regime category	lib	lib	con	lib	con	con	lib	con	lib	lib
ALMP expenditure (% of GDP)										
Placement and related services	0.2	0.09	0.03	0.11	0.2	0.05	0	0.28	0.04	0.2
Training	0.31	0.67	0.2	0.38	0.02	0.45	0.14	0.14	0.04	0.09
Employment incentives	0.1	0.32	0.27	0.07	0.01	0.06	0.15	0.02	0.21	0.52
Sheltered and supported employment, rehabilitation	0.03	0.66	0.08	0.11	0.01	0.01	0	0.48	0.21	0.24
Direct job creation	0.05	0	0.1	0.22	0.04	0.25	0.01	0.17	0.04	0
Start-up incentives	0.08	0	0.12	0.05	0	0	0.02	0	0.1	0.02
Total	0.77	1.74	0.8	0.94	0.28	0.82	0.32	1.09	0.64	1.07
Rank of spending item 'placement services'	2	4	6	3	1	4	5	2	4	3
Ideal-typical regime category	res	sol	sol	sol	res	sol	sol	res	sol	sol

Sources: Eurostat, OECD

Also on the residualism-solidarism axis of ALMP institutions, total ALMP expenditures are not compared inductively; instead, the ratio between placement services and other services in a country's activation portfolio is looked at, out of the rationale that ideal-typically residualistic activation systems should be characterised by a strong focus on workfarist and cheap job search monitoring whereas solidaristic activation systems should put more emphasis on enabling and expensive services such as training or wage subsidies. Hence, all activation systems where placement services make up the largest or second-largest item in the ALMP budget are characterised as residualistic, whereas all countries where other services predominate are labelled solidaristic. When seen from this angle, only three ideal-typically workfarist activation systems are contained in our sample: the UK, Germany and the Netherlands.[5]

Because the cultural and institutional regime characteristics of the 10 active welfare states investigated here are not measured on a uniform scale, a rough juxtaposition of regime labels must suffice for identifying frictions between the cultural and institutional activation regime dimensions as possible sources or triggers of activation regime change. The respective regime labels are summarised in Table 9.4. Whenever active welfare states differ between a residualistic pure type and a solidaristic variant on the residualism-solidarism axis, a first non-identity is counted. Whenever activation-related cultural attitudes and ALMP-institutional characteristics differ on the conservatism-liberalism axis, an additional non-identity is counted. As Table 9.4 shows, three active welfare states in our sample feature two non-identities, pointing either towards a solidaristic cultural backlash against a workfarist activation system (as possibly in the UK), or liberalising cultural resentment against paternalistic activation systems that privilege male breadwinners in obtaining qualitative employment (possibly in Spain and Ireland).

Table 9.4: Cultural versus institutional regime characteristics of 10 active welfare states

	DE	DK	ES	FR	UK	IE	IT	NL	PL	SE
Activation culture	R - L	S - L	R - L	R - L	S - L	R - L	R - L	R - L	R - L	S - L
ALMP institutions	R - L	S - L	S - C	S - L	R - C	S - C	S - L	R - C	S - L	S - L
Non-Identities	0	0	2	1	2	2	1	1	1	0

Notes: R = residualistic, S = solidaristic, L = liberal, C = conservative.

Hence, regime-inherent frictions may provide a fruitful starting point for explaining activation-cultural regime change in at least some of the cases discussed above, particularly Spain and the UK, where type-crossing regime changes were identified between 1991 and 2010.

Discussion

The main goal of this chapter has been to put flesh to the bones of the argument that Esping-Andersen's empirical welfare regime typology should be replaced by purely analytical, theory-derived ideal types. Using the example of ALMPs, it has been shown how an ideal-typical regime approach comprising two axes (conservatism-liberalism and residualism-solidarism) and three regime dimensions (culture, institutions and stratification) can be used as a heuristic device in comparing a wide array of welfare systems and programmes. In particular, three advantages of an ideal-typical welfare regime approach in empirical analysis were highlighted. First, ideal-typical regime comparisons provide more realistic insights into relative (that is, within-type) and absolute (that is, cross-type) differences between welfare entities than inductive mappings, which tend to overrate the importance of high and low indicator values. Second, an ideal-typical regime framework allows a reliable tracing of relative regime shifts and absolute regime changes over time. And third, welfare regime ideal types can serve as a fruitful tool for identifying frictions between two or more regime dimensions as signposts or possible explanations of regime changes.

It should be stressed here that using welfare regime ideal types in the place of empirically derived categories does not solve all methodological problems encountered in comparative social policy research. For instance, the validity and reliability of ideal-type-based regime mappings depends crucially on the quality of the indicators used, as well as on the diligence with which those indicators are tailored to the applicable regime axes. Nevertheless, the descriptive analysis above has hopefully demonstrated convincingly that regime ideal types can mitigate a number of shortcomings afflicting traditional regime comparisons, such as a distorting influence of outliers or inductively derived regime boundaries. Therefore, ideal type-based research could greatly enrich the comparative analysis of social policies and welfare systems at the supra-national, national, regional or local level, possibly supported by innovative research techniques such as fuzzy set analysis.

Notes

[1] Esping-Andersen used the term 'welfare state regime' in his initial work. From 1996 onwards, he switched to the term 'welfare regime'.

[2] The EVS is a representative longitudinal survey of basic human values. Four waves are currently available: 1981–83 (wave 1), 1991–93 (wave 2), 1999–2001 (wave 3) and 2008–10 (wave 4).

[3] Strictly speaking, full-time/part-time childcare coverage rates reflect not only childcare supply (a policy issue), but also labour market-induced childcare demand. However, for the current illustrative purposes, childcare coverage rates should suffice as a proxy of conservative versus liberal activation institutions.

[4] In 2005, the earliest year for which those statistics are available, the sample was still evenly divided between four liberal activation systems (Denmark, Italy, Poland, Sweden), four conservative activation systems (Ireland, the Netherlands, Spain, UK) and two mixed activation systems (France, Germany).

[5] In 2005, Germany still fell under the solidaristic activation regime category. All other regime labels remained unchanged between 2005 and 2010.

References

Arts, W. and Gelissen, J. (2001) 'Welfare states, solidarity and justice principles: Does the type really matter?', *Acta Sociologica*, vol 44, no 4, pp 283-99.

Arts, W. and Gelissen, J. (2002) 'Three worlds of welfare capitalism or more? A state-of-the-art report', *Journal of European Social Policy*, vol 12, no 2, pp 137-58.

Aspalter, C. (2011) 'The development of ideal-typical welfare regime theory', *International Social Work*, vol 54, no 6, pp 735-50.

Aurich, P. (2011) 'Activating the unemployed: directions and divisions in Europe', *European Journal of Social Security*, vol 13, no 3, pp 294-316.

Bambra, C. (2007) 'Going beyond *The three worlds of welfare capitalism*: regime theory and public health research', *Journal of Epidemiology and Community Health*, vol 61, no 12, pp 1098-102.

Bannink, D. and Hoogenboom, M. (2007) 'Hidden change: disaggregation of welfare state regimes for greater insight into welfare state change', *Journal of European Social Policy*, vol 17, no 1, pp 19-32.

Betzelt, S. (2008) *Activation policies from a gender-sensible citizenship perspective: A tentative analytical framework*, ZeS-Arbeitspapier 3/2008, Bremen: Centre for Social Policy Research.

Bolderson, H. and Mabbett, D. (1995) 'Mongrels or thoroughbreds: a cross-national look at social security systems', *European Journal of Political Research*, vol 28, no 1, pp 119-39.

Bonoli, G. (1997) 'Classifying welfare states: a two-dimension approach', *Journal of Social Policy*, vol 26, no 3, pp 351-72.

Clasen, J. and Clegg, D. (2006) 'Beyond activation: reforming European unemployment protection in post-industrial labour markets', *European Societies*, vol 8, no 4, pp 527-53.

Considine, M. and Lewis, J. (2003) 'Bureaucracy, network, or enterprise? Comparing models of governance in Australia, Britain, the Netherlands, and New Zealand', *Public Administration Review*, vol 63, no 2, pp 131-40.

Danforth, B. (2014) 'Worlds of welfare in time: a historical reassessment of the three-world typology', *Journal of European Social Policy*, vol 24, no 2, pp 164-82.

Da Roit, B. and Weicht, B. (2013) 'Migrant care work and care, care migration and employment regimes: a fuzzy-set analysis', *Journal of European Social Policy*, vol 23, no 5, pp 469-86.

Dingeldey, I. (2007) 'Between workfare and enablement – the different paths to transformation of the welfare state: a comparative analysis of activating labour market policies', *European Journal of Political Research*, vol 46, no 6, pp 823-51.

Donzelot, J. (1991) 'The mobilization of society', in G. Burchell, C. Gordon and P. Miller (eds) *The Foucault effect: Studies in governmentality*, London: Harvester Wheatsheaf, pp 169-79.

Esping-Andersen, G. (1990) *The three worlds of welfare capitalism*, Cambridge: Polity Press.

Esping-Andersen, G. (1996) 'After the golden age? Welfare state dilemmas in a global economy', in G. Esping-Andersen (ed) *Welfare states in transition: National adaptations in global economies*, London: Sage, pp 1-31.

Fenger, M. (2007) 'Welfare regimes in Central and Eastern Europe: incorporating post-communist countries in a welfare regime typology', *Contemporary Issues and Ideas in Social Sciences*, vol 3, no 2 (http://journal.ciiss.net/index.php/ciiss/article/view/45).

Ferragina, E. and Seeleib-Kaiser, M. (2011) 'Welfare regime debate: past, present, futures?', *Policy & Politics*, vol 39, no 4, pp 583-611.

Ferragina, E., Seeleib Kaiser, M. and Tomlinson, M. (2013) 'Unemployment protection and family policy at the turn of the 21st century: a dynamic approach to welfare regime theory', *Social Policy & Administration*, vol 47, no 7, pp 783-805.

Ferrera, M. (1996) 'The "southern model" of welfare in social Europe', *Journal of European Social Policy*, vol 6, no 1, pp 17-37.

Goodin, R.E. (2001) 'Work and welfare: towards a post-productivist welfare regime', *British Journal of Political Science*, vol 31, no 1, pp 13-39.

Hudson, J, (2012) 'Welfare regimes and global cities: a missing link in the comparative analysis of welfare states?', *Journal of Social Policy*, vol 41, no 3, pp 455-73.

Hudson, J. and Kühner, S. (2013) 'Qualitative comparative analysis and applied public policy analysis: new applications of innovative methods', *Policy and Society*, vol 32, no 4, pp 279-87.

Kasza, G.J. (2002) 'The illusion of welfare regimes', *Journal of Social Policy*, vol 31, no 2, pp 271-87.

Korpi, W. (1983) *The democratic class struggle*, London: Routledge & Kegan Paul.

Korpi, W. and Palme, J. (1998) 'The paradox of redistribution and strategies of equality: welfare state institutions, inequality, and poverty in the Western countries', *American Sociological Review*, vol 63, no 5, pp 661-87.

Koster, F. and Kaminska, M.-E. (2012) 'Welfare state values in the European Union, 2002-2008: a multilevel investigation of formal institutions and individual attitudes', *Journal of European Public Policy*, vol 19, no 6, pp 900-29.

Kvist, J. (2007) 'Fuzzy set ideal type analysis', *Journal of Business Research*, vol 60, no 5, pp 474-81.

Leibfried, S. (1992) 'Towards a European welfare state? On integrating poverty regimes into the European Community', in Z. Ferge and J.E. Kolberg (eds) *Social policy in a changing Europe*, Frankfurt am Main: Campus, pp 245-79.

Lewis, J. (1992) 'Gender and the development of welfare regimes', *Journal of European Social Policy*, vol 2, no 3, pp 159-73.

Lødemel, I. and Trickey, H. (2000) 'A new contract for social assistance', in I. Lødemel and H. Trickey (eds) *'An offer you can't refuse': Workfare in international perspective*, Bristol: Policy Press, pp 1-39.

O'Connor, J.S. and Robinson, G. (2008) 'Liberalism, citizenship and the welfare state', in W. van Oorschot, M. Opielka and B. Pfau-Effinger (eds) *Culture and welfare state: Values and social policy in comparative perspective*, Cheltenham: Edward Elgar, pp 29-49.

Pfau-Effinger, B. (2004) 'Socio-historical paths of the male breadwinner model: an explanation of cross-national differences', *British Journal of Sociology*, vol 55, no 3, pp 377-99.

Powell, M. and Barrientos, A. (2011) 'An audit of the welfare modelling business', *Social Policy & Administration*, vol 45, no 1, pp 69-84.

Rice, D. (2013) 'Beyond welfare regimes: from empirical typology to conceptual ideal types', *Social Policy & Administration*, vol 47, no 1, pp 93-110.

Rice, D. (2015) 'Building active welfare states: How policy shapes caseworker practice', PhD thesis, VU University Amsterdam.

Scruggs, L. and Allan, J. (2006) 'Welfare-state decommodification in 18 OECD countries: a replication and revision', *Journal of European Social Policy*, vol 16, no 1, pp 55-72.

Sellers, J.M. and Lindström, A. (2007) 'Decentralization, local government, and the welfare state', *Governance*, vol 20, no 4, pp 609-32.

Seo, M.-G. and Creed W.E.D. (2002) 'Institutional contradictions, praxis, and institutional change: a dialectical perspective', *Academy of Management Review*, vol 27, no 2, pp 222-47.

Siaroff, A. (1994) 'Work, welfare and gender equality: a new typology', in D. Sainsbury (ed) *Gendering welfare states*, London: Sage, pp 82-100.

Sihto, M. (2001) 'The strategy of an active labour market policy: an analysis of its development in a changing labour market', *International Journal of Manpower*, vol 22, no 8, pp 683-706.

Svallfors, S. (1997) 'Worlds of welfare and attitudes to redistribution: a comparison of eight Western nations', *European Sociological Review*, vol 13, no 3, pp 283-304.

Thelen, K. (2003) 'How institutions evolve: Insights from comparative historical analysis', in J. Mahoney and D. Rueschemeyer (eds) *Comparative historical analysis in the social sciences*, Cambridge: Cambridge University Press, pp 208-40.

TEN

What if we waited a little longer? The dependent variable problem within the comparative analysis of the welfare state revisited

Stefan Kühner

Introduction

Generally regarded as the main trigger for the 'welfare modelling business', Esping-Andersen's (1990) *The three worlds of welfare capitalism* incidentally also heralded the so-called dependent variable problem within the comparative analysis of the welfare state (henceforth, dependent variable problem). In what has become one of the most cited critiques, Esping-Andersen (1990, pp 19-21) stated that expenditure-based summary measures of welfare state effort 'are epiphenomenal to the theoretical substance of welfare states', and indicate neither a 'commitment to social citizenship and solidarity [nor] full employment.' Furthermore, Esping-Andersen (1990, pp 19-21) argued that 'if our aim is to test causal theories that involve actors [...] it is difficult to imagine that anyone struggled for spending per se'. Indeed, in my earlier study on the dependent variable problem covering 21 Organisation for Economic Co-operation and Development (OECD) countries and a time period between 1980 and 2001, I found that widely used expenditure-based summary measures of welfare state generosity produce inconsistent findings at the country level, and are hampered by conceptual limitations, missing values and imprecise operational definitions (Kühner, 2007). As for analyses of welfare state change, I showed that considerable asymmetries in the findings produced by different expenditure-based summary measures, but also increasingly between quantitatively informed research and qualitative comparative historical case analyses, persist.

At the same time, recent progress in the broad availability of social rights-based summary measures (see Scruggs and Allan, 2006, 2008; Scruggs et al, 2013) has enabled a seemingly preferable perspective on welfare state activity across time and space, but largely failed to bring about a decisive end to long-fought debates about best and second-best measures in comparative welfare state analysis. Instead, it is now commonplace to argue that scholars should take more seriously the multidimensional character of the welfare state and welfare state change, and perform analyses of different dependent variables whenever feasible. By doing so, the notion of broad welfare state retrenchment across high-income countries is overstated, but the same is true for claims of welfare resilience: while some countries have shown signs of sizeable cutbacks, some have remained stable and others have expanded welfare provision, noticeably since the 1980s. Importantly, my earlier study concluded by arguing that (1) Esping-Andersen's (1990) regime typology does not provide a sufficient explanation of these different reform processes and (2) the trajectories of disaggregated welfare state components are relatively independent. As a consequence, I argued that research that focuses on single programme areas and extends research frameworks beyond single-epistemology approaches should be encouraged (Kühner, 2007).

This chapter offers an update, revision and extension of my earlier study, and is largely inspired by Busemeyer's (2009) research note on the impact of globalisation on public social spending dynamics. Referring to Campbell (2004, p 167), Busemeyer asks: 'What if we waited a little longer', and finds evidence that the failure to identify a clear negative effect of globalisation on welfare effort can in some instances be explained by the particular time period covered in empirical applications, as international economic interdependence and liberalised trade and financial flows simply needed a little longer to show their *real* impact on the welfare state. This perspective is intriguing because my initial contribution was written just before the literature began to identify more consistent instances of unpopular welfare state reform across high-income countries (see, for example, Vis, 2007, 2010) – a momentum that can only be said to have increased since the 2008 financial crisis (see, for example, Farnsworth and Irving, 2011). Not least, a revision of my initial findings is now feasible as the key data sources of my earlier analysis – the OECD's *Social Expenditure Database* (SOCX) (2014a) and Scruggs et al's (2013) *Comparative Welfare Entitlements Database* (CWED I and II) – have recently been updated and make available time series spanning up to the years 2010–13 for the first time.

So, 'What if we waited a little longer?' Would expenditure-based summary measures of the welfare state paint a more consistent picture as unpopular welfare reforms had more time to play out, and time lags between policy implementation and outputs were better captured in available time series? Would inconsistencies between expenditure and social rights-based summary indicators persist, or would there be any signs of convergence of welfare trajectories across these two approaches? Does disaggregated analysis of single policy areas still present a preferable alternative to the use of summary measures? And finally, 25 years after the publication of Esping-Andersen's (1990) *The three worlds of welfare capitalism*, what can summary measures tell us about the validity of Esping-Andersen's (1990) original regime classification in the post-crisis era? What can they tell us about processes of welfare reform across different welfare regimes? It is these questions that this chapter addresses in turn. First, however, it is worth briefly summarising the dependent variable problem, and reviewing the most recent contributions to this still lively and evolving debate.

Dependent variable problem revisited

For the last 20+ years, comparative welfare state research has, in large parts, been preoccupied with devising ways to distinguish quantitative, incremental welfare state changes from more qualitative, structural ones (see, for example, Hall, 1993; Pierson, 1994; Kvist, 1999). There is a plethora of contributions that more specifically try to delineate key concepts such as welfare restructuring (Pierson, 2001), recommodification (Holden, 2003), or activation (Serrano Pascual, 2007; Eichhorst and Konle-Seidl, 2008). There have also been influential attempts to incorporate sophisticated processes of public policy change, namely institutional layering, conversion and drift, into the comparative analysis of social policies (Hacker, 2004; Streeck and Thelen, 2005). In the light of these debates, the dependent variable problem refers to the fact that there is often a lack of clarity when multidimensional concepts such as 'welfare state generosity' and 'welfare state change' are employed in empirical applications. Both of these concepts are multidimensional in nature and therefore cannot easily be reduced to a dichotomy of 'less' versus 'more', or 'retrenchment' versus 'expansion', and 'decommodification' versus 'recommodification' (Green-Pedersen, 2004; Clasen and Siegel, 2007; Howlett and Cashore, 2009; van Oorschot, 2012). To put it more simply: too many different things have been discussed under these headings – a prime example case of 'concept stretching' that has bedevilled other areas of comparative historical analysis for some time (Stiller and van Kersbergen, 2008). This theoretical ambiguity has tended to produce different conclusions on the subject matter, and led Green-Pedersen (2004, p 3) to conclude that ultimately the 'dependent variable problem is a problem of theoretical conceptualisation rather than a problem of data.'

Still, there is another facet of the dependent variable problem, which has primarily aimed to overcome limitations of expenditure-based summary measures by way of increasing their 'sophistication' in terms of data collection and operationalisation (Kühner, 2007). Despite a consistently strong empirical relationship between expenditure and social rights-based summary measures,[1] there has been a silent agreement that social rights-based measures are preferable for the comparative analysis of welfare state generosity and change (Wenzelburger et al, 2013; but see also Castles, 2004; Jensen, 2011, who present a useful defence of expenditure-based measures). The introduction and revision of Scruggs (2005) and Scruggs et al's (2013) welfare generosity index scores – mirroring Esping-Andersen's (1990) conceptualisation of old age, sickness and unemployment decommodification – has considerably reduced the dominance of expenditure-based approaches in the literature. Indeed, Scruggs (2014) already counts 100+ empirical applications of the data collected in CWED I and II respectively.

It is therefore not surprising that a whole range of contributions have repeated the notion that social expenditure data, as provided in the OECD's landmark SOCX, has continued to be marred by missing, estimated and imprecise data, which leaves out education spending and fails to account for variations of the tax system across time and space (see Adema et al, 2014). Others have uncovered inconsistencies in the classification of mandatory and voluntary private reform components for single countries (see de Deken and Kittel, 2007) or criticised operationalisations of specific expenditure-based measures for (1) not, or only inadequately, accounting for changing welfare needs (Castles, 2004), (2) for being prone to well-documented denominator problems – for instance, if increases in overall social spending measured as a share of GDP are due to a shrinking economy as seen in the wake of the 2008 financial crisis (Adema et al, 2011) – or (3) for not properly accounting for relative changes of single social policy programmes within nations (see, for example, Burgoon, 2001; Castles, 2008; Kuitto, 2011; for a more detailed discussion, see Table 10.1 and Kühner, 2007, pp 13-16).

More recently, however, much progress has also been made to enhance our understanding of the challenges facing social rights-based data as provided by CWED I and II. Importantly, the discourse has thereby moved beyond the initial criticisms of Esping-Andersen's (1990) conceptualisation of decommodification and the ensuing classification of welfare regimes (see, for example, Arts and Gelissen, 2002; Bambra, 2006; Scruggs and Allan, 2006). One of the more basic recent points of criticism brought forward is that, since they are largely based on net replacement rates, social rights data can only be collected for welfare programmes that actually replace incomes – this excludes various crucial social services in healthcare, housing and education, but also, to some extent, services for the long-term sick, people with disabilities and families with children (Olasoaga-Laurrari et al, 2009). Indeed, Jensen (2011) points out that those social rights-based studies that closely follow Esping-Andersen (1990) have almost entirely focused attention on old-age pensions, sick pay and unemployment benefits, and then directly inferred their findings on the welfare state in its entirety. By way of comparing index scores of CWED II and the other big social rights data collection exercise, namely, Korpi and Palme's *Social Citizenship Indicator Programme* (SCIP), Wenzelburger et al (2013) show that the treatment of taxation and income, means testing, decentralised programmes, assignment of benefits to years, and the nature of data sources differs to the extent that it leads to different evaluations of welfare state change as well as results on the determinants of change. In other words, there is now a better appreciation that utilisation of social rights data does not make studies immune from the impact of key data collection and operationalisation decisions.

More precise limitations of the current operationalisation on generosity scores within CWED I and II have been brought forward, arguably making differences to expenditure-based measures in terms of their reliability and validity appear less pronounced than often fully appreciated. Similar to expenditure-based measures, social rights-based generosity scores cannot account for changing welfare needs, but maybe more importantly, they suffer from their very own denominator problems. Several scholars have pointed out that net income replacement rates are sensitive to developments in real wages of the average production worker – that is, in the absence of any reform of old-age pension, sick pay or unemployment benefits an increase in the real wage of the average production worker will automatically lead to a reduction in 'generosity' even if no actual retrenchment of these policies has taken place (Schmitt and Starke, 2011; Wenzelburger et al, 2013). Danforth and Stephens (2014) add that CWED II fails to consider unemployment spells longer than 26 weeks as well as changes of family and work patterns, which make its reliance on the average production

Table 10.1: Limitations of expenditure and social rights-based measures

Expenditure data as provided by SOCX	*Social rights data as provided by CWED I and II*
General data collection issues	
Does not capture how money is spent	Difficult to obtain and update
Missing, estimated and imprecise data remain problematic	Net replacement rates can only be applied to benefits that replace income
Leaves out education spending	Treatment of taxation and income, means testing, decentralised programmes, assignment of benefits to years, and the nature of data sources differ
Does not account for variations of the tax system across time and space	Missing, estimated and imprecise data remain problematic
Classification of 'mandatory' and 'voluntary private' reform components can be inconsistent	
Further operational issues of specific measures	**Overall welfare generosity**
Public welfare state effort = social expenditure as % of GDP	Exclusively considers 'old risks': old-age pension, sick pay insurance and unemployment benefit programmes
Does not account for changing welfare needs	Does not account for changing welfare needs
Does not account for relative changes of single social policy programmes within nations	Sensitive to developments in real wages of the average production worker
Denominator problems as national economies grow to varying degrees	Does not consider unemployment longer than 26 weeks as well as change of family and work patterns
Welfare state downsizing	Present only a maximum payment available for specific circumstances
Does not account for changing welfare needs	Does not consider multiple recipiency and substitutability of benefits
Ignores increases in spending for single components (that is, cannot separate between 'retrenchment' and 'restructuring')	Considerable time-lags between policy implementation and impact on net replacement rates
Does not account for the relative size of single components	
Structural transformation	
Does not account for changing welfare needs	
Ignores the direction of change of single social policy components	
Low number of degrees of freedom (makes outlier problems likely)	
Welfare state generosity = standardised social expenditure as ratio of GDP	
Does not account for relative changes of single social policy programmes within nations	
Denominator problems as nation's economies and wages grow to varying degrees	
Limits delivery of the welfare state to only two kinds of recipients (elderly and unemployed)	
Disregards significance of early retirement schemes and non-take-up of old-age pensions	
Cannot account for possible 'socio-political' reasons (that is, growing coverage rates) behind growing unemployment figures	

Extended from Kühner (2007: 15) – all listed indicators discussed below (Table 10.2 and Table 10.3).

worker increasingly problematic. Not least, the failure to consider 'new model workers' creates a theoretical problem, since other available data suggests a de-coupling of reform dynamics for old and new social risks (see also below).

At the same time, Caminada et al (2010) stress that net replacement levels only present maximum payment available for specific circumstances that do not necessarily correspond with distributional outcomes. Olaskoaga-Laurrari et al (2009) point in a similar direction, when they suggest substitutability of welfare benefits may lead to misleading interpretations of social rights-based generosity dynamics. For instance, standard pension benefits may simply be lower in one country than another because more is provided in this country in terms of care. The likelihood of multiple recipiency thereby varies with the degree of fragmentation of social security systems as a whole, and threatens to bias results of individual countries to a varying extent (van Oorschot, 2012). Finally, social rights indicators are also no better than expenditure-based measures at capturing time-lags between policy implementation and output, that is, the impact on benefit levels and eligibility criteria. This is particularly an issue for pension reforms, which are often specifically designed to have an impact on future pensioners more strongly than current ones (see, for example, Myles and Pierson, 2001). For this reason, Allan and Scruggs (2004) and Vis (2010), for instance, refrained from including old-age pension generosity in their respective studies on welfare reform activities, but this issue is not absent in the other two policy areas covered in CWED I and II.

Since Esping-Andersen's (1990, pp 19-20) initial criticisms of expenditure-based measures as 'epiphenomenal to the theoretical substance of welfare states', considerable progress has been made in regards to our understanding of the promises and perils of *both* expenditure and social rights-based measures as part of the discourse on the dependent variable problem. While interesting new investments into data collection are continuously devised – see, for example, Adema et al (2014) and their net social spending measure; Olaskoaga-Laurrari et al's (2009) synthetic relative standards of social protection; de Deken and Clasen (2013) who propose the use of caseload data; and Knotz and Nelson's (2013) attempt to quantify conditionality – it is fair to say that this progress has blurred the lines between traditional *best* (social rights) and *second-best* (expenditure-based) measures, and enhanced further the necessity to move beyond single indicator approaches in quantitatively informed comparative welfare state analysis. Keeping these limitations in mind, we now explore whether a simple consideration of longer time series has an impact on substantive findings regarding processes of welfare state change (see Kühner, 2007). To this end, the remainder of this chapter provides a comprehensive descriptive analysis of OECD's SOCX, CWED II and other social rights data covering 21 OECD countries, and a time period roughly between 1980 and 2013, to address its key question: 'What if we waited a little longer?'

Country-level comparisons of summary measures of welfare state change

Only one of the 21 observed countries shows an actual decrease in public welfare state effort between 1980 and 2013 (see Table 10.2). Social spending in the Netherlands decreased from an above average 24.8 per cent of GDP in 1980 to 20.9 per cent in 2008; social spending increased noticeably in the wake of the 2008 financial crisis, but remained just short of 1980 levels in 2013. Ireland was the only other country which showed a reduction in total social expenditure in the earlier study (Kühner, 2007): total public social expenditure levels went from a comparatively low 17 per cent of GDP in 1980 to 13.8 per cent of GDP in 2001, but increased markedly to 19.7 per cent in 2008 and 21.6 per cent in 2013. One has to be careful not to read too much into these figures. The reduction in total public welfare state effort in the Netherlands is more pronounced if public and mandatory private social spending figures are considered – yet, this is at least partly due to the treatment of the 1996 reform of Dutch pensions funds, which have been classified in SOCX as 'voluntary private' (de Deken and Kittel, 2007).[2] Similarly, the extent of welfare expansion in Ireland is exaggerated due to a combination of a shrinking economy and considerable increases of unemployment during and after the 2008 financial crisis. This problem affects the majority of countries, albeit to a varying extent. Still, the overall picture continues to be one of a general increase in total public welfare state effort, with some countries, namely, Finland, France, Greece, Italy, Japan, Portugal and Spain, showing slightly higher average annual percentages growth rates than others. There are then signs of upward convergence of public social welfare effort as the mean average and median level of spending increased alongside decreasing standard deviations between 1980–2013. All of these findings are pretty commonplace and have featured in the literature for quite some time now (see, for example, Castles, 2004).

What is more, high scores of Castles' (2002) welfare downsizing indicator continue to coincide with high degrees of his structural transformation measure in Belgium, Denmark, Ireland, Netherlands,

New Zealand, Sweden and the UK. Welfare downsizing considers the sum of negative changes in the nine social expenditure components in OECD's SOCX,[3] whereas regressing the values of these components for a given country in 2009 on the values for the same country in 1980 attains structural transformation scores. Contrary to downsizing, the structural transformation measure therefore also accounts for simultaneous increases in single components of social spending. Indeed, there are several countries, namely Japan, Portugal, the UK and the US, which combine low scores of welfare state downsizing with relatively high scores of structural transformation, indicating that single social spending components in these countries grew faster than others. The issue with all of these measures is that they are 'unstandardised' in the sense that they do not control for changing welfare needs. Castles' (2004) welfare state generosity measure 'standardises' public social spending by dividing it by the unemployment rate plus the percentage of people aged 65 and older. Although limited by the implication that the welfare state delivers benefits and services exclusively to these two groups of beneficiaries, standardised social expenditure indicators typically produce more evidence for welfare state change than unstandardised measures. This is also the case here: nine of the 21 observed countries show negative average annual percentages growth of this indicator suggesting – at first glance – more instances of welfare cutbacks. However, similar to my earlier findings (Kühner, 2007), the majority of negative changes continue to be below −0.5, with only the Netherlands, New Zealand and Sweden exceeding this figure.

While it would be an exaggeration to make the case for large-scale welfare state retrenchment out of these summary figures, looking at disaggregated policy areas provides a better perspective on where exactly cuts have concentrated. Olaskoaga-Larrauri et al (2009) introduce separate old age and unemployment protection measures by dividing the total spending on old age benefits and services by the number of people aged 65 and older and unemployed, respectively, and expressing this standardised spending figure as a percentage of the average wage of a manual worker. Following this principle, an additional family protection measure was calculated by dividing the total family spending benefits and services by the number of young people aged 19 or below as percentage of the average wage of a manual worker.[4] Again, and not too surprisingly, comparison of these three disaggregated measures suggests that unemployment protection was subject to cuts in more countries, and that cuts were deeper in this policy area compared to the old age and family functions. Again, Sweden stands out, with an annual average

Table 10.2. The dynamics of social expenditure based measures in 21 OECD countries (1980–2013)

	Public Welfare State Effort					Welfare State Downsizing	Degree of Structural Transformation	Welfare State Generosity	Old age protection	Unemployment protection	Family protection
	1980	2008	2013	1980-2013[a]	1980-2013[b]			1980-2013[b]	1990-2010[b]	1990-2010[b]	1990-2010[b]
Australia	10.3	17.8	19.5	9.2	2.0	5.8	9.7	1.3	2.2	-1.5	5.5
Austria	22.4	26.8	28.3	5.9	0.8	1.8	3.8	-0.2	0.7	-2.7	0.4
Belgium	23.5	27.3	30.7	7.2	0.9	9.8	19.6	0.5	0.2	0.5	1.6
Canada	13.7	17.6	18.2	4.5	1.0	6.6	2.2	0.1	-0.5	-3.6	5.8
Denmark	24.8	26.8	30.8	6.0	0.7	10.5	20.3	0.3	0.5	-0.3	1.0
Finland	18.1	25.3	30.5	12.4	1.8	0.0	12.4	0.3	1.0	-2.0	0.5
France	20.8	29.8	33.0	12.2	1.5	4.3	8.7	0.4	0.6	-0.3	2.0
Germany	22.1	25.2	26.2	4.1	0.6	3.2	6.5	-0.5	-0.3	-0.4	0.4
Greece	10.3	22.2	22.0	11.7	2.5	0.0	3.9	-0.3	1.4	8.7	5.6
Ireland	16.5	19.7	21.6	5.1	1.1	7.9	25.5	0.0	2.0	0.9	6.9
Italy	18.0	25.8	28.4	10.4	1.4	0.0	3.8	0.1	1.4	4.9	6.7
Japan	10.3	19.8	22.3	12.0	2.7	1.0	23.8	-0.5	1.8	-3.6	9.1
Netherlands	24.8	20.9	24.3	-0.5	0.0	21.4	40.9	-0.6	0.5	1.9	2.2
New Zealand	17.0	19.8	22.4	5.4	0.9	15.9	34.4	-0.6	..	..	..
Norway	16.9	19.8	22.9	6.0	0.5	3.6	2.4	0.6	2.5	0.1	2.3
Portugal	9.9	23.1	26.4	16.5	3.1	0.0	18.3	1.2	11.1	0.3	8.0
Spain	15.5	22.9	27.4	11.9	1.8	0.0	4.9	-0.1	0.9	0.9	13.3

	Public Welfare State Effort					Welfare State Downsizing	Degree of Structural Transformation	Welfare State Generosity	Old age protection	Unemployment protection	Family protection
	1980	2008	2013	1980-2013[a]	1980-2013[b]			1980-2013[b]	1990-2010[b]	1990-2010[b]	1990-2010[b]
Sweden	27.1	27.5	28.6	1.5	0.2	10.3	8.9	-1.0	0.9	-7.7	-0.8
Switzerland	13.8	18.5	19.1	5.3	0.8	2.5	7.9	-0.5	-0.3	0.8	2.2
United Kingdom	16.5	21.8	23.8	7.3	1.2	17.6	20.3	0.6	2.4	0.6	5.3
United States	13.2	17.0	20.0	6.8	1.3	3.0	18.6	0.8	0.7	4.1	3.8
Mean	17.4	22.6	25.2	7.7	1.3	6.0	14.1	0.1	1.5	0.1	4.1
Median	16.9	22.2	25.3	6.8	1.1	3.6	9.7	0.1	0.9	0.2	3.1
Std. Deviation	5.3	3.8	4.4	4.1	0.8	6.3	10.8	0.6	2.4	3.4	3.6

Notes: aFirst difference; baverage annual % growth; public welfare state effort = total public social expenditure as a percentage of GDP; Welfare state downsizing = the sum of negative changes in social expenditure components between 1980 and 2009 measured as percentages of GDP divided by the total social expenditure of the year 1980 (see: Castles, 2002); Degree of structural transformation = 100 – (100 * the adjusted R2 obtained by regressing the values of the social expenditure components for a given country in 2009 measured as percentages of GDP on the values for the same country in 1980) (see: Castles, 2002); Welfare state generosity = social expenditure/ GDP divided by the unemployment rate plus the percentage of people aged 65 and older (see: Castles, 2004); Old age protection = total spending on old age pensions and services divided by the number of people aged 65 and older expressed as a percentage of the average wage of a manual worker (see: Olaskoaga-Larrauri et al., 2009); Unemployment protection = total spending on unemployment benefits divided by the number of unemployed people expressed as a percentage of the average wage of a manual worker (see: Olaskoaga-Larrauri et al., 2009); Family protection = total spending family benefits and services divided by the number of people aged 19 and younger expressed as a percentage of the average wage of a manual worker (following Gornick and Meyers, 2001). All average annual growth rates calculated as the sum of the annual growth rates for each year divided by the number of years within each given time period. *Sources:* OECD Social Expenditure Database (2014), OECD.STAT. Shaded cells identify countries that show 'retrenchment' according to the criteria defined in **Table 10.4** below.

percentage growth of −7.7, but Austria, Canada, Finland and Japan show sizeable reductions too. The mean and median growth rates of family protection are considerably higher than for old age protection, which supports the point made earlier about different growth trajectories for policy areas catering for 'old' versus 'new' risks.

This latter point holds true if we move beyond expenditure-based measures and consider social rights-based indicators more closely (see Table 10.3). Scruggs (2005) prominently saw signs of sizeable welfare state retrenchment and reductions in overall welfare generosity in a number of countries. Indeed, absolute reductions in overall welfare generosity are considerable in Denmark, Germany, Sweden and the UK, according to CWED II. However, once we look at average annual percentage growth rates, it is again only one of these countries, namely Sweden, that exceeds a score of −0.5. The majority of countries have in fact seen increases in overall generosity levels since 1980s, or at least feature a great deal of resilience with average annual percentage growth rates between 0.0 and 0.5. There is a more equal number of countries characterised by reductions in unemployment benefit and old age generosity according to CWED II, but again, the reductions in unemployment benefit generosity are on the whole more extensive. Single countries standing out in regards to this measure are Germany, Sweden and the UK, with sizeable reductions of unemployment benefit generosity, and Finland, Greece, Ireland, Italy and Portugal, with considerable expansions. As for the old age benefit generosity, it is again Sweden that shows the largest reduction, with an annual average percentage growth of −0.6, closely followed by Greece, Denmark, Germany and New Zealand, with scores between −0.4 and −0.1 respectively.

As discussed above, one criticism of CWED II unemployment benefit score is that it does not account for unemployment of 26 weeks or more; it also does not account for multiple recipiency, for instance, when people receive unemployment benefits alongside housing assistance or social assistance top-ups (see Table 10.1). The OECD's *Benefits and Wages* (2014b) series makes available alternative net unemployment replacement data for short and long-term unemployment (and for different family and income groups), which paints an even starker image of the extent of cutbacks of unemployment and social assistance systems. The OECD's data is only available from 2001, but even in this shorter time period, 11 of our 21 observed countries have seen reductions in short-term net unemployment replacement rates (calculated as the average for six family types at 100 per cent average production worker wage); 11 of our 21 countries also saw reductions in the long-term net

Table 10.3: The dynamics of social rights-based measures in 21 OECD countries (1980-2011)

	Overall welfare generosity					Unemployment benefit generosity	Old-age pension benefit generosity	Unemployment net replacement rates		Family income protection	Family leave provision
						1980-2011[c]	1980-2011[c]	2001-11[b]		1980-2008[b]	1980-2008[b]
	1980	2008	2010	1980-2010[a]	1980-2010[b]			Short-term	Long-term		
Australia	20.5	20.8	20.9	0.4	0.1	0.0	0.3	-0.9	-2.5	1.7	n.a.
Austria	32.5	34.2	34.3	1.8	0.2	-0.1	0.3	-0.1	-0.3	0.1	0.4
Belgium	37.4	41.6	42.6	5.2	0.4	0.1	1.2	0.7	1.7	1.3	4.5
Canada	24.6	25.8	25.7	1.1	0.1	-0.2	0.5	0.3	-0.6	0.8	5.3
Denmark	40.0	33.3	34.1	-5.9	-0.5	0.1	-0.2	-0.4	-0.4	1.1	2.2
Finland	29.3	33.5	34.1	4.8	0.5	1.1	0.3	-0.5	-1.4	-1.5	7.0
France	34.2	37.9	38.0	3.8	0.4	0.0	1.1	-0.2	-0.9	-1.4	10.1
Germany	35.8	32.2	32.0	-3.8	-0.3	-0.5	-0.1	-0.1	-2.0	2.1	2.5
Greece	24.5	29.6	29.2	4.7	0.4	1.7	-0.4	1.6	na	0.0	1.3
Ireland	25.8	36.2	35.3	9.5	1.4	1.2	1.7	1.7	0.7	1.3	12.1
Italy	24.9	30.0	29.6	4.7	0.7	2.2	0.6	0.8	na	3.7	0.6
Japan	23.6	25.5	25.7	2.1	0.4	0.2	0.4	-0.4	1.0	2.1	6.9
Netherlands	38.1	37.8	38.6	0.5	0.0	-0.3	0.3	0.7	0.2	-0.5	3.8
New Zealand	22.4	21.4	21.4	-1.0	-0.1	-0.2	-C.1	-1.1	-1.7	-1.1	2.1
Norway	40.7	43.1	43.9	3.2	0.2	0.7	0.2	0.2	1.6	-2.5	5.1

	Overall welfare generosity					Unemployment benefit generosity	Old-age pension benefit generosity	Unemployment net replacement rates		Family income protection	Family leave provision
								Short-term	Long-term		
	1980	2008	2010	1980-2010[a]	1980-2010[b]	1980-2011[b]	1980-2011[b]	2001-11[b]		1980-2008[b]	1980-2008[b]
Portugal	29.4	31.7	35.1	5.7	1.3	1.6	3.0	-0.2	0.5	5.3	2.3
Spain	28.0	34.8	35.6	7.6	0.9	0.8	0.8	-0.6	0.0	2.1	1.6
Sweden	44.1	36.2	35.2	-8.9	-0.7	-0.6	-0.6	-2.5	-1.5	-1.3	2.6
Switzerland	36.4	37.1	37.1	0.7	0.1	0.2	0.1	0.1	-0.9	1.8	0.0
United Kingdom	31.5	28.2	27.5	-4.0	-0.1	-0.9	0.0	1.6	-0.7	-1.0	-0.5
United States	21.3	21.3	21.7	0.4	0.1	0.1	0.0	-1.1	1.4	2.0	n.a.
Mean	30.7	32.0	32.3	1.6	0.3	0.3	0.5	0.0	-0.3	0.8	3.7
Median	29.4	33.3	34.1	1.8	0.2	0.1	0.3	-0.1	-0.4	1.1	2.5
Std Dev	7.1	6.4	6.6	4.5	0.5	0.8	0.8	1.0	1.2	1.9	3.4

Notes: a First difference; b average annual growth (%); for overall welfare generosity, unemployment benefit generosity and old-age pension benefit generosity, see Scruggs et al (2013); short term unemployment net replacement rates = average for six family types at 100% AW [[in full?]], family does not qualify for cash housing assistance or social assistance top-ups (see OECD, 2014); Long term unemployment net replacement rates = for single earner, no children at 67% AW, including cash housing assistance and social assistance "top ups" if available (see: OECD, 2014 [[not in refs]]); family income protection = additional disposable income ('take-home pay' after taxes and cash transfers) of a one-earner-two-parent-two-child family as compared to the disposable income of a childless single earner, expressed as a percentage of the disposable income of the childless single earner (see Gauthier, 2011); family leave provision = sum of full-time equivalent paid maternity, paternity and childcare leave (see Gauthier, 2011). All average annual growth rates calculated as the sum of the annual growth rates for each year divided by the number of years within each given time period. Shaded cells identify countries that show 'retrenchment' according to the criteria defined in Table 10.4 below.

unemployment replacement rates (for single earners with no children at 67 per cent AW [average wage], including cash housing assistance and social assistance 'top-ups' if available). Short-term replacement rates were reduced most markedly in Sweden, New Zealand and the US, whereas Australia, Germany and Finland stand out alongside Sweden and New Zealand in terms of their reductions in average annual percentage growth rates for long-term unemployment.

Finally, we consider social rights-based data on family income protection and family leave provision collected by Gauthier (2011). Family income protection considers the additional disposable income ('take-home pay' after taxes and cash transfers) of a one-earner-two-parent-two-child family as compared to the disposable income of a childless single earner, expressed as a percentage of the disposable income of the childless single earner. Interestingly, the previous picture of predominant expansion based on the standardised expenditure-based family protection measure (see Table 10.1) is not confirmed as several countries, namely, Finland, France, New Zealand, Norway, Sweden and the UK, have seen sizeable reductions since 1980. There are, however, an equal number of countries that show very marked expansions during the same time period (see Germany, Italy, Portugal, Spain, Japan and the US). Family leave provision is computed as the sum of full-time equivalent paid maternity, paternity and childcare leave. The annual average growth rates of this measure suggest a much more unified expansion across the observed countries. Here it is Finland, France and Ireland that show the largest levels of average annual percentage growth, whereas Austria, Italy, Switzerland and the UK clearly lag behind the development of this particular family policy area.

What if we waited a little longer?

As stated previously, this chapter aims to revisit the key findings of an earlier analysis (Kühner, 2007), which employed time series of key expenditure and social rights-based summary measures up to the early 2000s. More specifically, the stated aim of this chapter was to ask whether state-of-the-art summary measures of the welfare state paint a more consistent picture once time series are extended. While there is an increased understanding of the challenges faced by social rights-based measures (see above), it also asks whether major inconsistencies in the results produced by the different expenditure and social rights-based indicators persist. By extending our analysis to include different disaggregated measures for old-age pension, unemployment and family

Table 10.4: Results for expenditure and social rights-based measures compared

	Suggests [...] for the following countries		
	[Retrenchment]	[Resilience]	[Expansion]
Public welfare state effort		Net, (Nor), Swe	Aus, Aut, Bel, Can, Den, Fin, Fra, (Ger), Gre, Ire, Ita, Jap, NZ, Por, Spa, Swi, UK, US
Welfare state downsizing	Bel, Den, Ire, Net, NZ, Swe, UK	Aus, Aut, Can, Fra, Ger, Nor, Swi, US	Fin, Gre, Ita, Jap, Por, Spa
Welfare state generosity	(Net), (NZ), Swe	Aut, (Bel), Can, Den, Fin, Fra, (Ger), Gre, Ire, Ita, (Jap), Spa, (Swi)	Aus, (Nor), Por, (UK), US
Overall welfare generosity	Swe	Aus, Aut, Bel, Can, (Den), Fra, Ger, Gre, Jap, Net, NZ, Nor, Swi, UK, US	(Fin), Ire, Ita, Por, Spa
Old age protection		Bel, (Can), (Den), Ger, Swi	Aus, Aut, Fin, (Fra), Gre, Ire, Ita, Jap, (Net), Nor, Por, Spa, Swe, UK, US
Old age benefit generosity	Swe	Aus, (Can), Den, Fin, Ger, Gre, Jap, Net, NZ, Nor, Swi, UK, US	Aut, Bel, Fra, Ire, Ita, Por, Spa
Unemployment protection	Aus, Aut, Can, Fin, Jap, Swe	(Bel), Den, Fra, Ger, Nor, Por	Gre, Ire, Ita, Net, Spa, Swi, (UK), US
Unemployment benefit generosity	Swe, UK	Aus, Aut, Bel, Can, Den, Fra, (Ger), Jap, Net, NZ, Swi	Fin, Gre, Ire, Ita, Nor, Por, Spa
Short-term unemployment net replacement rates	Aus, NZ, Spa, Swe, US	Aut, Can, Den, Fin, Fra, (Fin), Ger, Jap, Nor, Por, Swi	Bel, Gre, Ire, Ita, Net, UK
Long-term unemployment net replacement rates	Aus, (Can), Fin, Fra, Ger, NZ, Swe, Swi, UK	Aut, Den, Net, (Por), Spa	Bel, Ire, Jap, Nor, US
Family protection	Swe	Aut, (Fin), Ger	Aus, Bel, Can, Den, Fra, Gre, Ire, Ita, Jap, Net, Nor, Por, Spa, Swi, UK, US
Family income protection	Fin, Fra, NZ, Nor, Swe, UK	Aut, Gre, (Net)	Aus, Bel, Can, Den, Ger, Ire, Ita, Jap, Por, Spa, Swi, US
Family leave provision		Aut, Swi, (UK)	Bel, Can, Den, Fin, Fra, Ger, Gre, Ire, Ita, Jap, Net, NZ, Nor, Por, Spa, Swe

Notes: All measures as presented in Tables 10.2 and 10.3; average annual growth rates classified based on a five-point scale: average annual percentage growth rates <−1.00 are labelled as '[retrenchment]'; >−0.99 and −0.51 by '[[retrenchment]]'; >−0.5 and <0.5 by 'resilience]'; >0.51 and <0.99 by '[(expansion)]', and >1.00 by '[expansion]'; 'borderline' countries given in brackets; countries with negative average annual growth rates in italics.

benefits and services, we also explore whether disaggregated analysis of single policy areas continue to present a more preferable alternative to the use of summary measures.

The utilised measures continue to support claims of a slowdown of budgetary welfare expansion, rather than broad-scale cutbacks of welfare provision. Issues surrounding the translation of numerical information into theoretical concepts such as 'retrenchment', 'resilience' and 'expansion' continue to loom large (see above). Nevertheless, Table 10.4 attempts to directly compare the results of the expenditure and social rights-based measures discussed previously along a one-dimensional spectrum bordered by 'welfare retrenchment' and 'welfare expansion'. Although cut-off points are admittedly chosen arbitrarily, it enables us to learn some important lessons and answer – albeit tentatively – our key research questions. We find that there are only a limited number of countries that have seen an overall retrenchment according to the different summary measures of welfare state change. Interestingly, however, compared to my earlier analysis (see Kühner, 2007), a relatively small set of countries has emerged that indicate more or less consistent retrenchments between 1980-2013. Sweden has seen very limited increases in total public welfare effort, and marked decreases across the various standardised and unstandardised expenditure as well as the social rights-based measures. Although less pronounced, the Netherlands and New Zealand also show consistent reductions according to the welfare state downsizing and welfare state generosity measures; however, the findings regarding the public welfare state effort and overall welfare generosity point in a slightly different direction for these two countries. Several countries, such as Belgium, France and Switzerland, have seemingly changed course and managed to recuperate earlier cutbacks since publication of my earlier study (Kühner, 2007). Similarly, there is now also a comparatively clearer set of countries showing consistent signs of welfare expansion. Although it remains to be seen to what extent these developments will be thwarted by the ongoing political consequences of 2008 financial crisis, it is Portugal, Spain, Italy and, with some distance, Greece, which are characterised with the most significant expansion of welfare state generosity across our time series.

At the same time, conflicting evidence does persist for several countries. Despite appreciable Pearson correlations between the average annual percentage growth rates of the unstandardised expenditure and social rights-based summary measures of around 0.5 ($p<0.01$), the standardised spending measure is not correlated with any of the other summary measures. Ireland – possibly due to the before mentioned denominator problem and increased welfare needs – stands out as a case in point, showing a sizeable expansion of unstandardised public welfare effort, a high score of unstandardised welfare state downsizing, but relative increases of overall welfare generosity according to CWED II. The UK and Denmark's trajectory seems equally difficult to capture: while both unstandardised and standardised social spending suggest a process of welfare expansion, welfare state downsizing and – to a lesser extent – overall welfare generosity indicate a welfare state dynamic in the opposite direction. Considering again the high degrees of structural transformation in all of these countries – indeed, together with the Netherlands, Denmark, Ireland and the UK show the highest scores of this measure (see Table 10.2) – we would suggest that these erring results are at least partly caused by the inability of *summary* measures to account for the dynamics of individual welfare policy areas.

Table 10.4 confirms, at least in the bird's eye perspective, the previous assessment that cutbacks across our sample have disproportionately been concentrated on unemployment benefits. Only one country, namely Sweden, shows sizeable reductions of old age benefit generosity. Sweden is also the only country that shows sizeable reductions according to the family protection measure – a finding that is corroborated by looking at Sweden's family income protection score. There is no country in our sample that is listed as retrenching family leave provision according to our criteria of classification, although the UK is a borderline case. Compared to this, Australia, Canada, New Zealand and Sweden show the most consistent evidence of unemployment benefit cutbacks across the different measures. There are few countries, eg Japan, that appear to have concentrated cutbacks on short-term unemployment replacement rates, and others, namely Finland, France and Germany, that show clear signs of retrenchment of combined benefits for the long-term unemployment while benefits for other categories of the unemployed have proved more resilient to change.

It should be pointed out that Pearson correlations between the disaggregated expenditure and social rights-based measure are stronger than for the different summary measures: the correlation between average annual percentage growth rates of standardised old age protection and old age benefit generosity scores is 0.7 ($p<0.01$); between the standardised unemployment protection and unemployment benefit generosity 0.6 ($p<0.05$); and between standardised family protection and family income protection 0.6 ($p<0.05$). Comparing these findings with the ones from the summary measures above, one may suggest that at least empirically speaking, standardisation according to rough categories of welfare needs, that is, the young, the elderly, the unemployed, remains more promising if computed for disaggregated rather than aggregated analysis.

Finally, this chapter also promised to reconsider whether summary measures tell us more about processes of welfare reform across different welfare regimes. There have been many studies suggesting that welfare state dynamics should be mediated by welfare state structures. For instance, it has been argued that welfare institutions in corporatist/ conservative nations should be more robust against radical welfare state change compared to targeted, basic security and encompassing models as the specific mode of financing through earnings-related contributions leads to benefits generally being perceived as deferred wages or 'earned rights' (Korpi and Palme, 2003; Kangas, 2004); adverse policy changes are said to be particularly unpopular in this context, and tend to be associated with high electoral costs (see also Vis, 2010). We would therefore expect to find that targeted, basic security and encompassing models – or, to use Esping-Andersen's (1990) more familiar terminology, liberal and social-democratic types – should be prone to higher degrees of negative welfare state change than is the case in corporatist/conservative ones. Yet, correlations between overall welfare generosity in 1980 – a proxy for welfare regime membership – and the various summary measures introduced earlier continue to suggest merely a ceiling effect, where those welfare states that were relatively generous in 1980 have simply experienced less growth compared to welfare laggards – at least for two of the summary measures, public welfare state effort and overall welfare generosity (see Table 10.5).

Interestingly, the emerging data pattern nevertheless suggests a certain clustering of welfare regime types (see Figure 10.1). With the exception of the liberal welfare types, which broadly cluster together at the lower left corner in both scatter graphs, and Japan, which is out of sync with the other corporatist/conservative countries (for possible explanations, see Holliday, 2000; Scruggs, 2005), overall welfare generosity scores in 1980 explain a notable percentage of the variance of average annual percentage growth rates of social democratic, corporatist/conservative and Latin Rim countries since 1980. While these observations do not capture the theoretical accounts about self-reinforcing welfare state structures, and largely disappear when repeated for disaggregated data, it is the case that members of the same regime types have experienced broadly similar rates of welfare state change between 1980–2013 according to these measures. There is, of course, a certain irony in the fact that 25 years after publication of Esping-Andersen's (1990) *The three worlds of welfare capitalism* and the ensuing debate on the dependent variable problem, we

Table 10.5: Expenditure and social rights-based measures and the ceiling effect

Measure (average annual % growth)	Correlation with overall welfare generosity, 1980
Public welfare state effort	Yes Adj R^2=0.35, p<0.03
Welfare state generosity	No Adj R^2=0.02, p<0.25
Welfare state downsizing	No Adj R^2=0.03, p<0.21
Overall welfare generosity	Yes Adj R^2=0.14, p<0.05

Notes: All scores used as provided in Tables 10.2 and 10.3.

end up with a finding that suggests that at least at crude bird's-eye level the oft-criticised unstandardised expenditure-based measure provides us with a very similar graphic illustration of longer-term welfare dynamics than the now generally preferred, but equally imperfect, social rights data.

Conclusion

Considerable progress has been made in regards to our conceptual and methodological understanding of the promises and perils of *both* expenditure and social rights-based measures since Esping-Andersen's (1990, pp 19-21) criticism of expenditure-based summary measures as 'epiphenomenal to the theoretical substance of welfare states.' This chapter's brief review of the literature suggests that this progress has blurred the lines between traditional *best* (social rights) and *second-best* (expenditure), but nevertheless identified clear avenues for further data investments, some of which are already underway and promise important additional insights. There are those, of course, who have long lamented an 'output focus' of comparative welfare state analysis, and the regained interest in distributional and labour market outcomes, primarily inequality and the precariatisation of labour, may well overshadow further progress in regards to the conceptualisation and measurement of welfare state inputs in the short and medium term. In short, there is much to suggest that the dependent variable problem continues to be a problem of theoretical ambiguity as much as it is a problem of data collection and operationalisation.

This additional facet of the dependent variable problem potentially has important empirical implications for Esping-Andersen's (1990) *The three worlds of welfare capitalism*. Despite a general 'ceiling effect', where those

Figure 10.1: Summary measures and the clustering of welfare regime types

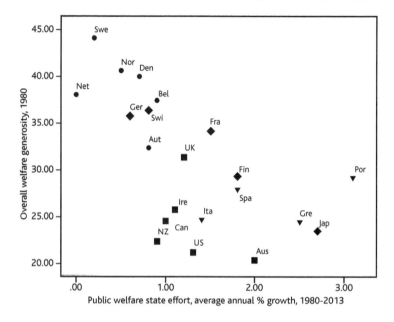

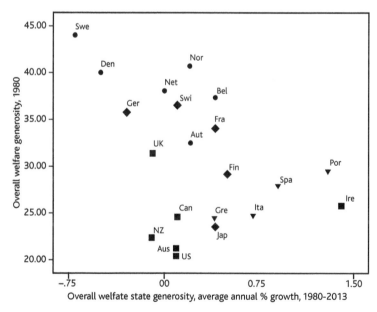

welfare states which were relatively generous in 1980 have expanded welfare generosity less noticeably compared to welfare laggards, summary measures still struggle to teach us about the precise dynamics of welfare reform across different welfare regime types. Conflicting evidence for a considerable number of countries persists and continues to make it difficult to derive meaningful lessons from 'less or more' or 'retrenchment or expansion' approaches employing multiple indicators measuring identical concepts. Having said that, there is now a small set of countries where more or less consistent retrenchments are indicated across the board. One of the prime examples appears to be Sweden, famously labelled by Esping-Andersen (1990) as the social-democratic regime ideal-type, which appears to have experienced sizeable retrenchments for no less than 10 of our 13 observed indicators (Table 10.4). Analysis of disaggregated data highlights several additional countries, primarily Germany, New Zealand, the Netherlands and the UK, that have received a lot of attention in the welfare modelling business, yet equally show trajectories that raise questions about whether they are still adequately captured by Esping-Andersen's (1990) original classification.

This chapter does not intend to overturn regime-based interpretations, but its findings should give pause to those (including myself!) who have continued to determine empirical case selection strategies or organise teaching curricula simply based on Esping-Andersen's (1990) *The three worlds of welfare capitalism*. Competing theories on welfare state development and change are plentiful, and often to the detriment of theoretical clarity continue to explain the same data equally well. What we have learned by '*waiting a little longer*', then, is not a radical departure, but further confirmation that – in the words of Wenzelburger et al (2013, p 1229) – 'future research needs to be more programme-specific, more data-conscious and more humble in its claims.'

Notes

[1] For instance, the Pearson correlation coefficient for public welfare state effort (see Table 10.2) and overall welfare state generosity (see Table 10.3) for the 21 observed countries is $r=0.751$ ($p<0.00$) for 1980 and $r=0.574$ ($p<0.01$) for 2010.

[2] Although intended as an update and revision of Kühner (2007), this chapter focuses only on public social spending rather than public and mandatory private social spending due to the fact that the latter data was only available up to 2009 at the time of writing. The analysis has been replicated with public and mandatory private social spending figures: although mandatory private social spending is considerable in countries

like Germany, Italy, Norway and particularly Switzerland, no major changes in terms of general social spending trajectories became apparent.
[3] That is, old age, survivors, incapacity-related, health, families, unemployment, active labour market programmes (ALMPs), housing, social assistance and other.
[4] Scores for New Zealand cannot be included here because of missing data for average annual wages.

References

Adema, W., Fron, P. and Ladaique, M. (2011) *Is the European welfare state really more expensive?*, OECD Social, Employment and Migration Working Papers, no 124, Paris: OECD.

Adema, W., Fron, P. and Ladaique, M. (2014) 'How much do OECD countries spend on social protection and how redistributive are their tax/benefit systems?', *International Social Security Review*, vol 67, no 1, pp 1-25.

Allan, J.P. and Scruggs, L. (2004) 'Political partisanship and welfare state reform in advanced industrial societies', *American Journal of Political Science*, vol 48, no 3, pp 496-512.

Arts, W. and Gelissen, J. (2002) 'Three worlds of welfare capitalism or more? A state-of-the-art report', *Journal of European Social Policy*, vol 12, no 2, pp 137-58.

Bambra, C. (2006) 'Research note: Decommodification and the worlds of welfare revisited', *Journal of European Social Policy*, vol 16, no 1, pp 73-80.

Burgoon, B. (2001) 'Globalization and welfare compensation: disentangling the ties that bind', *International Organization*, vol 55, no 3, pp 509-51.

Busemeyer, M. (2009) 'From myth to reality: globalisation and public spending on OECD countries revisited', *European Journal of Political Research*, vol 48, no 4, pp 455-82.

Caminada, K., Goudswaard, K. and van Vliet, O. (2010) 'Patterns of welfare state indicators in the EU: is there convergence?', *Journal of Common Market Studies*, vol 48, no 3, pp 529-56.

Campbell, J.L. (2004) *Institutional change and globalization*, Princeton, NJ: Princeton University Press.

Castles, F.G. (2002) 'Developing new measures of welfare state change and reform', *European Journal of Political Research,* vol 41, pp 613-41.

Castles, F.G. (2004) *The future of the welfare state. Crisis myths and crisis realities*, Oxford: Oxford University Press.

Castles, F.G. (2008) 'What welfare states do: a disaggregated expenditure approach', *Journal of Social Policy*, vol 38, no 1, pp 45-62.

Clasen, J. and Siegel, N.A. (eds) (2008) *Investigating welfare state change: The 'dependent variable problem' in comparative analysis*, Cheltenham: Edward Elgar Publishing.

Danforth, B. and Stephens, J.D. (2013) 'Measuring social citizenship: achievements and future challenges', *Journal of European Public Policy*, vol 20, no 9, pp 1285-98.

de Deken, J. and Clasen, J. (2013) 'Benefit dependency: the pros and cons of using "caseload" data for national and international comparisons', *International Social Security Review*, vol 66, no 2, pp 53-78.

de Deken, J. and Kittel, B. (2007) "Social expenditure under scrutiny: the problems of using aggregate spending data for assessing welfare state dynamics', in J. Clasen and N.A. Siegel (eds) *Investigating welfare state change: The 'dependent variable problem' in comparative analysis*, Cheltenham: Edward Elgar Publishing, pp 72-105.

Eichhorst, W. and Konle-Seidl, R. (2008) *Contingent convergence: A comparative analysis of activation policies*, Institute for the Study of Labour Discussion Paper Series No 3905, Bonn: IZA.

Esping-Andersen, G. (1990) *The three worlds of welfare capitalism*, Cambridge: Polity Press.

Farnsworth, K. and Irving, Z. (2011) *Social policy in challenging times: Economic crisis and welfare systems*, Bristol: Policy Press.

Gauthier, A.H. (2011) Comparative Family Policy Database, Max-Planck-Institute for Demographic Research (www.demogr.mpg.de/cgi-bin/databases/FamPolDB/index.plx).

Gornick, J.C. and Meyers, M.K. (2001) 'Lesson-drawing in family policy: media reports and empirical evidence about European developments', *Journal of Comparative Policy Analysis*, vol 3, pp 31-57.

Green-Pederson, C. (2004) 'The dependent variable problem within the study of welfare-state retrenchment: defining the problem and looking for solutions', *Journal of Comparative Policy Analysis*, vol 6, pp 3-14.

Hacker, J.S. (2004) 'Privatizing risk without privatizing the welfare state: the hidden politics of social policy retrenchment in the United States', *American Political Science Review*, vol 98, no 2, pp 243-60.

Hall, P.A. (1993) 'Policy paradigms, social-learning, and the state – the case of economic policy-making in Britain', *Comparative Politics*, vol 25, no 3, pp 275-96.

Holden, C. (2003) 'Decommodification and the workfare state', *Political Studies Review*, vol 1, pp 303-16.

Holliday, I. (2000) 'Productivist welfare capitalism: social policy in East Asia', *Political Studies*, vol 48, no 4, pp 706-23.

Howlett, M. and Cashore, B. (2009) 'The dependent variable problem in the study of policy change: understanding policy change as a methodological problem', *Journal of Comparative Policy Analysis: Research and Practice*, vol 11, no 1, pp 33-46.

Jensen, C. (2011) 'Less bad than its reputation: social spending as a proxy for welfare effort in cross-national studies', *Journal of Comparative Policy Analysis: Research and Practice*, vol 13, no 3, pp 327-40.

Kangas, O. (2004) 'Institutional development of sickness cash-benefit programmes in 18 OECD countries', *Social Policy and Administration*, vol 38, no 2, pp 190-203.

Knotz, C. and Nelson, M. (2013) 'Quantifying "conditionality": a new database on conditions and sanctions for unemployment benefit claimants', Paper prepared for the 2013 ESPAnet Conference, Poznan, 5-7 September.

Kühner, S. (2007) 'Country-level comparisons of welfare state change measures: another facet of the dependent variable problem within the comparative analysis of the welfare state?', *Journal of European Social Policy*, vol 17, no 1, pp 3-16.

Kuitto, K. (2011) 'More than just money: patterns of disaggregated welfare expenditure in the enlarged Europe', *Journal of European Social Policy*, vol 21, no 4, pp 348-64.

Kvist, J. (1999) 'Welfare reform in the Nordic countries in the 1990s: using fuzzy-set theory to assess conformity to ideal types', *Journal of European Social Policy*, vol 9, no 3, pp 231-52.

Myles, J. and Pierson, P. (2001) 'The comparative political economy of pension reform', in P. Pierson (ed) *The new politics of the welfare state*, Oxford: Oxford University Press, pp 305-33.

OECD (Organisation for Economic Co-operation and Development) (2014) *Social expenditure database*, Paris: OECD (www.oecd.org/social/expenditure.htm).

OECD (Organisation for Economic Co-operation and Development) (2014) *Benefits and wages*, Paris: OECD (www.oecd.org/els/benefitsandwagesstatistics.htm).

Olaskoaga-Larrauri, J., Aláez-Aller, R. and Díaz-de-Basurto, P. (2009) 'Measuring is believing! Improving conventional indicators of welfare state development', *Social Indicators Research*, vol 96, no 1, pp 113-31.

Pierson, P. (1994) *Dismantling the welfare state? Reagan, Thatcher and the politics of retrenchment,* Cambridge: Cambridge University Press.

Pierson, P. (2001) 'Coping with permanent austerity: welfare state restructuring in affluent democracies', in P. Pierson (ed) *The new politics of the welfare state*, Oxford: Oxford University Press, pp 410-56.

Schmitt, C. and Starke, P. (2011) 'Explaining convergence of OECD welfare states: a conditional approach', *Journal of European Social Policy*, vol 21, no 2, pp 120-35.

Scruggs, L. (2005) Comparative Welfare Entitlements Dataset (http://sp.uconn.edu/~scruggs/#links).

Scruggs, L. (2014) *Social welfare generosity scores in CWED 2: A methodological genealogy*, CWED Working Paper Series WP 01, February (accessed at: http://cwed2.org/Data/CWED2_WP_01_2014_Scruggs.pdf)

Scruggs, L. and Allan, J. (2006) 'Welfare-state decommodification in 18 OECD countries: a replication and revision', *Journal of European Social Policy*, vol 16, pp 55-72.

Scruggs, L. and Allan, J. (2008) 'Research Note: Social stratification and welfare regimes for the twenty-first century. Revisiting the three worlds of welfare capitalism', *World Politics*, vol 60, July, pp 642-64.

Scruggs, L., Jahn, D. and Kuitto, K. (2013) Comparative Welfare Entitlements Dataset 2, Version 2013-08 (http://cwed2.org/).

Serrano Pascual, A. (2007) 'Reshaping welfare states: activation regimes in Europe', in A. Serrano Pascual and L. Magnusson (eds) *Reshaping welfare states and activation regimes in Europe*, Brussels: Peter Lang, pp 11-34.

Stiller, S. and van Kersbergen, K. (2008) 'The matching problem within comparative welfare state research: how to bridge abstract theory and specific hypotheses', *Journal of Comparative Policy Analysis: Research and Practice*, vol 10, no 2, pp 133-49.

Streeck, W. and Thelen, K. (2005) *Institutional change in advanced political economies*, Oxford: Oxford University Press.

van Oorschot, W. (2012) 'Comparative welfare state analysis with survey based benefit recipiency data: the "dependent variable problem" revisited', Paper presented at SOFI, Swedish Institute for Social Research, Stockholm University, 14 November.

Vis, B. (2007) 'States of welfare or states of workfare? Welfare state restructuring in 16 capitalist democracies, 1985-2002', *Policy & Politics*, vol 35, pp 105-22.

Vis, B. (2010) *Politics of risk-taking: Welfare state reform in advanced democracies*, Amsterdam: Amsterdam University Press.

Wenzelburger, G., Zohlnhöfer, R. and Wolf, F. (2013) 'Implications of dataset choice in comparative welfare state research', *Journal of European Public Policy*, vol 20, no 9, pp 1229-50.

ELEVEN

The welfare modelling business in the East Asian welfare state debate

Gyu-Jin Hwang

Introduction

Since Esping-Andersen's (1990) *The three worlds of welfare capitalism* was published in 1990, many aspects of his work have been debated, criticised and reinvigorated (see, for example, Abrahamson, 1999; Arts and Gelissen, 2002; Powell and Barrientos, 2011). Of the many great welfare state scholars, he is undoubtedly one of the most widely cited and talked about. Particularly pertinent is his argument that welfare states cluster around certain distinct regime types. This practice of typologising, despite being criticised as 'the lowest form of intellectual endeavour' (Baldwin, 1996, p 26), has had an enduring influence in academic circles. While Esping-Andersen was not the first person to develop a welfare regime typology, his has been so influential that almost any discussion regarding the issue of welfare state modelling cannot be carried out without referring to his work as a starting point.

This chapter discusses the influence of Esping-Andersen's work in comparative analyses of the welfare state in East Asia. There are a number of good reasons for approaching the question of how his work has influenced debates from this angle. Arguably, the most obvious is the simple fact that East Asia is now a fully industrialised region and its countries rich enough to be part of the world(s) of welfare capitalism. This was not so at the moment Esping-Andersen undertook his study using data from 1980. Any retrospective on the contribution of *The three worlds of welfare capitalism* can gain much from looking at new members of the 'welfare capitalism club' in order to test, extend and, indeed, challenge the welfare models debate. We might add, too, the fact that rapid economic growth in the East Asian region means it has been at the heart of a growing interdisciplinary interface between comparative social policy and international development, facilitating exchange of theory between the two disciplines. Finally, and most importantly perhaps, these factors mean East Asia might provide a testing ground for new theoretical developments in the welfare modelling debate.

This chapter makes two distinct arguments concerning the influence of *The three worlds of welfare capitalism* on debates about social policy in East Asia. First, since publication of the book there has been an enormous increase of social scientific interest beyond the once dominant intellectual terrain of economic development. This not only includes an increasing number of single country case studies of welfare systems, but also comparative studies on specific social policy sectors, leading ultimately to a substantial literature debating whether there is a coherent welfare regime in East Asia. Second, this regime-oriented focus in the East Asian welfare debate has been a mixed blessing. On the one hand, we now know much more about the East Asian welfare systems and their uniqueness and similarities than before. On the other hand, this debate has not led to a more nuanced theory-building process. Limited in ambition, perhaps, little is available about East Asian welfare development that can parallel some of the path-breaking contributions concerning the development of welfare states in the West. As such, the focus on typologising that has been prompted by *The three worlds of welfare capitalism* might have produced a blind alley at the expense of the bigger and arguably more important question of why welfare regimes develop.

Modes of welfare studies in East Asia

Prior to publication of *The three worlds of welfare capitalism*, studies about social welfare in East Asia were almost non-existent. A small number of exceptions existed, including John Dixon and Hyung-Shik Kim's edited volume *Social welfare in Asia* (1985) and James Midgely's article 'Industrialization and welfare' (1986). Despite their contributions introducing East Asian welfare to the wider world, work remained either very descriptive or confined within the practice of enlarging 'N' for the testing of existing theories. For instance, James Midgely's study was not so much about finding the logic behind social policy development in East Asia, but more about emphasising the inadequacy of existing theories of welfare that were abstracted from Western experiences to new 'third world' cases. Hence, little was presented regarding what would explain social policy development in the region except the argument that all four little tigers (Hong Kong, South Korea, Singapore and Taiwan) had developed their provisions in a rather incremental fashion.

This began to change rather dramatically around the same time as Esping-Andersen's publication created an unprecedented level of academic interest in welfare provision in the region of East Asia. Prior to the publication, discussion about social policy in East Asia had been confined within the terrain of economic development. Given that hardly any country, with a possible exception of Japan, could qualify as a welfare state in the region, this was not surprising. Yet a critical turn in academic interest to the way the countries in East Asia were doing social policy began to emerge in the 1990s, arguably not as a result of what Esping-Andersen said about them, but rather as a result of what he did not, as suggestions East Asia may be the home of the fourth world of welfare missed by Esping-Andersen began to generate international debate beyond the domain of the economic performance of the tigers.

A pioneering study that suggested that there was uniqueness as well as commonality in East Asian welfare systems came from Catherine Jones (1990, 1993). Her early work on Hong Kong, Singapore, South Korea and Taiwan led her to conclude that East Asian countries made up their 'own brand' of welfare states, first termed as 'Oikonomic' (1990), and later revised as Confucian welfare states (1993). With a cultural factor as a central explanatory tool, the development of social policy in East Asia was no longer put aside as irrelevant. An increasing number of scholars, particularly within the region, soon began to engage in the question of how to explain social policy development in East Asia (see, for example, Ku, 1997; Takahashi, 1997; Tang, 1998; Kwon, 1999).

For a field of study that was much less developed than that on economic development and initially presented out to the world by the Western scholars, perhaps it was logical to expect that there should be more country-specific case studies in order to enrich our understanding of these societies before any explicit comparative material began to appear. Researched during the early and mid-1990s, and mostly conducted as part of their PhD research outside their home countries, a number of East Asian scholars published their own case study accounts of social policy development (for an excellent summary, see Ku with Jones, 2007). As far as English writing was concerned, these authors could be seen as pioneers in the study of social policy in individual countries in East Asia (see, for example, Takahashi, 1997; Ku, 1997; Tang, 1998; Kwon, 1999). These country-specific case studies were particularly welcomed, not least because they then led to the enrichment of more explicit comparative material in the next decade. Speaking of Takahashi's contribution, for instance, Ito Peng (2000, p 498) stated that '[d]espite enormous interest both within and outside Japan, there is very little written material on Japanese social welfare or social policy in English today.'

With little doubt, these studies established the groundwork for the development of more explicit comparative approaches as evidenced by an increasing volume of publications that began to deal with the region as a whole. Some were case specific either at a country level or at a system level or both. Others engaged more closely with the notion of welfare regimes, largely inspired by Esping-Andersen's typology (for a review, see Abrahamson, 2011). Esping-Andersen himself has not explicitly debated the East Asian welfare regime question. His first engagement with East Asia, apart from his inclusion of Japan in his original classification and Roger Goodman and Ito Peng's contribution in his edited volume (Esping-Andersen, 1996), seemed to be found in his responses to the criticisms raised on the possibility of adding a fourth regime to his three-way classification. In his 1999 book (Esping-Andersen, 1999), Esping-Andersen provided some arguably compelling reasons against the addition of a possible fourth world. Yet his argument that East Asia did not warrant an additional fourth regime was almost exclusively based on his prior analysis of the Japanese welfare regime where he concluded that there was nothing unique about it (Esping-Andersen, 1997). Instead of paying more attention to other neighbouring countries in East Asia, Esping-Andersen (1999) chose to investigate the centrality of families to welfare regimes as an additional measure to address the issues raised by both feminist theorists and those suggesting an East Asian fourth regime could be identified.

Perhaps the first systematic attempt to look at the possibility of an 'East Asian welfare model' was found in the publication of the same title by Roger Goodman and his colleagues (1998). Of many important points presented there, two key arguments seem to stand out. First, there does not seem to be a single, homogeneous welfare model in East Asia. Second, East Asia seems to present the case of the West's past rather than its future (Goodman et al, 1998). However, others have been keen to argue that there *is* indeed an identifiable and distinct welfare model in East Asia. In an ideal-typical sense, where smaller and larger variations from the norm can occur but still the greater picture remains intact and valid, Christian Aspalter (2006, p 298) suggests East Asia forms a conservative welfare regime where the market and family play a vital role in welfare provision. Different from Esping-Andersen's conservative welfare regime – Aspalter terms that a 'Christian democratic' welfare regime – he saw East Asia as placing emphasis on productive, economy-friendly welfare programmes with redistribution limited to immaterial resources such as health and education, demonstrating a 'commanding example of how to square the welfare circle' (2006, p 300).

East Asian welfare states are therefore understood by some to be distinctive since particular forms of productive welfare that do not slow down or obstruct economic growth are central (Aspalter, 2006, p 298). This relationship between economic and social policy was more clearly configured by Ian Holliday earlier, when he developed the productivist welfare capitalism thesis (2000). In fact, while much earlier work explored what was distinctive about East Asian welfare systems, Ian Holliday's approach was more directly engaged with the ways in which Esping-Andersen developed his typology. His starting point was to argue that the sphere of welfare capitalism should not be restricted to 'those capitalist states so strongly affected by their social policy as to be identifiable as welfare states' (2000, p 707). In fact, it should be extended to those 'capitalist states that do engage in social policy, while also subordinating it to other policy objectives' (2000, p 708). For him, East Asian welfare systems were distinctive, not because they had an ultimately different objective compared to their Western counterparts, such as the goal of nation-building or regime legitimation, but because it was the 'ways in which they pursue that objective that set them apart' (Holliday, 2000, p 716). His work has been highly influential and much cited. In fact, if Esping-Andersen's *The three worlds of welfare capitalism* is the work that is most frequently cited in the field of comparative welfare state research, Holliday's is its equivalent in the field of East Asian welfare state debate.

Productivist welfare capitalism and welfare state restructuring in East Asia

By directly engaging with Esping-Andersen's welfare state regime debate, Ian Holliday's productivist welfare capitalism thesis has attracted a great deal of attention. Yet his thesis was not the only one that identified the instrumental role of social policy in the promotion of economic growth. Taking cues from the notion of the developmental state originally developed by Chalmers Johnson (1982), a whole range of developmental welfare state literature emerged in relation to how the developmental state promoted growth-oriented strategies within which social policy was used to achieve economic growth, nation-building and political legitimacy (Deyo, 1992; Tang, 2000; Kwon, 2005b). In this tradition, a good deal of attention was paid to the making of the link between development studies and social policy, where the United

Nations Research Institute for Social Development (UNRISD) played an important role (Mkandawire, 2004; Kwon, 2005b). However, the question of whether East Asia forms a distinct welfare regime received much less attention, with more emphasis given to the logic behind the development of welfare systems. In comparison, Holliday's thesis added a missing dimension to Esping-Andersen's typology, with East Asia identified as a model.

According to Esping-Andersen (1999, p 35), a welfare regime can be defined as 'the combined, interdependent way in which welfare is produced and allocated between state, market, and family.' In his original typology, he used the term 'welfare state regime' instead of 'welfare regime'. In his definition of welfare regime, the state is only one of three key actors (the others being the market and the family). In his original classification, the state refers to a welfare state, and consequently, the three worlds of welfare capitalism refers to three welfare state regimes. Hence, the position of social policy as an organising principle of social order is either privileged, as is the case in social democratic regime, or not, as in liberal and corporatist welfare regime. For Holliday, this misses out those capitalist economies that subordinate social policy to other public policies while still doing social policy. Here, he is not claiming the addition of a fourth 'welfare *state* regime'. Rather his identification of a fourth, productivist world is as part of the world of *welfare capitalism* as a broader entity to include other welfare regimes.

Ian Gough and his colleagues made this point clear (Gough et al, 2004). By expanding the scope of analysis well beyond the Organisation for Economic Co-operation and Development (OECD) countries, they saw welfare state regimes as one of the three welfare regime types (the other two being informal security regimes and insecurity regimes). In their analyses, many East Asian countries were seen as transforming from productivist regimes to productivist welfare state regimes (Gough, 2004), the role of the state in protecting citizens against the common social risks increasing (hence the term welfare state), although the nature of social policy remains largely intact in promoting economic growth in this analysis. More than anything, this point about whether East Asian countries have undergone a significant regime shift has attracted a great deal of attention (see, for example, Ramesh, 2004; Kwon, 2005a, 2005b; Walker and Wong, 2005; Kim, 2008).

In his analysis of the Japanese welfare regime, Esping-Andersen (1997) was cautious of its nature, for it was not seen to have reached the point of crystallisation. As welfare regimes are a moving target rather than a static entity, then equal, if not more, caution should be applied to other countries in the region where growth has been more rapid in recent decades. Yet while the term 'transitional' can easily be applied to all the countries of the region, whether East Asian countries have undergone 'transformation' requires a close examination. By definition, transformation indicates a fundamental shift in underlying logic. This temporal dimension of welfare state variability (that is, the degree to which states have experienced change over time) began to put pressure on existing classifications of the East Asian welfare regime. Particularly notable is the challenge against the validity of Holliday's productivist thesis, partly because of conceptual ambiguity embedded in his theorising, and partly because of significant changes to social policy that have taken place in the region.

First, the productivist world of welfare capitalism is seen by Holliday to be the polar opposite of the social democratic world. Yet Nordic 'productivism' maximises the productive potential of the citizenry too. This is, of course, unlike workfare in the US, which refers to conditional welfare rather than providing necessary resources and motivation to work (Esping-Andersen, 1999, p 80). Still, all welfare states are deeply productivist as they are 'all centrally concerned to ensure a smooth supply of labour to productive sectors of the formal economy and they are all anxious that the welfare state not get too badly in the way of that' (Goodin, 2001, p 14). Enhancing productivity and economic growth has always been the important feature for consideration when social provisions are debated elsewhere too (Bonoli and Shinkawa, 2005, p 21). Indeed, social policy has increasingly become subsumed under economic policy, and this subordination of social policy to economic considerations is becoming a defining characteristic within the standard welfare state model (Jessop, 1993). For this reason, the productivist assumptions may not be uniquely East Asian.

Second, the passage of time has suggested that East Asian countries are now deviating from the functional imperatives for economic development, the possibility of which is by definition ruled out by the productivist argument. A number of significant signs, albeit arguably inconclusive, indicated this. First, the growth of social provision in East Asia shares a similar pattern of coverage extension found elsewhere (Pierson, 2004, pp 223-32), while the sweeping dominance of insurance-based provision is improving its risk-pooling functions both by merging multiple insurance funds to one and by achieving near-universalism, thereby making the distinction between different occupational categories more or less meaningless (Hwang, 2012, p 4). Even the institutional intention or purpose behind the introduction of social provision is changing from legitimacy gaining and economic growth to democratic responses and social and economic justice (Peng and Wong, 2008, p 74).

Subsequently, this second point has raised some important questions. What accounts for this process of welfare deepening? Has this change led to a fundamental regime shift in East Asia? Rigorous debates began to emerge by examining a number of important factors including labour market change, dramatic socioeconomic shifts, political realignments and financial crisis. Of particular importance has been the process of democratic transition, either in the form of power alternation (as in Taiwan and South Korea) or in the form of the end of one-party dominance (as in Japan). The ultimate foundation that provided these countries with strong state autonomy in governing the economy has come to an end. Through democratisation, truly meaningful political competition finally came to the scene. As a result, the process of social policy-making has opened up its channels to a wide range of constituent groups at an unprecedented level. 'Democracy is clearly not a necessary condition for expansion of social commitments', Stephan Haggard argues, 'but democratic governments have greater incentives to respond to total pressures than authoritarian ones, *ceteris paribus*' (2005, p 156). In fact, this very process is what differentiates the Northeast Asian countries of Japan, South Korea and Taiwan from their Southern counterparts of Hong Kong and Singapore (Kwon, 2005a). Social policy institutions have increasingly become much more symbiotic with, rather than subordinate to, economic objectives (Peng, 2004; Kwon et al, 2009).

For all these reasons, many commentators are very optimistic about the prospects of East Asia moving away from the developmental or productivist assumptions (Hort and Kuhnle, 2000; Ramesh, 2004; Kwon, 2005a). In the cases of South Korea and Taiwan, Ito Peng and Joseph Wong (2008, p 75) argue that 'unlike under authoritarian developmentalism, [during] which the extension of social policy was targeted for the purposes of meeting productivist imperatives, social provision during the democratic era was in fact intended to be universal, a de facto right of social citizenship rather than a social benefit exchanged for productivity.' For the Korean experience, in particular, where the extent of welfare expansion has been most dramatic (Hwang, 2012), Paul Wilding (2008, p 29) argues that it is 'probably much more of a hybrid' case of somewhere between purely productivist and a 'pure' welfare state, while Young-Jun Choi (2012, p 289) sees it as 'moving towards the liberal welfare state regime.' Stein Kuhnle (2004, p 61), after examining Korea's productive welfare, has gone as far as to claim that 'tentatively it looks as if the Korean welfare system may in due time have more in common with the "Nordic" or Scandinavian, "social-democratic" welfare regime than any of the other European and Western types.'

Nonetheless, many of those who identified a clear productivist outlook in East Asia continue to hold their earlier position. For instance, Huck-Ju Kwon (2005a, p 494) notes that 'the change in the overall goal of economic policy, and a shift toward democratic politics, has made the developmental welfare state more inclusive in both Korea and Taiwan. What remains unchanged is that social policy is set and used for economic development, even though social inclusion is now considered an important social policy goal.' Responding to the critiques of his original productivist thesis, Holliday (2005; see also Kwon and Holliday, 2007) points to the resilience of strong productivist traits found in welfare reforms including cuts in old-age pensions, limited coverage of healthcare, and a strong emphasis on workfare in social assistance. Aspalter (2011, p 741), too, maintains his earlier views, stating that in East Asia, 'redistribution takes on a more indirect form – it is directed toward growth-generating investment.... East Asian governments have come to appreciate the fact that social policy not only provides the essential ingredients for political peace and power maintenance, but also the key ingredient to stable and continuous economic growth.'

To date, therefore, the question of how far expansion of welfare marks a triumph of social policy over economic policy remains a moot point. Out of this debate of whether East Asia has a different model of welfare and whether it has changed over time, we also see parallel debates about different forces shaping welfare development in the region. Here, political and social reforms are intertwined, while economic forces that are part of the mix continue to influence social policy development in East Asia. Indeed, welfare reforms were initiated not only to correct dysfunctions that had emerged over the period of fast economic development, but also to lay new foundations for future growth and to address deep concerns regarding the survival of the economy. Despite the fact that we have not yet reached a concrete conclusion, largely because East Asia is a fast moving target undergoing a process of welfare state regime crystallisation, East Asian experience has sparked some theoretical consolidation on a number of aspects. Importantly, this is the area where East Asia could be a testing ground for existing theories of welfare. At the same time, this is the area that East Asia could be the context within which new theories of welfare could develop too. Although at the margins of the debate to date, a theoretical innovation may be made via robust theory building that is more explicitly derived from the East Asian experience; it is this to which we now turn.

Theories of welfare state development in East Asia

Comparative welfare state research is almost always about finding similarities and differences. For Esping-Andersen, it is not so much about his successful identification of similarities between the countries under the umbrella of social democratic, liberal and corporatist welfare regimes; it is more about three distinct clusters that have followed three institutionally distinct pathways over a stretched period of time. Behind the construction of regime typology, there is a clear process of theory building. Of the well-known theories of welfare state development, power resources theory (or class mobilisation thesis) seeks to explain broad cross-national differences in welfare states. Operationalised through the strength of Social Democratic parties, this approach explains the origins of welfare states as well as their expansion and nature (see, for example, Korpi, 1983; Esping-Andersen and Korpi, 1984; Hicks, 1999; Huber and Stephens, 2001). Strong leftist parties and labour unions have the political resources to enact their redistributive visions into public policy, creating large and generous welfare states. Where they are weak, welfare provision is stingier and less redistributive. Critiques of this theory, however, argue that it overlooks the role and indeed power of non-leftist parties, cross-class alliances as well as extra-parliamentary organisations in policy development (Iversen et al, 2000; Swenson, 2002). As an early advocate of this theory, Esping-Andersen's typology has its foundation in this theory. However, through the analysis of cross-class coalitions and various power-mobilising groups, greater nuance was introduced to form three worlds, reflecting the power of liberal, labour or conservative political forces.

Building on established theories, whether flawed or not, is often the starting point of a new theoretical innovation. By the nature of social science, comparative research provides an excellent avenue to provide this opportunity. Unlike the volume and quality of literature available for the developmental pathways to welfare states in the West, however, there is a notable deficit of the intellectual progress on the development of welfare in East Asia. Not only is there a lack of explicit comparative attempts to suggest, test and modify the multiplicity of various factors at work with varying degrees of influence and intensity over an extended period of time; there is also a shortage of coherently and systematically managed single-authored – or meaningful collaborative – efforts to address the emergence and development of welfare in East Asia similar to the work of Douglas Ashford (1986), Peter Baldwin (1990) and, of course, Esping-Andersen (1990). Indeed, much of the comparative welfare state research on East Asia is written by authors in (or specialising on) the different countries, often with different specialities, thereby lacking consistency and coherence at a cross-national level. Given the fact that the academic inquiry into these issues is relatively recent, this is perhaps understandable. Lack of comparable datasets for East Asian countries, many of which are not even part of the OECD world, and, in the case of Taiwan, excluded from some international databases due to diplomatic tensions, makes it particularly difficult for individual researchers to produce a broader, deeper and more well-rounded treatment of comparative research agendas.

Some exceptions are out there, such as Kwong-Leung Tang's (2000) work on social development in East Asia, and Christian Aspalter's (2001) on conservative welfares state systems in East Asia. As rare single-authored books, they cover all four or more countries in the region. Impressive and ambitious they may seem, the theoretical progress out of these attempts is rather limited. Tang (2000) suggests that each of the four little tiger economies has unique social welfare development, but there is no overarching theoretical framework that accounts for their development. Instead of examining the question of what determines welfare state development in the region, he paid more attention to the nature of East Asian welfare, identifying each with a distinct name such as the capital investment state of Singapore, the authoritarian social insurance state of Taiwan, the authoritarian developmental state of Korea and the capital investment state of Hong Kong. Aspalter (2001), in comparison, paid more attention to historical as well as institutional factors to account for East Asian welfare. By examining a number of political determinants including political institutions, political legitimisation, and party and electoral competition, he concluded that the label 'conservative welfare state systems' characterised East Asia. Yet apart from his central point that political factors matter, no clear theoretical proposition is advanced here.

More recently, Stephan Haggard and Robert Kaufman (2008) provided a more explicit explanatory account for distinctive welfare trajectories in East Asia, along with Latin America and Eastern Europe. Key to their explanatory account is 'an extended historical consideration of how critical realignments, development strategies, and regime type interacted in altogether different regional settings' (2008, pp 19-20). Similar to the previous studies, the key set of analytical factors is largely drawn from the factors that identified the experiences of the advanced welfare states. They found that no single determining factor explains welfare state expansion, retrenchment and change. But they validate the positivity between the labour power and the progressivity of the welfare state, the benefits of democracy, and the possibility of a broader range of economic alternatives in a wider context (Haggard and Kaufman, 2008, pp 21-4). Perhaps the most valuable lesson that can be drawn from their work is that all of those powerful explanatory variables – the merits of the power resource approach, the effects of economic structure and performance on welfare commitments, and the enduring effects of institutions – will continue to enter the new testing ground.

Systematic, comparative research to advance a new theory-building process has been lacking. Nonetheless, the East Asian experience has sparked some theoretical challenges and possible consolidation on a number of aspects. First, with little doubt, shortage of readily available comparative data has been a major obstacle in the process of theory building. While Esping-Andersen's work has prompted the development of even more extensive datasets on welfare in his original 18 countries (see, for example, Scruggs et al, 2014), the progress of building comparable datasets for East Asia has been slow and is still in its infancy (for further discussion, see Park and Jung, 2013). Nonetheless, some notable attempts have been made, for instance, to test the hypothesis of whether the developmental welfare state truly exists (Lee and Ku, 2007). Fifteen indicators were developed to represent the assumed characteristics of developmental welfare states, nine of which were selected in particular to refer to developmentalism (2007, p 205). The research concludes that 'an East Asian welfare regime does exist, quite separate from the three classical groupings' (2007, p 206). Yet the demonstrated characteristics including family supports, non-coverage in pension, gender wage lag, social investment and self-reliance in retired life may not necessarily be found uniquely in East Asia. In other words, there is a boundary problem in theoretical terms for what should or should not be included as 'developmental'.

In part, this boundary problem has been addressed by using a fuzzy set ideal-type analysis, this time in order to examine whether there exists a clear case of unique East Asian productive welfare capitalism (Hudson and Kühner, 2012). Here four dimensions are identified to indicate productive-protective dimensions including education investment, training investment (as a share of the total active labour market policy [ALMP] budget), income protection and employment protection. Included are 23 OECD countries as well as seven East Asian economies. The research finds that there does not seem to be a coherent East Asian model of welfare, while the US and New Zealand fit better to the productive welfare type than any other East Asian countries. Only

Singapore and Malaysia come close as a weak-productive type (Hudson and Kühner, 2012, pp 55-6).

Despite the utilisation of fuzzy set analysis that offers a 'bridge between quantitative and qualitative approaches' (Hudson and Kühner, 2012, p 41), there still remains the question of exactly what should be considered as productivist elements. For one, what differentiates them from neoliberal economy-friendly welfare restructuring elsewhere is unclear in Holliday's proposition (Kim, 2008). Indicators such as a share of the total ALMP budget may be undisputable, not least because the Swedish invention of an ALMP in the 1930s was a typical productive strategy to contribute to economic development. Yet the productivist argument in the East Asian context is conceptualised in a different form. Holliday (2000), for instance, explains that the extent to which social rights extend beyond the productive elements in society is what differentiates a more or less pure form of productivist welfare type. Here, Singapore is a purer form, while Japan is less so, for in the latter social rights are extended, albeit limited. Education is often seen as the vanguard of productive approach in 'social policy as social investment' literature (Deeming and Smyth, 2015). Yet universal education is an extension of social rights too, and at the same time it is a strategy of generating a productive workforce.

Some more concrete examples could highlight the productivst intention of social policy in East Asia, such as the introduction of national pensions and their funds as a source of capital accumulation in order to accelerate industrialisation. The problem is that this is found elsewhere too. In Sweden, for instance, supplementary pension funds were used to provide housing in urban areas, while the national pension funds in Finland were used to build up national basic infrastructure (Kangas and Palme, 2005). This, then, makes the distinction ambiguous between what Esping-Andersen (1997, p 181) calls 'Sweden's celebrated productivistic social policy' and Holliday's notion of social policy being subordinate to economic policy (for further discussion, see Kim, 2008). This relationship between social policy and economic policy is further confused by the emerging literature on social investment strategies. This time, the distinction is between the Nordic 'heavy' (egalitarian and protective) and the liberal 'light' (pro-market). In this dichotomy, the East Asian version of productivist welfare seems to lie in the 'tendency for the productivist values of social investment to be promoted at the expense of, rather than as a complement to, the value of social protection' (Deeming and Smyth, 2015, p 302; see also Kwon and Holliday, 2007).

Inspired by Esping-Andersen's typology, the welfare modelling business in general and the productivist thesis in particular has made an important contribution to the East Asian welfare debate. Yet we might have been too obsessed with the regimisation exercise rather than examining how different types have come about in the first place, overlooking the central question of why we have these different paths. This not only applies to Esping-Andersen's typology, but also to Holliday's. As an explanatory model, the productivist thesis has been criticised for placing functionalism at its theoretical core, hence, 'almost everything unique in the Korean welfare state is reduced to the functional prerequisites for economic development' (Yang, 2013, p 460). Yet Holliday's analysis was much less about providing 'systemic' or explanatory accounts in relation to social policy development in the region, and more about the missing 'productivist' dimension in Esping-Andersen's (1990) original typology. Even in his later analysis Holliday's (2005) emphasis on policy continuity was more about the limited characteristic of social policy reform rather than how the structural constraints imposed by the economy influenced the directions of social policy reform (Hwang, 2012). In other words, the problem was not so much about his proposition of an explanatory account – it was much more about the lack thereof. In this sense, literature derived from the developmental state logic seems to have a more robust theoretical foundation.

A way forward

In the search for reasons why particular nations developed their welfare provision along one particular path or another, the developmental approach emphasised the intense political process East Asia has undergone. The productivist account adds the systemic or structural dimension to this to enhance our understanding. In this mix of political and socioeconomic accounts, however, surprisingly little systematic attention has been paid to the three factors that Esping-Andersen (1990, p 29) identified as critical: the nature of class mobilisation; class political coalition structures; and the historical legacy of regime institutionalisation. For the nature of class mobilisation, especially of the working class, the weak political power of the working class in East Asia might have been the reason why it was not given sufficient attention and subsequently understood as the reason why these countries lag in developing a welfare state. Yet the working class in the region, arguably even the most militant Korean one at its peak in particular, did not fight for class solidarity and the building of the welfare state. In fact, Esping-

Andersen (1990, p 29) states that 'there is absolutely no compelling reason to believe that workers will automatically and naturally forge a socialist class identity; nor is it plausible that their mobilisation will look especially Swedish.'

What appears to be more important is 'the history of political class coalitions'. In fact, Esping-Andersen himself, distancing away from his earlier preference of a power resources model, argues that working–class strength itself does not help explain much of the history of welfare state development: 'It is a historical fact that welfare state construction has depended on political coalition-building. The structure of class-coalitions is much more decisive than are the power resources of any single class' (1990, p 30). Until recently, however, conservative political dominance in East Asia has made this important enquiry rather difficult to unpack. It is since the late 1990s that the emerging democratic class struggle has signalled a change in political dynamics and its intensity, thereby opening up the possibility of investigating this much more historically. The East Asian experiences validate that organised labour should no longer be assumed to pursue class solidarity and social welfare. Rather, its behaviour is presumed to be self-interest-oriented and heavily influenced by the existence of cross-class alliances as well as the institutional rules of the game (see, for example, Yang, 2013). Indeed, the success of emerging class coalitions in East Asia depends increasingly on the support of the new middle classes, the sort of analysis that has so far been lacking in the region despite the fact that this 'history of political class coalitions is the most decisive cause of welfare state variations' (Esping-Andersen, 1990, p 1).

While the previous developmental and productivist accounts focus more on Esping-Andersen's third element – the historical legacy of regime institutionalisation – the system immaturity has made a thorough investigation of this difficult. Fast-changing political dynamics and socioeconomic structures also have complicated matters. In other words, the entwining of past welfare reforms and existing welfare arrangements with the institutionalisation of class preferences and political behaviour is an ongoing process that has yet to crystallise. Social policies, once legislated and implemented, create new popular constituencies favouring extensive welfare programmes, and shape the political process from which social policies emerge. This notion of path dependency and policy feedback effects should be more prominent in scholarly work as East Asian welfare systems mature.

At the same time, East Asia is likely to be an important testing ground for how the crystallisation of its welfare regime will be configured and affected by newly emerging challenges. Many of the new risks emerging in the region are not necessarily unique, but they are coming at an unprecedented speed, as evidenced in the rapid ageing of the population. No country has ever experienced anything like this yet, which places the East Asian welfare debate at the forefront of new theoretical building ground. Not surprisingly, Esping-Andersen (et al, 2002; Esping-Andersen, 2009) discussed these challenges in his later work, but only within his comfort zone of the standard welfare states. Against the risks of an ageing population, the emerging relevance of family policy, which has long been seen as irrelevant in East Asia, is gaining momentum. The processes of industrialisation as well as de-industrialisation are unfolding simultaneously, complicating the directions of the labour market policy. Due to the compressed, intense and unprecedented speed of structural transformation, social policy responses may have to be innovative rather than path-dependent. Here, East Asia provides a context within which new theories of welfare development can be developed.

All in all, a more direct engagement with theoretical challenges derived from the construction of regime typology is crucial if we wish to move the East Asian welfare debate further forward. As Peter Baldwin (1996, p 29) argues, it is 'the theory that creates the typology, not the typology the theory'. Despite numerous criticisms, Esping-Andersen's typology has proven to be remarkably robust, even 25 years after its creation. What makes Esping-Andersen's analysis most compelling is his insistence that, in Paul Pierson's words (2000, p 809), 'welfare states be seen as parts of complex, historically generated configurations. The three worlds did not result from more or less of a few discrete, independent master variables but from the cumulative effects of a number of interdependent causal factors.' Esping-Andersen's typology is an amalgamation of historically informed theoretical work. In order to configure a distinctive East Asian welfare model, a theoretical debate should precede typology. This seems particularly significant, not only because the debate on the nature of an East Asian welfare model seems to have reached a deadlock ever since Holliday's contribution, but also because little serious theoretical advancement has been made in the debate concerning the pathways of welfare state development. Unintended, perhaps, the typologies might have been a distraction from the real debate Esping-Andersen would have liked us to have about welfare in East Asia. In this sense, he might have created a Frankenstein's monster.

References

Abrahamson, P. (1999) 'The welfare modelling business', *Social Policy & Administration*, vol 33, no 4, pp 394-415.

Abrahamson, P. (2011) 'The welfare modelling business revisited: the case of East Asian welfare regimes', in G.-J. Hwang (ed) *New welfare states in East Asia: Global challenges and restructuring*, Cheltenham: Edward Elgar, pp 15-34.

Arts, W. and Gelissen, J. (2002) 'The three worlds of welfare capitalism or more? A state-of-the-art report', *Journal of European Social Policy*, vol 12, no 2, pp 137-58.

Ashford, D.E. (1986) *The emergence of the welfare states*, Oxford: Basil Blackwell.

Aspalter, C. (2001) *Conservative welfare state systems in East Asia*, Westport, CT: Praeger.

Aspalter, C. (2006) 'The East Asian welfare model', *International Journal of Social welfare*, vol 15, no 4, pp 290-301.

Aspalter, C. (2011) 'The development of ideal-typical welfare regime theory', *International Social Work*, vol 54, no 6, pp 735-50.

Baldwin, P. (1990) *The politics of social solidarity: The class basis of the European welfare states, 1875-1975*, Cambridge: Cambridge University Press.

Baldwin, P. (1996) 'Can we define a European welfare state model', in B. Greve (ed) *Comparative welfare systems: The Scandinavian model in a period of change*, London: Palgrave Macmillan, pp 29-44.

Bonoli, G. and Shinkawa, T. (2005) 'Population ageing and the logics of pension reform in Western Europe, East Asia and North America', in G. Bonoli and T. Shinkawa (eds) *Ageing and pension reform around the world*, Cheltenham: Edward Elgar, pp 1-23.

Choi, Y.-J. (2012) 'End of the era of productivist welfare capitalism? Diverging welfare regimes in East Asia', *Asian Journal of Social Science*, vol 40, no 3, pp 275-94.

Deeming, C. and Smyth, P. (2015) 'Social investment after neoliberalism: policy paradigms and political platforms', *Journal of Social Policy*, vol, 44, no 2, pp 297-318.

Deyo, F.C. (1992) 'The political economy of social policy formation: East Asia's newly industrialised countries', in R. Applebaum and J. Henderson (eds) *States and development in Asian Pacific Rim*, London: Sage, pp 289-306.

Dixon, J. and Kim, H.S. (eds) (1985) *Social welfare in Asia*, London: Croom Helm.

Esping-Andersen, G. (1990) *The three worlds of welfare capitalism*, Cambridge: Polity Press.

Esping-Andersen, G. (ed) (1996) *Welfare states in transition: National adaptations in global economies*, London: Sage.

Esping-Andersen, G. (1997) 'Hybrid or unique? The Japanese welfare state between Europe and America', *Journal of European Social Policy*, vol 7, no 3, pp 179-89.

Esping-Andersen, G. (1999) *Social foundations of postindustrial economies*, Oxford: Oxford University Press.

Esping-Andersen, G. (2009) *The incomplete revolution: Adapting to women's new roles*, Cambridge: Polity Press.

Esping-Andersen, G. and Korpi, W. (1984) 'Social policy as class politics in post-war capitalism: Scandinavia, Australia, and Germany', in J.H. Goldthorpe (ed) *Order and conflict in contemporary capitalism: Studies in the political economy of Western European nations*, Oxford: Clarendon Press, pp 179-208.

Esping-Andersen, G. with Gallie, D., Hemerijck, A. and Myles, J. (2002) *Why we need a new welfare state*, Oxford: Oxford University Press.

Goodin, R.E. (2001) 'Work and welfare: towards a post-productivist welfare regime', *British Journal of Political Science*, vol 31, no 1, pp 13-39.

Goodman, R., White, G. and Kwon, H.-J. (eds) (1998) *The East Asian welfare model: Welfare orientalism and state*, London: Routledge.

Gough, I. (2004) 'East Asia: the limits of productivist regimes', in I. Gough et al (eds) *Insecurity and welfare regimes in Asia, Africa, and Latin America: Social policy in developmental contexts*, Cambridge: Cambridge University Press, pp 169-201.

Gough, I., Barrientos, A., Bevan, P., Davis, P. and Room, G. (eds) (2004) *Insecurity and welfare regimes in Asia, Africa, and Latin America: Social policy in developmental contexts*, Cambridge: Cambridge University Press.

Haggard, S. (2005) 'The political economy of the Asian welfare state', in R. Boyd and T.-W. Ngo (eds) *Asian States: Beyond the developmental perspectives*, London: Routledge Curzon, pp 145-71.

Haggard, S. and Kaufman, R. (2008) *Development, democracy, and welfare states: Latin America, East Asia, and Eastern Europe*, Princeton, NJ: Princeton University Press.

Hicks, A. (1999) *Social democracy and welfare capitalism: A century of income security politics*, Ithaca, NY: Cornell University Press.

Holliday, I. (2000) 'Productivist welfare capitalism: social policy in East Asia', *Political Studies*, vol 48, no 4, pp 706-23.

Holliday, I. (2005) 'East Asian social policy in the wake of the financial crisis: farewell to productivism?', *Policy & Politics*, vol 33, no 1, pp 145-62.

Hort, S.O. and Kuhnle, S. (2000) 'The coming of East and South-East Asian welfare states', *Journal of European Social Policy*, vol 10, no 2, pp 162-84.

Huber, E. and Stephens, J.D. (2001) *Development and crisis of the welfare state: Parties and policies in global markets*, Chicago, IL: University of Chicago Press.

Hudson, J. and Kühner, S. (2012) 'Analysing the productive dimensions of welfare: looking beyond East Asia', in G.-J. Hwang (ed) *New welfare states in East Asia: Global challenges and restructuring*, Cheltenham: Edward Elgar, pp 35-60.

Hwang, G.-J. (2012) 'Explaining welfare state adaptation in East Asia: the cases of Japan, Korea and Taiwan', *Asian Journal of Social Science*, vol 40, no 2, pp 174-202.

Iversen, T., Pontusson, J. and Soskice, D. (eds) (2000) *Unions, employers, and central banks: Macroeconomic coordination and institutional change in social market economies*, Cambridge: Cambridge University Press.

Jessop, B. (1993) 'Towards a Schumpeterian workfare state? Preliminary remarks on post-Fordist political economy', *Studies in Political Economy*, vol 40, pp 7-39.

Johnson, C. (1982) *MITI and the Japanese miracles: The growth of industrial policy 1925-75*, Stanford, CA: Stanford University Press.

Jones, C. (1990) 'Hong Kong, Singapore, South Korea and Taiwan: Oikonomic welfare states', *Government and Opposition*, vol 25, no 4, pp 446-62.

Jones, C. (1993) 'The Pacific challenge: Confucian welfare states', in C. Jones (ed) *New perspectives on the welfare state in Europe*, London: Routledge, pp 198-217.

Kangas, O. and Palme, J. (eds) (2005) *Social policy and economic development in the Nordic countries*, Basingstoke: Palgrave Macmillan.

Korpi, W. (1983) *The democratic class struggle*, London: Routledge & Kegan Paul.

Kim, Y.-M. (2008) 'Beyond East Asian welfare productivism in South Korea', *Policy & Politics*, vol 36, no 1, pp 109-25.

Ku, Y.-W. (1997) *Welfare capitalism in Taiwan: State, economy and social policy*, Basingstoke: Macmillan.

Ku, Y.-W., with Jones, C.F. (2007) 'Developments in East Asian welfare studies', *Social Policy & Administration*, vol 41, no 2, pp 115-31.

Kuhnle, S. (2004) 'Productive welfare in Korea: moving towards a European welfare state type?', in R. Mishra, S. Kuhnle, N. Gilbert, and K. Chung (eds) *Modernizing the Korean welfare state: Towards the productive welfare model*, New Brunswick, NJ: Transaction Publishers, pp 47-64.

Kwon, H.-J. (1999) *The welfare state in Korea: The politics of legitimation*, Basingstoke: Macmillan.

Kwon, H.-J. (2005a) 'Transforming the developmental welfare State in East Asia', *Development and Change*, vol 36, no 3, pp 477-97.

Kwon, H.-J. (ed) (2005b) *Transforming the developmental welfare state in East Asia*, London: Palgrave Macmillan and UNRISD.

Kwon, H.-J., Mkandawire, T. and Palme, J. (2009) 'Introduction: social policy and economic development in late industrializers', *International Journal of Social Welfare*, vol 18, no 1, pp 1-11.

Kwon, S. and Holliday, I. (2007) 'The Korean welfare state: a paradox of expansion in an era of globalization and economic crisis', *International Journal of Social Welfare*, vol 16, no 3, pp 242-8.

Lee, Y.-J. and Ku, Y.-W. (2007) 'East Asian welfare regimes: testing the hypothesis of the developmental welfare state', *Social Policy & Administration*, vol 41, no 2, pp 197-212.

Midgely, J. (1986) 'Industrialization and welfare: the case of the four little tigers', *Social Policy & Administration*, vol 20, no 3, pp 225-38.

Mkandawire, T. (ed) (2004) *Social policy in a development context*, London: Palgrave Macmillan and UNRISD.

Park, C.-U. and Jung, D. (2013) 'Challenges and directions: building a comparative quantitative dataset for East Asian social policies', in M. Izuhara (ed) *Handbook on East Asian social policy*, Cheltenham: Edward Elgar, pp 334-69.

Peng, I. (2000) 'Review, *The emergence of welfare society in Japan* by Mutsuko Takahashi and *Poverty, equality, and growth: The politics of economic need in postwar Japan* by Deborah J. Milly', *Journal of Japanese Studies*, vol 26, no 2, pp 498-502.

Peng, I. (2004) 'Postindustrial pressures, political regime shifts, and Social policy reforms in Japan and South Korea', *Journal of East Asian Studies*, vol 4, no 3, pp 389-425.

Peng, I. and Wong, J. (2008) 'Institutions and institutional purpose: continuity and change in East Asian social policy', *Politics and Society*, vol 36, no 1, pp 61-88.

Pierson, C. (2004) 'Late industrializer and the development of welfare regimes', *Acta Politica*, vol 40, no 4, pp 395-418.

Pierson, P. (2000) 'Three worlds of welfare state research', *Comparative Political Studies*, vol 33, no 6/7, pp 791-821.

Powell, M. and Barrientos, A. (2011) 'An audit of the welfare modelling business', *Social Policy & Administration*, vol 45, no 1, pp 69-84.

Ramesh, M. (2004) *Social policy in East and Southeast Asia: Education, health, housing and income maintenance*, London: Routledge.

Scruggs, L., Jahn, D. and Kuitto, K. (2014) Comparative Welfare Entitlements Dataset 2, Version 2014-03, University of Connecticut and University of Greifswald.

Swenson, P.A. (2002) *Capitalists against markets: The making of labor markets and welfare states in the United States and Sweden*, Oxford: Oxford University Press.

Takahashi, M. (1997) *The emergence of welfare society in Japan*, Aldershot: Avebury.

Tang, K.-L. (1998) *Colonial state and social policy: Social welfare development in Hong Kong 1842-1997*, Lanham, MD: University Press of America.

Tang, K.-L. (2000) *Social welfare development in East Asia*, London: Palgrave.

Walker, A. and Wong, C.-K. (eds) (2005) *East Asian welfare regimes in transition: From Confucianism to globalisation*, Bristol: Policy Press.

Wilding, P. (2008) 'Is the East Asian welfare model still productive?', *Journal of Asian Public Policy*, vol 1, no 1, pp 18-31.

Yang, J.-J. (2013) 'Parochial welfare politics and the small welfare state in South Korea', *Comparative Politics*, vol 45, no 4, pp 457-75.

TWELVE

The role of regime-type analysis in OECD work on social policy and family

Dominic Richardson[1]

Introduction

For over two decades, social policy researchers have turned to regime classifications to summarise how countries organise their social protection systems, in order to aid comparisons and to explain findings of a range of empirical analyses. But although work on policy typologies, such as *The three worlds of welfare capitalism* (Esping-Andersen, 1990), and other more recent influential pieces (see, for example, Korpi and Palme, 1998; Ferrarini, 2006), are favoured citations in the academic literature, questions remain about how this work has fed into discussions among policy-makers. In particular, how has it been used in the discussions of policy transfer between policy-makers in the countries compared?

This chapter explores this question from the perspective of the work of the OECD Social Policy Division, and in particular, the work on child and family policy analysis and evaluation undertaken there.

The main message is that, although welfare regimes have not been used comprehensively, systematically, or indeed consistently in OECD policy discussions, reference to geographic classifications with implicit and sometimes explicit welfare regime messages (such as 'social democratic regimes of continental Europe' [OECD, 2005, p 453]) are common. Geographic or linguistic classifications (Anglophones) are used to imply shared historic welfare 'cultures' which resonate in present practice. These types of classification references have regularly found their way into descriptive analysis, sometimes in theoretical propositions (see, for example, Considine, 2006), but had not been used in more complex empirical analysis until recently (the type of analysis designed to evaluate policy effects, such as OECD, 2015c, although these are new classifications 'built' as part of the analysis). Although there is no obvious justification for the lack of more sophisticated analysis using regime types, it is likely to be due to insufficient data for undertaking macro-level analyses of sufficient detail to supersede available evaluative evidence undertaken at the micro level.

Following an introduction to the work of the OECD Social Policy Division, and how policy is being discussed and debated within it, the remainder of the chapter is structured as follows: the subsequent section focuses on the stream of work on child and family policy and wellbeing, and how regime types have featured in this work; it is followed by a section that introduces new work where regime types have led new empirical analysis built on data availability; and the penultimate section reflects on the potential developments of regime-type analysis for ongoing policy discussions. The final section concludes.

How policy is discussed and debated in the OECD Social Policy Division

Child and family policy analysis in the OECD Social Policy Division refers specifically to work on social protection policies and wellbeing. From the inaugural *Babies and Bosses* series (see, for example, OECD, 2002a), through *Doing better for children* and *Doing better for families* (OECD 2009, 2011a), and the OECD Family database (OECD, 2015a), to more recent analysis comparing the effectiveness and efficiency of cash versus in-kind family benefits (OECD, 2015c: forthcoming), the OECD Social Policy Division has contributed to recent debates on work–family balance, child poverty and wellbeing, social protection for non-traditional family types, child protection policies, youth activity, fertility and more.

In the Social Policy Division, as with other divisions and directorates in the OECD, the work undertaken is communicated directly to policymakers through reports, but also through presentations, reviews and discussion of the various work streams. Annual or twice-yearly meetings are held with OECD country delegations, made up of social protection[2] ministry representatives that oversee the work undertaken, and every five years ministerial meetings are held for, and attended by, ministers from the social protection departments of each OECD country. In these meetings, discussions focus on the main messages of the projects (for individual countries as well as generalisable findings) and on proposals for future work. These meetings also provide a forum for countries themselves to showcase recent or successful policies and programmes.

During the development of the child and family stream of work – and OECD publications in general are no different – country categories and classifications have been regularly used to summarise results of descriptive analysis of child and family policies. Two points are important to make, however. First, country classifications are by no means expected when analysing the data; these are often considered broad 'first-stage' reflections on findings that require further explanation and/or justification. And second, welfare regimes based on policy choices are not commonly used, at least when compared to more simplified/inferential categories – and arguably less useful categories for policy evaluation, such as geographic (for example, Nordic countries) or linguistic (for example, Anglophone countries) classifications.[3]

Key limitations with applying the regime types

Although country classifications or welfare regimes are used for descriptive work, there are a number of potential limitations to their application in policy evaluation, and therefore in turn, to their role for informing policy-makers. In particular, for social policy evaluation between OECD countries:

- Not all OECD countries have been included in the welfare regime classifications, and these and new member countries can be difficult to place (new countries members, Central and Latin American countries).
- There is no single classification (geographic, linguistic or welfare regime type) used across the OECD as a common reference. The use of geographical and/or linguistic categorisations is most common and likely to be due to non-relative and universally understood points of reference for classification (even if conceptually, analytically *and* in terms of potential policy responses, 'where you are' will have weaker effects and be less malleable to policy interventions than 'what you do').
- Regime typologies are necessarily simplified nominal categorisations of complex systems – often based on one part of the policy cycle and operationalised using available data (spending, policy structures or choices, governance structures, or social outcome measures – the fifth section of this chapter discusses these in more detail) – and at a glance cannot communicate the nuances necessary for best informing policy change, including:
  - the types of public social protection (cash, tax break, services, leave and job protection rights, or conditional cash transfers), the timing of interventions in welfare regimes (cash transfers to families can increase, decrease or remain stable as children age),

and the accumulation of aggregate social spending within these streams;

- potential complementarities or trade-offs in spending and policy delivery choices in a given regime over time (through path dependency and accumulated spending) and in a given context (for example, through 'active' and 'passive' social protection policies, or the balance between services provision and cash transfers or tax breaks);
- implementation strategies, which inform policy-makers of how to make changes, once the plans for policy reforms are agreed.

- Due to data on spending and structures being most readily available in comparable series, classifications are often simply synonyms for high spender or low spender, or for a universal or a means-tested approach – and not for more effective/efficient or less effective/ efficient systems:

  - the inferred link between spending and policy structures (and indeed outcomes) is complicated, as in reality, interactions are sometimes counterintuitive – for example, in the context of the Great Recession and family policies, which saw increased demand for means-tested spending put some countries in the high spender bracket, despite targeted welfare approaches (for example, Ireland and the UK; see OECD, 2015a).

- A final, and perhaps a less objective limitation for many OECD countries, is that policy-making is often about progress in policy change and development. Welfare regime classifications give a sense of permanence that is necessarily subject to debate (geography and official language are less arguable!) and change. Debate about accuracy of classifications, on the one hand, inevitably limits the 'take-up' of policy findings and recommendations using regime types, whereas change, on the other, is dependent on sufficiently nuanced messages – bringing into question the use of simplified regime categories.

Together the limitations of regime types, which are often incomplete and inferential (across the policy cycle), generalised (aggregated, compounding policy efforts and effects), and rigid (that do not account for the interaction between spending types, time and methods, changes to the options, or accumulated or path-dependent spending) create serious challenges to the use of such descriptive tools in policy evaluation and policy-making. Most policy-makers are also funders of research at the national and international level, as well as having access to administrative statistics, evaluative evidence, as well as the detailed policy descriptions over time. This means that simplified categorisation of countries into groups is of limited value when compared to detailed country-specific or micro-level evidence.

The following section goes on to highlight the use of country classifications in recent child and family social protection policy work in the OECD, before introducing a new method designed to build on recent work while overcoming some of the limitations outlined above.

Family and child policy and child wellbeing

Although child poverty analysis has been a mainstay of the empirical work undertaken in the Social Policy Division dating back over a decade (see *Society at a Glance* [OECD, 2002b] and the Income Distribution database [OECD, 2015e]), the first attempt to establish child policy and wellbeing analysis in the Social Policy Division came with the *Babies and Bosses* series. The OECD was already undertaking work on child policy in the Education directorate, including work on early years education and care in the *Starting Strong* series (OECD, 2001a), and country-specific background reports (dating back to 1999), as well as the Programme for International Student Assessment (PISA) from 1999 onwards (for details, see OECD, 2015d).

The Directorate for Employment, Labour and Social Affairs, in which Social Policy is a division, had previously evaluated family policy from the perspective of employment (the OECD's *Employment Outlook* produced a chapter on work–family balance [2001b], and Social Policy's work was limited to the production of working papers – see Kamerman et al [2003] and Pylkkänen and Smith [2003]).

OECD Family database, Doing better for children and Doing better for families

Following the *Babies and Bosses* series, an important development in establishing a stream of work on family and child policy in the OECD Social Policy Division has been the creation and expansion of the OECD Family database. Initially designed to house the data collected as part of the various projects, the Family database now houses over 70 indicators, covering the structure of families, labour market status of families, public policies for families and children, and child outcome indicators/child wellbeing module.

The purpose of the database is to meet demand for cross-national indicators on family outcomes and policies; to allow for cross-national comparison across OECD countries, partner countries and European Union (EU) member states; to outline similarities and differences across countries and over time; and to provide a framework for future assessments of family policies. Each indicator typically presents the data on a particular issue as well as relevant definitions and methodology, comparability and data issues, and information on sources. In discussion of the data, which is descriptive or inferential in almost all cases, the use of country classifications is rare and used in shorthand to reflect country clusters in the results (see the fertility rates indicator SF2.1, or public spending on family benefits indicator PF1.1).

In 2007, with the Family database still in its infancy, the OECD began work on its first report on child wellbeing – *Doing better for children* (OECD, 2009). This report included an index on child wellbeing (the OECD's first wellbeing index of any kind) as well as chapters on net social expenditure (by type and timing – in the age-spending profiles), a review of policies from conception to kindergarten, a report on the intergenerational transmission of poverty risk, and a meta-analysis of findings from the more sophisticated research exploring the link between sole parenthood and child wellbeing. Nordic and Anglophone country groupings were commonly highlighted in descriptive work of social outcomes in the wellbeing chapter (even to the point of highlighting where the groups did not cluster; see OECD, 2009, p 49, for child mortality rates). In the meta-analysis of sole parenthood, country groupings were used to summarise findings as part of the main results table (OECD, 2009, Table 5.2), but used only to highlight a 'counterintuitive' finding that negative effect sizes, after controls, of growing up in a sole-parent household were larger than in Anglophone and Western European countries!

The main developments from *Doing better for children* did not directly effect a change in how OECD child and family policy used classifications, but did influence work that would create possibilities for the change. For instance, the report contributed to the debate on indicator development for measuring child wellbeing outcomes (as well as review of available data and its quality from the international survey of children; see Richardson and Ali, 2014), and a proposal for a child wellbeing module being added to the OECD Family database. More importantly for this discussion, the breakdown of net social expenditure by type and timing in the age-spending profiles led to demand for comparisons of the relative effectiveness of spending by type (cash versus service spending, versus tax breaks) and comparisons of 'when public monies should be spent', that contributed to the burgeoning discussion on social investment versus social consumptions (later led by the European Commission).

In 2011, the OECD published *Doing better for families*, covering the evolution of family outcomes, the 'balance' of net social expenditure, fertility, parental employment, child development and wellbeing, sole parenthood and child protection. The publication itself is entirely without reference to 'regimes'; however, the use of country classifications is very common, and appears for the first time in the second paragraph of the executive summary. This first reference, as with remaining references (except for the occasional reference to Anglophone countries) refers to geographic regions, including 'Nordic countries', 'Asian countries' and various European groups – again, building on implicit messages of welfare typologies through shared historic welfare 'cultures'. Country classifications are used to facilitate social outcome descriptions as well as policy similarities and/or converging practices, but now the link between policy efforts and outcomes in given country groupings is being made explicitly (see OECD, 2011a, p 28, for an example of a link made between advance on maintenance payments and divorce rates in Nordic countries).

Over the development of the stream of work on family and child policy there has been a change in the use of country classification, moving from a shorthand description of clusters in social outcomes and policy approaches separately (with inferences accepted) to the direct linking of commonalities in policy approaches and outcomes in groups of countries. In particular, *Doing better for families* highlighted new questions about the order and complementarity of specific policies within regimes, and over time, that are more or less favourable to producing different social outcomes.

Across the work as a whole, the combination of new net social expenditure breakdowns and a broader range of child wellbeing outcomes (beyond poverty) – and greater confidence in linking policies and practices to measured outcomes over time – directly contributed to further proposals of work to OECD country delegations that would ask which policy structures are most effective and efficient for producing various socially desirable family and child outcomes. But it is following the publication of *Doing better for families* and the maturation of the Family database (time series of various spending and social outcomes were being produced) that the Social Policy Division could specifically propose the use of country classifications in its work on family policy evaluations.

Assessing family policy efficiency and effectiveness using welfare typologies: the example of female employment

Work to be released in 2015 covers the Social Policy Division's first attempt at using policy 'regime typologies' in evaluative research. Proposed to the country delegations in 2012, the purpose of the work was to add a macro perspective to analysis of the effectiveness and efficiency of family policy choices in light of the stimulus and austerity in response to the Great Recession. Using a series of family outcomes and net social expenditure data from the OECD Family database and Social Expenditure database in a macro-pooled time series regression of policy effort to family outcomes, this work also involved the collection of a new database: the OECD Family Policy Structures database (see OECD, 2015a).

Changes to a range of family policy structures were recorded form 1996 onwards in order to provide a moderating factor to the family spending to family outcomes associations. Due to an inability to systematically disaggregate the spending (a restriction on the model sample sizes and therefore degrees of freedom), data for the Family Policy Structures database on key family cash policy structures[4] and service policies[5] were subject to Qualitative Comparative Analysis (QCA), to generate clusters of cash and service ideal types (for details, see OECD, 2015c: forthcoming). Table 12.1 provides an overview of the types developed for the study.

To explore the effect of family spending levels on family outcomes *within* different policy regime settings, and thereby assess which regimes are most effective and efficient – all other things being equal – the regressions employed interaction terms. These are commonly used to test whether the effect of an independent variable on an outcome (spending on poverty) varies by the values of a third variable (in this case, policy regime types). Specifically, regime-type interaction terms are used to see whether a family spending increase in one macro-policy setting produces a lesser or greater impact on a chosen family outcome than the same increase in family spending in another regime type. In other words, interactions between the levels of spending and policy design choices should illustrate how marginal returns to increases in cash and in-kind spending vary in different family policy settings – and thereby inform about the efficiency of investment by macro-policy structures.

Table 12.1: Cash and service ideal types

Cash benefit ideal types				Service benefit ideal types		
Main Child Benefit is not means-tested	Tax Breaks	Sole-parent Supplement	Extensive Leave Structures	Childcare is Universal ?	Childcare Payment ?	Other in-kind birth services FPC?
Comprehensive universal				*Public*		
Yes	Yes	Yes	Yes	Yes	Yes	Yes
Yes	No	Yes	Yes	Yes	No	Yes
Universal				*Social Market*		
Yes	Yes	No	Yes	Yes	Yes	No
Yes	Yes	No	No			
Comprehensive targeted				*Subsidy*		
No	Yes	Yes	No	No	Yes	No
No	No	Yes	No			
Targeted				*Private*		
No	Yes	No	No	No	No	No
No	No	No	No	No	No	Yes
Hybrid				*Hybrid*		

The effect of cash and in-kind spending on female civilian employment

The new regime type analysis discussed above focused on three types of family outcomes: child poverty, female employment and total fertility rates. This section just looks at one of the examples: how cash and in-kind policy decisions at the national level (including levels of spending and forms of delivery) separately correlate to rates of female civilian employment (in the 15-64 age group). Results show that for family cash policies, policy regimes with comprehensive and universal support for families, and for services regimes with public provision of childcare services, are the most effective and efficient systems for helping women into work (OECD, 2015c: forthcoming).

Initial tests of associations between the country cash policy groupings and female employment – independently of spending levels – showed that countries without strong parental leave systems or universal benefits, but *with* sole parents' conditions in family benefits, have significantly lower rates of female employment compared to other policy settings. Historically long-length sole parent benefits and disincentives to work may explain this finding when compared to more targeted systems (only paying benefits to working women through tax breaks), and universal systems (where child benefits are paid to all families, and therefore have lower marginal effective tax rates for women entering employment). Initial tests for in-kind policy groupings did not produce significant results, suggesting that there is no evidence for an *independent* service policy effect on female employment (OECD, 2015c: forthcoming).

In reality, the effectiveness of public expenditure on family policies will depend on how resources are transferred, so the analysis mapped spending patterns *within* each of the family policy groups (cash and in-kind separately) to explore associations with rates of female employment (Figure 12.1). The axes in each graph in Figure 12.1 record the standard deviation change in outcomes and spending in different policy types. Zero on each figure is average spending, '1' and '–1' are one standard deviation above and one standard deviation below the mean respectively. The length of the thick part of each line represents the boundaries of observed data. The position of the line on the y-axis represents the effectiveness of spending in each setting. Take the 'zero' or average line on the spending axis in the top panel on cash spending. In this example, the comprehensive universal line 'A' crosses zero at around +4 standard deviations below the average FLMP (female labour market participation) rate, Comprehensive targeted line 'C' crossed this line around 10 standard deviations below the average. Therefore, at average spending – all other things being equal – the comprehensive universal setting is more effective than the comprehensive targeted settings at average spending levels. The angle of the lines can be used to interpret the efficiency of different policy settings: the steeper the angle in the direction of interest (up for increases to female employment), the larger the change in the outcome for each standard deviation increase in spending. Steeper lines represent higher social returns on investment, or greater levels of efficiency.

In cash policy groupings (top panel), money is most effectively spent through the most comprehensive universal systems (systems with universal family benefits, tax breaks, sole parent payments and strong parental leave policies): the upward slope, higher up in the chart, shows higher average rates of female employment at average spending levels (0 on the x-axis), and larger increases to female employment when more family cash spending is invested in these systems. Although targeted settings also have positive outcomes-to-spending trends, targeted systems

Figure 12.1: In most cash systems, and in service systems with more public supports, increased spending is associated with increases in female employment rates after controls

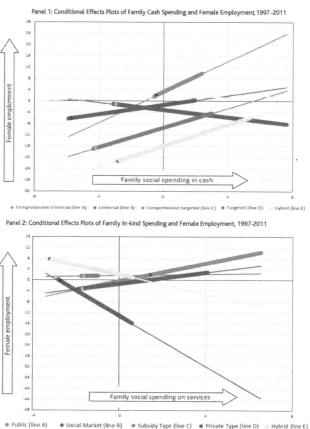

Panel 1: Conditional Effects Plots of Family Cash Spending and Female Employment, 1997-2011

Panel 2: Conditional Effects Plots of Family In-kind Spending and Female Employment, 1997-2011

Note: The interaction terms between in-kind family spending and different in-kind family types on child poverty and fertility (with the exception of hybrid systems), and both family spending types by ideal types on female civilian employment, are only statistically significant at the 0.1 level. Caution is warranted when interpreting these findings. For regression models, see Richardson et al. (forthcoming), Annexes A4 and A5.
Source: OECD, 2015c, forthcoming.

are only more effective than comprehensive systems in low-spend settings (where FLMP outcomes would remain below average levels internationally), and there are higher returns to increasing spending comprehensive universal settings. In-kind policy groupings (see bottom panel) with more than one type of childcare support have the steepest upward slope in the chart, and are highest in the chart at average spending of the four defined typologies (hybrid systems are those that do not fit in the classifications). Returns to increases in in-kind spending in public and social market systems are greater than returns in settings with lower levels of public involvement (private systems are counter-productive on this measure as spending increases – as the slope goes downwards). These public and social market settings are distinguished by having universal childcare systems and childcare payments for families who have enrolled their children in childcare.

Compared to previous regime typologies used by OECD specifically, this new work moved from descriptive uses to analytical and particularly evaluative use of regime typologies. In particular, policy-makers can take several direct and clear messages from these results:

- Comparing results within each of the tests (each of the charts), depending on similarities between settings, can be used to decide whether countries would be better off increasing spending levels *or* reforming spending patterns, *or* undertaking a mix of the two for the purposes of achieving a change in that outcome.
- Based on other countries' experience of spending changes within similar systems, the results can also be used to predict the change in outcomes associated with reduced spending, or reforms for purposes not related to the outcome measure at hand.
- Comparing effectiveness and efficiency between each of the tests (again, each of the charts) by outcome can be used to provide recommendations for increasing or decreasing spending in cash or in-kind to the greatest or least social cost.

The usefulness of regime typologies: some recommendations for development

The recent application of regime types for evaluating family policy in OECD countries leads the discussion into the final section which will build on selected limitations highlighted earlier, and on real examples of recent research demand from policy-makers (OECD, 2105b, 2015c), to recommend ways in which the regime-type literature might develop in order to become more applicable in policy discussions.

This section covers a number of issues, including complexity and complementarity in spending patterns; the governance of public benefits and budgets; the need to understand what drives the differences; the development of social expenditure measures: welfare effort; the need for consistency, or flexibility, in typologies; and the need for clear policy messages.

Complexity and complementarity in spending patterns

What countries do, in terms of spending, is one factor in a complex equation of policy achievement. Spending levels have been used as a factor in many efforts to assess policy generosity and to define regime typologies in past decades – in many cases these typologies including spending commitments have only looked at parts of the total social protection budget (Ferrarini, 2006), social policy budget (Esping-Andersen, 1990), or total government expenditure (OECD, 2015c). Figure 12.2 maps total government expenditure by type for a selection of OECD countries. It is clear from this picture that typologies that miss education, health and housing miss large social investments that could have an impact on the effectiveness of a given regime (around 35 per cent in total across the OECD, and making up shortfalls in total government expenditure overall). Moreover, what is missed is not consistent across countries, as the balance of social spending by type varies widely.

What is achieved by spending in a given year is further complicated by issues of path dependency (monies following previous spends, invested in maintaining infrastructures perhaps, reducing liquidity of public funds and reform recommendations) and the cost of the administration of systems (which vary from cash to services – some services spending is almost entirely administration; and cash spending total in net social expenditure figures do not include administrative costs). Service delivery (a large part of education, housing and health) has investment properties in some countries above and beyond the 'welfare' transfer – either acting as banks of public goods (trained professionals, public services settings) or opportunities for 'indirect social transfers', such as job creation. Annual spending figures miss the effects of accumulated public investment, indirect social investment (job creation, security, local area infrastructure and investment) and locked public resources that have implications for social impacts and policy reform opportunities.

Figure 12.2: The allocation of total government expenditure: social polices account for around 70% of total OECD-wide

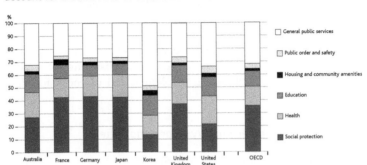

Source: OECD National Accounts Statistics (database). Data for Australia are based on Government Finance Statistics provided by the Australian Bureau of Statistics.

Note: General public services include Defence, Environmental protection and Recreation, Culture and Religion. Data are not available for Canada. OECD average is for 30 countries (Chile, Mexico and New Zealand also missing).

Beyond spending: governance of public benefits and budgets

Some of the more recent demands of policy-makers in OECD countries have been to look beyond the standard social protection cash payments, and to explore the role of services, both intensive services for high-need social groups, but also how personal and household services (childcare, housing, out-of-school care and so on) can facilitate improved living standards, gender equity and work–family balance (see OECD, 2012, 2015b). Service delivery is often undertaken by sub-central levels of government (local, regional or state), and within countries, as across types, the governance picture is a complicated one, which has an impact on the evolution of social policy in a country alongside policy design and levels of spending within regimes.

Figure 12.3 maps the different levels of governments involved in the delivery of services in the sectors of social protection, employment services, housing, health, education and public order. Where data is available, each country row records the level of governance at which social services are managed by sector. At first glance this figure highlights the complexity of social protection within a set of OECD countries.

The importance of, yet complexity in, the delivery of social services creates several policy challenges for regime typologies:

Figure 12.3: The governance of social services is complex and varied across countries

	Social protection		Employment		Housing		Health			Education			Public order	
	Social Assistance	Family cash benefits	Job centres (& Job training)	Cash benefits	Institutions (homeless, children in care)	Social Housing	Secondary health services	Primary health services	Mental health / counselling services	Compulsory	Childcare	Adult Education (lifelong learning)	Policing	Prisons
Australia	C/F	C/F	C/F	C/F	CF, R	CF, R	R	R	R	R	R	R	CF, R	R
Canada	R	CF, R	C/F (from 2017)	C/F	...	R	R	R	R	R	R	R	CF, R, L	C/F
France	R, L	CF, R	L	C/F, L	R	C/F	R*	R*	R**	C/F	R, L	C/F	C/F, L	C/F
Germany	R	C/F	L	CF, R	L	R, L	R, L	R, L	R, L	R	L	R	C/F	C/F
Italy	R, L	C/F	R	C/F	...	L	R	R	R	R, L	R, L	...	C/F, L	C/F
Japan	L	L	...	C/F	...	...	C/F, L	C/F, L	C/F	L	L	C/F	C/F, L	C/F
United Kingdom	C/F	C/F	C/F	C/F	L	L	CF, R	CF, R	CF, R	C/F, L	C/F, L	...	R	C/F (Pr).
United States	CF, R, L	CF, R	CF, R	CF, R	CF, R, L	CF, R, L	Pr. with CF, R***	Pr. with CF, R***	Pr. with CF, R***	CF, R, L	CF, R, L	C/F, L	R, L	CF, R (Pr.)

Note: C/F is central or federal, R is regional (referring to states, provinces or counties), L is local (municipalities, local governments, city governments), Pr. denotes private provider involvement. Data is provisional.

Source: OECD (2015b).

- First, policy-makers, particularly in the federal countries of the OECD (Austria, Australia, Canada, and so on), and those with particularly active (high-spending) local governments (Nordic countries), are sensitive to the limitations of macro-spending figures, knowing, as they do, that full expenditures are not always accounted for.
- Second, for policy too, different electoral cycles and elected bodies can lead to conflicting policy regime types in a given setting, and confound any idea of a singular, established and sustainable regime type.
- Third, and related, is the transfer of executive power from central to local government, and/or related social budgets. Central governments may or may not control final policy decisions in cash or in-kind and when monies are devolved (policies are amended – note state top-ups to federal policies, such as Brazil's *Bolsa Família*). Evidence from the most recent version of *Governance at a Glance* (OECD, 2013) shows on average that although only around 20 per cent of total public monies are raised at the sub-central level, almost 30 per cent of total spending is managed by local or regional authorities. Across the OECD local governments manage between 5 per cent (Greece) and 67 per cent (Canada) of total government revenue, which shows the potential, in practice, for 'national regime

types' to be actively influenced by local government policies and local 'welfare cultures' to varying degrees.

- Fourth, this shift of funds creates transaction costs that could confound the 'generosity' of a given country in a given setting (transaction and additional administrative costs need to be accounted for), or may result in multiple experiences of different 'generosity' levels across more devolved countries.
- Finally, changes to governance are not simple to achieve, and budgeting and planning needs to 'fit' into pre-existing public models, and any evolution of delivery would produce very different models country-to-country.

Development of social expenditure measures: welfare regimes and welfare effort

Esping-Andersen, 10 years after his 'three worlds' work, reiterated the challenge of understanding how some countries manage the impact of global social forces (globalisation and its economic and social demand) better than others: 'despite the ubiquity of these "driving forces", they do not seem to result in convergent social and economic outcomes [across countries]' (Esping Andersen, 2001, p 135). In doing so he put an implicit emphasis on the role of welfare regimes in managing the risk. In a later paper, Esping-Andersen states that the 'total welfare package' of an individual is derived from three inputs – government, markets and family (2005, p 180) – and it is this that defines the regime, not public spending alone.

This is undoubtedly true, and a challenge for regime-type analysts. First, it means that the role of the family in providing welfare as well as that of social enterprise should contribute to regime-type discussions – with equivalent care to that taken by public interventions. The former has found its way into discussions (for example, through the 'southern European' type); the latter, however, is harder to define and measure in ways equivalent to public investment and policy effort.[6] Addressing this shortfall will become increasingly important in future work.

Regime typology analysis needs to respond to new methods in measuring welfare effort, as well as new demands of welfare efforts (note the role of social enterprises, for instance). Esping-Andersen is a supporter of the net social expenditure measures (see Esping-Andersen, 2005) produced by the OECD, as these account for private investment as well as tax breaks (and taxes on cash benefits), all of which have changed the face of the measurement of welfare effort since the publication of the earliest typologies.

Moreover, with reference to social outcomes, Esping Andersen argues that for social indicators to be useful for policy, they need to capture the dynamics of the issue (Esping Andersen, 2005), as headcounts have limited use. Annual expenditure figures could be argued to have the same limitations, as annual spending is an annual 'headcount' and does not attempt to link the spending to previous efforts or future promises. The appreciation of cumulative effects in social need can be reflected in the cumulative effects of social spending (investment or consumption), perhaps changing the appreciation of investment strategies and policy choices, and limiting the applicability of 'politically defined' regimes based on a series of annual figures (accumulated effects are hard to account for, and have not been covered in the new OECD work).

Esping-Andersen also notes how social expenditure is increasingly being discussed in terms of social investment and social consumption (or, in other words, movement from passive to active social policies). This resonates with the argument relating to service policies above – that some policies are designed to create returns, directly or indirectly, and as such, aggregate amounts used in regime typologies are not fully capturing the dynamic and indirect aspects of spending. This can lead to misclassification in 'spending-based' or politically defined typologies – a problem that will lead to many policy-makers immediately rejecting the findings of the work.

Finally, the evolution from passive to active social policy noted in much research since the turn of the century shows the willingness of welfare regimes to evolve, and the fluidity of category membership. And it highlights the need for flexibility in the research of welfare typologies.

Need for consistency, or flexibility, in categorisations

As noted in the limitation of typologies in the second section of this chapter, the flexibility of typologies is an important factor for policy-makers, who view their systems as dynamic and fluid, rather than inflexible. The new OECD work is a good example of how to achieve such flexibility, as it allows countries to move between welfare categories as policies are reformed (OECD, 2015c).

Also, as with any discipline, communication is facilitated with consistent use of terminology. Even the experts can get this wrong; Esping-Andersen's (2001) work on emerging risk profiles to social cohesion makes reference to the 'Nordic' group and the Mediterranean group in the first paragraph, switches quickly to southern Europe in the next sentence, and then continental Europe on page 139 (all of this must be quite confusing for non-Europeans). When looking at Europe alone, in the exclusion section of the paper, Scandinavia is referenced (which is now challenging for Europeans, who might not be able to conceptually distinguish this group from the Nordics – in the OECD context, what does the inclusion of Finland and Iceland really mean?). Across the paper, some classifications are more helpful for the policy-minded, as the classification turns to policy choices (from mixed linguistic [Anglophone] and varied geographic ones) with references to 'deregulated economies' and low-wage deregulated economies.

The classification should depend on the knowledge and needs of the audience – for policy-makers, who like policy-amenable information, regime types might be better served by policy specific titles.

Clear policy messages – applied and implementable

The extent to which policy regime/typology analysis can be designed to produce disaggregated results, and therefore the most transferable forms of policy advice, will define the extent of its policy influence. Policy recommendations are most attractive when they can be applied, are implementable, and active. Suggesting a country changes regime/type will not have the same traction as suggesting a country might change a policy, or indeed, a practice. Complexity in spending, and specifically in governance, serve to highlight the need for effective implementation advice to complement the promotion of programmes and practices. If typologies cannot develop to achieve such outputs, they will inevitably be subject to exclusion from policy-makers' discussions.

Conclusion

Simplification in comparative research is both a blessing and a curse, and regime typologies experience this well. Typologies can simply communicate the commonalities in findings, while giving some starting point for explaining why countries have the spending levels or social outcomes that they do (they also provide the researcher with some sort of face validity – based on expectations of how countries should cluster). In reality, and to the frustration of policy-makers, typologies commonly provide too few 'directives' and too many possible 'directions'.

It is clear that comparative social policy analysis is pushing the use of country regime-type categorisation in two ways:

- First, as policy-makers are asking for more detailed evaluations of social policy, relative to predetermined, measurable and desirable social outcomes (often multiple social outcomes), this requires specific identification of policies and programmes that do specific tasks. Clearly there is limited room for standard regime typologies here.
- Second, data availability is providing opportunities for more sophisticated regime typology work. The availability of data series, in terms of outcomes measures, inputs, policy choices and contextual information, has come to a point at which numbers are high enough to undertake more sophisticated analyses. With such data more can be learned through analysing longer-term trends, as well as undertaking macro-pooled time series analysis.

Finally, since the publication of the seminal *The three worlds of welfare capitalism*, social policy analysis, and particularly comparative child policy, has seen a shift in the types of policies being prioritised, for what purposes, how much is spent, and what is being achieved. In his work on 'Indicators and social accounting for 21st century social policy', Esping Andersen puts his weight behind this change, noting a need for new measures and a priority on purpose over practice (that is, that social policies should be defined by their objectives, and equity in pursuit of the objectives, and that using measures based on limits of social expenditure 'is like putting the cart before the horse' [Esping-Andersen, 2005, p 181]). For regime types to have a meaningful impact on policy-makers, analysts must keep the focus on the objectives and effectiveness of policy, the development of these objectives and appropriate data developments, detail of programmes and policy implementation strategies within those regimes, and remember that 'policy inputs', such as regime types and their total spending levels, are seen as a means to an end, rather than an end in themselves.

Notes
[1] Organisation for Economic Co-operation and Development (OECD) Social Policy Division. The views expressed in this chapter are those of the author, and do not necessarily reflect those of the OECD or its member countries.

[2] Social protection is the common thread here, although the names and exact remit of ministries can vary country to country, and can include, for example, joint remits with health, housing and employment alongside social protection.

[3] See, for example, the early work by Kamerman et al (2003), who use the term 'Nordic' and 'Anglo-American'.

[4] Including universality of the main child allowance, the length and generosity of paid parental leave schemes, sole parent benefits and tax breaks to families with children.

[5] Including childcare provision, conditional childcare subsidies, and free-to-access primary healthcare services for children.

[6] How far public services, by sector, are open to third party contributions can be estimated by the extent to which the public sector is co-producing in these sectors. An OECD survey of 26 countries in 2011 (OECD, 2011b; Brazil, Egypt, Russia and the Ukraine, plus 22 OECD countries) mapped 'significant' civil society involvement in the delivery of public services, and showed that of 58 examples of co-production, 19 per cent were in social protection, 16 per cent were in housing and community amenities, and 10 per cent were in each of the areas of environmental affairs, economic services, education and health. In each sector, co-production in service delivery was found at all levels of governance (local, state and federal or national levels; OECD, 2011b, p 23). However, the effectiveness, range and type of investment were not comprehensively covered in the report.

References

Considine, M. (2006) 'Local partnerships: different histories, common challenges – a synthesis', in OECD (Organisation for Economic Co-operation and Development), *Managing decentralisation: A new role for labour market policy*, Paris: OECD Publishing (http://dx.doi. org/10.1787/9789264104716-17-en).

Esping-Andersen, G. (1990) *The three worlds of welfare capitalism*, Cambridge: Polity Press.

Esping-Andersen, G. (2001) 'A new challenge for social cohesion? Emerging risk profiles in OECD countries', in OECD (Organisation for Economic Co-operation and Development), *What schools for the future?*, Paris: OECD Publications, pp 135-43.

Esping-Andersen, G. (2005) 'Indicators and social accounting for 21st century social policy', in OECD (Organisation for Economic Co-operation and Development), *Statistics, knowledge and policy: Key indicators to inform decision making*, Paris: OECD Publishing, pp 176-86.

Ferrarini, T. (2006) *Families, states and labour markets. Institutions, causes and consequences of family policy in post-war welfare states*, Cheltenham: Edward Elgar.

Kamerman, S.B., Neuman, M., Waldfogel, J. and Brooks-Gunn, J. (2003) *Social policies, family types and child outcomes in selected OECD countries*, OECD Social, Employment and Migration Working Papers, No 6, Paris: OECD Publishing (http://dx.doi.org/10.1787/625063031050).

Korpi, W. and Palme, J. (1998) *The paradox of redistribution and strategies of equality: Welfare state institutions, inequality and poverty in the Western countries*, Luxembourg Income Study Working Paper Series, No 174, Luxembourg: LIS

OECD (Organisation for Economic Co-operation and Development) (2001a) *Starting Strong: Early childhood education and care*, Paris: OECD Publications.

OECD (2001b) 'Balancing work and family life', in OECD, *Employment Outlook*, Paris: OECD Publications.

OECD (2002a) *Babies and Bosses: Reconciling work and family life in Australia, Denmark, and the Netherlands*, Paris: OECD Publications.

OECD (2002b) *Society at a Glance, 2002*, Paris: OECD Publications.

OECD (2005) 'The social market and social democratic countries of continental Europe', in OECD, *Statistics, knowledge and policy: Key indicators to inform decision making*, Paris: OECD Publishing.

OECD (2009) *Doing better for children*, Paris: OECD Publications.

OECD (2011a) *Doing better for families*, Paris: OECD Publications.

OECD (2011b) *Together for better public services: Partnering with citizens and civil society*, Paris: OECD Publications.

OECD (2012) *Closing the gender gap: Act now*, Paris: OECD Publishing.

OECD (2013) *Government at a Glance*, Paris: OECD Publishing.

OECD (2015a) *OECD Family database*, Paris: OECD Publishing.

OECD (2015b) *Integrated service delivery for vulnerable groups*, Paris: OECD Publishing.

OECD (2015c: forthcoming) *Cash or services: What works best for families?*, Paris: OECD.

OECD (2015d) Programme for International Student Assessment (PISA) (www.oecd.org/pisa/home/).

OECD (2015e) *OECD Income Distribution database*, Paris: OECD Publishing.

Pylkkänen, E. and Smith, N. (2003) *Career interruptions due to parental leave: A comparative study of Denmark and Sweden*, OECD Social, Employment and Migration Working Papers, No 1, Paris: OECD Publishing (http://dx.doi.org/10.1787/048564246616).

Richardson, D. and Ali, N. (2014) *An evaluation of international surveys of children*, OECD Social, Employment and Migration Working Papers (No 146), Paris: OECD Publishing (http://dx.doi.org/10.1787/5jxzmjrqvntf-en).

Richardson, D., Hudson, J., Kühner, S., Frey, V., Patana, P. and Ali, N. (2015: forthcoming) *Comparing effectiveness and efficiency of cash benefits and in-kind childcare services on family outcomes,* OECD Social, Employment and Migration Paper, Paris: OECD Publishing.

Index

Note: Page numbers in italics refer to figures and tables. Page numbers followed by the letter *n* refer to chapter endnotes.